The Voices ... on *The New Village Green*

What if we change the story? What if, instead of the landfill being the place we take our garbage, we make it our repository of wealth?

— from the Preface

Man is a part of nature, and his war against nature is, inevitably, a war against himself.

—*Rachel Carson*, Silent Spring

A small shift in one thing can produce big changes in everything.

— Donella Meadows, scientist, author, and cheese maker

But even the widespread adoption of solar power would not put an end to the threat of global warming.

— Bill McKibben, author & activist

When a decision is made to cope with the symptoms of a problem, it is generally assumed that the corrective measures will solve the problem itself. They seldom do.
Bioregionalism, in combination with deep ecology, is the most important ecological idea of our time.

— Kirkpatrick Sale, author and director of the Middlebury Institute

All historians understand that they must never, ever talk about the future.
— *Stewart Brand, jack of all trades, master of more than a few*

The anti-nature attitude in our culture comes from some very respectable sources.
— *Euell Gibbons, forager*

The New Village Green is a testament that life endures, even flourishes... Do we know the factors that support community, enhance civility, and achieve sustainability. Read this book and find out.

— *Paul Freundlich, Founder and President Emeritus of Co-op America*

THE NEW VILLAGE GREEN

living light,
living local,
living large

STEPHEN MORRIS
AND THE EDITORS OF
GREEN LIVING

NEW SOCIETY PUBLISHERS

CATALOGING IN PUBLICATION DATA:

A catalog record for this publication is available
from the National Library of Canada.

Cover design: Diane McIntosh
Cover image: iStockphoto.com

Printed in Canada. First printing June 2007.
Paperback ISBN: 978-0-86571-599-8
Inquiries regarding requests to reprint all or part of
The New Village Green
should be addressed to New Society Publishers at the address below.
To order directly from the publishers, please call toll-free (North America) 1-800-567-6772,
or order online at www.newsociety.com
Any other inquiries can be directed by mail to:

New Society Publishers
P.O. Box 189, Gabriola Island, BC V0R 1X0, Canada
(250) 247-9737

New Society Publishers' mission is to publish books that contribute in fundamental ways to
building an ecologically sustainable and just society, and to do so with the least possible impact
on the environment, in a manner that models this vision. We are committed to doing this not just
through education, but through action. We are acting on our commitment to the world's remaining ancient forests by phasing out our paper supply from ancient forests worldwide. This
book is one step toward ending global deforestation and climate change. It is printed on acid-
free paper that is 100% old growth forest-free (100% post-consumer recycled), processed chlorine free, and printed with vegetable-based, low-VOC inks. For further information, or to browse
our full list of books and purchase securely, visit our website at: www.newsociety.com

NEW SOCIETY PUBLISHERS   www.newsociety.com

contents

6 : Small is Beautiful

7 : Whole Earth Catalog

8 : The Good Life

To Donella Meadows,
who took complex ideas
and gave them a human face,
and it was a face with a smile

acknowledgments

The New Village Green is a unique intersection of many places and communities. I look out my window to the left of my laptop and see a squabbling flock of bluejays. The birdseed they squander will be cleaned up later by the chickadees, juncos, and doves. Through the window on my right I see tracks where a flock of turkeys marched up the hill and into the woods. There were no wild turkeys in the state when I moved here in 1979. Now there are almost daily stately processions.

I gaze back into my laptop and wonder who might show up today. Will it be a high school buddy with a new joke? A YouTube.com video from my son in New York? An updated tour schedule from my son, the musician, or an email from my partner, Sandy Levesque, working out of her own home office on the other side of the house, wanting to know when we might break for a walk or a ski. I wonder if, besides her, I will talk to another human being today?

The day will have its share of small dramas as I connect with other citizens on the New Village Green. I am thankful for all of them.

My *Green Living* associates are regulars. I thank Amelia Shea, Dede Cummings, Carolyn Kasper, Linda Pinkham, and Kathleen James for keeping this light boat afloat. A tip of the hat to Marshall Glickman for launching this enterprise in 1990 and steering it so ably for many years.

I thank my various mates from Co-op America with whom I have been aligned for so many years. Alisa Gravitz, Denise Hamler, Dennis Greenia, and Paul Freundlich have been parts of my world for many years and will continue to be, hopefully forever.

A new sphere of associates are the folks from New Society — Chris and Judith Plant, Ingrid Witvoet, Sara Reeves, and others — who have made the distance between Gabriola Island and Vermont seem very small.

I thank those who have been willing to play along with this venture by sharing their ideas, words, opinions, Rolodexes, and address books. Insofar as this book is successful it is due to your willingness to play along. Rochelle Elkan deserves thanks for her stalwart role in seeking permissions and preparing the manuscript. Special thanks to Michael Potts, co-founder of The Public Press and co-conspirator in so many ventures. Michael wears so many hats — from data wrangler to designer to writer — that it is difficult to cite his single most important contribution.

These are but a few of the characters who are part of *The New Village Green*. Many more will appear on the following pages.

Radiolarian

The images between articles (except where noted) are the
work of Ernst Heinrich Haeckel (1834–1919). A meticulous
scientific illustrator as well as a philosopher-biologist,
Haeckel held that all life is continuous and related.

My Friend The Beast
by Stephen Morris, Editor

Dan Chiras lives in Evergreen, Colorado. He doesn't have a Wikipedia page (yet), and Oprah has never featured one of his books, but quietly and methodically over the past 20-odd years he has churned out more than two dozen environmental books, including *The Homeowner's Guide to Renewable Energy*, *The New Ecological Home*, *The Solar House*, *The Natural House*, *Superbia! 31 Ways to Create Sustainable Neighborhoods*, and *The Natural Plaster Book*. Within the world of green building he's a superstar.

I first encountered Dan when he submitted a proposal to Chelsea Green, where I was publisher, for a survey book on green building techniques called *The Natural House*. This became a successful book that was named Book of the Year by our state publishing association. Dan's next proposal was quickly accepted and resulted in a second successful project.

Although no one at the company had met Dan in person, he quickly acquired the nickname, The Beast, in recognition of his prolific output. He came East on a family trip, and we finally had a chance to meet The Beast in person. It was clear from the moment he arrived that Dan was a card-holding member of our little clan. In addition to our intertwined business relations, he shared our beliefs, our attitudes and values, even our companywide love of music. It was my personal pleasure to host Dan and his sons at my home overnight.

Not all of Dan's projects were dead center for us, and inevitably he submitted something we had to reject. We suggested a rival publisher, New Society Publishers located on Gabriola Island, British Columbia, and even offered to put in a good word. It wasn't needed, and Dan soon found himself with two publishers.

My relationship with Dan continued on a professional and personal level even as I moved on to new ventures. When I sent him a copy of *Stripah Love*, the inaugural offering from my experimental publishing venture called The Public Press, I was gratified when he responded with genuine enthusiasm and even agreed to write a review on Amazon. I was even happier when, some months later, Dan approached The Public Press about publishing his first venture into fiction, a novel called *Here Stands Marshall*. This book was published in 2005.

By now Dan and I were colleagues, with an established relationship that had roots in producing successful products, exchanging money, and (all too infrequently) breaking bread. Our personal encounters were few, brief, and warm. We connected briefly at events like SolFest in Hopland, California, and it was always like encountering a long-lost treasured friend.

I am fortunate to have other professional connections where the contact is as much about collegiality as about business. Two people with whom I always enjoy crossing paths are Chris and Judith Plant. When they came to Burlington to attend the BALLE Conference in June 2006, we huddled over lunch to swap industry gossip, exchange notes on common acquaintances (such as Dan Chiras), and exchange publishing war stories. I told them about my recent acquisition of *Green Living Magazine* and my goal to merge it with the interests of The Public Press. They mentioned casually that if I ever wrote a book that explained the ideas and practices of "green living" they'd be interested in seeing a proposal.

"Who's got time to write a book?" I protested. "I'm already the busiest guy in the world!"

It took several weeks for the extent of the opportunity to become apparent to me. Maybe I could take on the project if I could enlist a little help from my friends. Towards that end I contacted a number of friends and friends of friends, Dan included, and asked them to jumpstart the process by identifying the seminal books, ideas, events, and people that have defined our current world view.

As usual, Dan did not let me down. He wrote back:

> I don't believe that any single book or idea has influenced the human-environment relationship — how we think about our place in the natural world and how we act. Rather, it seems to me that our understanding, and to a lesser extent our way of life, has evolved over time, thanks to several key books and seminal ideas.
>
> Rachel Carson's *Silent Spring*, of course, had a profound influence early on. It helped us understand just how dramatically humans could influence the environment through the application of pesticides. This book was a wake up call that many claim gave birth to the environmental movement.
>
> Then came Paul Ehrlich's *Population Bomb*. This book broadened our understanding of another key issue, notably overpopulation. I think that it started an important debate and considerable action throughout the world.
>
> Then came Schumacher's *Small is Beautiful*. This marvelous book got many of us to begin thinking about technology, notably appropriate technology. This idea helped sow the seeds of sustainability.
>
> *Limits to Growth* by Dana Meadows, her husband Dennis, and Jorgen Randers, arrived on the scene with much fanfare, and deservedly so. This seminal work showed us that our current way of

thinking and our current patterns of growth and development had no chance of success — that they were fundamentally unsustainable. It showed us that our future was profoundly influenced by pollution, resource demand, and population growth.

Our Common Future by the World Commission on Environment and Development was yet another influential book that raised the level of discussion on the human-environment interaction — specifically outlining a hopeful strategy for sustainable development. It has sparked a considerable amount of thinking and action aimed at creating an enduring human presence.

Thus, an organizing principle was born. Although our book list and sequence differs from Dan's, the principle remains the same. This new Village Green is just like its predecessor, but in a constant state of evolution. It extends from Vermont to Gabriola Island to Evergreen, Colorado to parts beyond. It is joined by electrons and personal connections. It features colorful characters from Chellis Gendinning of New Mexico, who inquired if I had run into her ex-husband in my Vermont travels, to Albert Bates of The Farm in Tennessee, who extended my regards to an old mate who lives there.

The New Village Green proves that the world is a small, but beautiful place. It's a place of colorful characters, interesting ideas, and even delicious food. What has been lost as the human species careens forward has found a new expression. Let's hope the best ideas are likely those still to come.

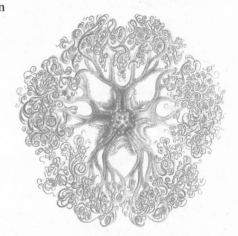

Gorgon-headed starfish

About this book

This book is designed to be read in any order. Our goal has been to enlighten and entertain. There has been thought given to grouping and sequencing, but sometimes the rationale for including a specific piece in a specific chapter will be not be apparent. This book is a reader, bringing together many voices from a wide range of individuals. Some are famous; some are being published here for the first time. Some are academic; some have dirt under their fingernails. The goal is not a symphony, but the harmonious cacophony of coyote pups baying at a full moon or a chevron of honkers in flight.

Typography

Ragged-right text (like this) is written by us — the Editor or one of his collaborators at *Green Living Journal*.

Justified text (like this) is previously published material, contributed by others, that deserves, in our view, renewed exposure.

Terminology

We use the latinate version of the neologism *locavore*; it means "eating locally." In Vermont, this is unaccountably spelt "localvore."

Since neither "starfish" nor "jellyfish" are fish, we use the preferred terms sea-star and sea-jelly.

We use the initials BCE (Before Common Era) rather than BC.

A Landfill Fantasy

Welcome to *The New Village Green*, or ... A Landfill Fantasy.

Methane, a simple hydrocarbon consisting of one atom of carbon and four of hydrogen, is a greenhouse gas that is more than twenty times more damaging than carbon dioxide in terms of its impact of global warming. It is formed naturally whenever organic matter ferments anaerobically, that is, in an environment that contains no oxygen. Methane is created when ancient forests decompose deep beneath the earth's surface, when last night's dinner is digested in your intestines, and at the local landfill when the community garbage is mixed together and buried.

When burned in the presence of oxygen, methane releases one molecule of carbon dioxide and two of water. At the local landfill, especially if it's lined, society's refuse is transformed by wild yeasts into sludge and methane that is often flared off (ignited). Although it seems wasteful, the rationale is that we are better off with carbon and water than methane.

The last time I recycled, the "eternal flame" of flared methane struck me as a monument to our ability to create malodorous trash, I had a thought: What if we changed the story? What if, instead of the landfill being the place where we take our garbage, we make it our repository of wealth?

It can become our own "locavore" Saudi Arabia, teeming with riches below the surface that improve life above. Through the miracle of anaerobic respiration, we could enjoy a new resource for food, energy, and community.

The penny dropped, and I was seized by a big picture solution to planetary problems. Let's begin by building a greenhouse over the methane flare. Voila! Heated greenhouse. The north side of the greenhouse could be constructed of straw bales to improve the R-value. We could then lease out greenhouse space to the local, organic farmers and gardeners who could cultivate seeds much earlier, preserve late season harvests, and supply us with fresh greens year-round.

What the heck, since we're at the landfill anyway, let's start a composting operation next door. People are bringing their wet garbage and lawn clippings anyway. We could give people an incentive for bringing their organic waste: one pound of finished compost for every fifty pounds of raw material.

As people flock to the landfill for free compost, we've got the traffic for a farmers' market where the community gathers for fresh produce, yummy foods, and demonstrations by local craftsfolk. We could build a little amphitheater out of straw bales to listen to local musicians. And, of course, there would have to be one of those outdoor bread ovens for making flatbread pizzas.

In fact, we should have a complete community kitchen to encourage small-scale food ventures.

And a root cellar. We definitely need a community root cellar.

And a masonry oven for making breads. Now should the masonry oven be inside or outside the greenhouse? And if it is inside, is it too fanciful to imagine a related sauna? A sauna will necessitate a pond with all the related aquaculture, but why wouldn't we want a pond?

While we're at it, we need one of those "living machines" that processes toxins by using natural systems to extract nutrients that can be used to nourish crops of flowers and medicinal herbs. Imagine giant, fragrant tropical flowers growing by the edge of the small pond that doubles as the fish farm for Tilapia and brine shrimp, which will eventually be harvested and served at the barbecue stand.

Is a banana plantation out of the question?

I forgot the barbecue. In addition to the grilled fish and shrimp, the barbecue will serve the free range chicken and grass-fed beef that graze on the hillsides of the landfill. We'll also need a few sheep and goats for milkers to provide material for the local cheese makers and ice creamery. There needs to be an outdoor pond for ice skating in the winter and swimming in the summer. As opposed to the interior pond, this one will be populated by crayfish that keep the waters pristine, while providing culinary focus for both the annual Crayfish Festival and the signature Landfill Bouillabaisse.

"Landfill Bouillabaisse" doesn't have quite the right ring. Let's change the landfill to *The New Village Green*.

This will quickly become THE place to be. Teenagers will hang out just to be seen by members of their own species. Singles will abandon MySpace and Match.com in favor of taking their pets down to *The New Village Green* for a stroll.

Dads will bring their meticulously sorted recycling, while Moms will use their skills and resources to launch fledgling businesses selling innovative products ranging from horseradish jelly to doggy bandanas. Thanks to free community WiFi, they can process orders from all over the globe in between chats with the neighbors.

Such a confluence of humanity will, in turn, attract local politicians who will be confronted with the overwhelming community fabric. As they stroll from booth to booth, enterprise to enterprise, they suddenly understand their dual duty to lead and represent the interests not of special interests, but rather of the commons.

By this time I can barely see the flared methane in my rear view mirror. How difficult could it be to get from here to there?

— Stephen Morris
Editor

The New Village Green
by Paul Freundlich

Even in ancient times and the most primitive villages, there was a place where commerce and community met: the crossroads, the commons, the square, the piazza, the village green. It was a place for the exchange of goods and gossip, the mix of classes, strangers and neighbors, entertainment, public speeches, courting, market day.

In a world where it seems there is a Starbucks on every corner, and the internet only a WiFi'd laptop away, it is easy to ignore the billions who lack electricity, with potable water growing scarce. For them, the explosion of expectations and affluence that seemed about to rescue humanity from grinding poverty in the 19th and 20th centuries remains a dream denied. For them, it still matters that there is a crossroads, a commons, a square, a piazza, a place where there is a bench and a patch of green that all can claim as their right.

Yet this book will argue that for all of us it matters. Just the rush of events and distractions compromise the choices we make. Years ago, I briefly lived on a one-block section of Court Street in New Haven, Connecticut. Some of the first federal rehab money had been distributed. What they simply accomplished was to widen the sidewalks so that there was only one lane for traffic, with a few wider areas for cars to drop off groceries. With safe sidewalks and no parking, the life of the neighborhood moved from the backyard to the front stoop. Folks visited, kids played.

On a larger scale, shopping malls and superstores have destroyed too many towns. Corporate decisions about pricing result in virtual slave labor in the southern hemisphere so we can save a few pennies in Northern countries. A drug war against marijuana has had the unexpected consequence of elevating crack cocaine.

When I traveled as a filmmaker for the Peace Corps in the 60s, I documented the lives of entitled young Americans, who via a government initiative, found themselves teaching and learning in barrios, slums, and outlying rural areas. What did they learn? What did they accomplish? Who did they affect?

Whatever happened occurred because the program was in place, because the US had accumulated resources and political capital. We are always making choices as individuals, as communities, as nations.

In the 70s and 80s, many of us struggled against a rising tide of what we perceived as greed. I was editing *Communities* magazine for a decade, then founded and led Co-op America for another. It looked to me as though a set of values focused on cooperation, community, social and environmental responsibility were being undercut by exploitation.

In the 21st century, with privatization and pollution made synonymous with progress, where is our village green, and what worthwhile do we hold in common? The Romans respected private property and public structures, yet recognized *res communes:* "that there was the air and water, flora and fauna which were no one's property."

Not too long ago, I attended a meeting at a modern crossroads, the United Nations. Present were leading environmental groups, and representatives of pension funds and financial institutions holding more than $3 trillion in assets. The subject was climate risk, and INCR, the Investor Network on Climate Risk, committed itself, far beyond the resources of the usual demonstrations and campaigns, to preserving the health of this planet.

These are strange days for those who knew which side we were on. On the Stakeholder Council of the Global Reporting Initiative, as we struggle with defining the guidelines for worldwide corporate accountability, my fellow travelers include business, labor, public interest groups, and the financial industry. Whether from Europe, Asia, North and South America, Africa or Oceania, the common specter of the disaster we face is more compelling than our differences.

The time for platitudes and greenwashing is past. For too long, the basis for accountability has been too short: Companies valued on the basis of the next quarterly earnings; politicians by the next election; media by ratings and advertising; education by test scores; health by insurance premiums. We need practical answers to compelling questions, answers that are more than Band-aids.

The ability to extrapolate from present circumstances and trends gives us an ability denied to other species. We can see the future and prepare for it. We have the capacity to look at the past and learn from it. We can look around at the many varieties of human experience and select the best and most relevant.

There is a city in Brazil that has made public transport so attractive and easy that the absence of cars in the central area is judged a benefit by most of the population. In Chinese hospitals, families of the ill camp on the grounds and participate in the care. Fed up with excuses about a badly educated citizenry? Headstart demonstrated four decades ago the cost-benefit of bringing children into a supportive, educational environment early.

There are hundreds of towns, even a few cities, that are high on any measure of livability. How do they do it? Ask them. Can we deliver health care and social services efficiently to all? There are hundreds of community health centers that provide excellent primary care at a reasonable cost. How do they do it? Ask them.

When the survivors of Hurricane Katrina visited Holland, they were embarrassed, shocked, and angry to see what serious preparation for flooding looked like.Thirty years ago, Francis Moore Lappé wrote *Diet for a Small Planet*, explaining how starvation and malnutrition were artifacts of bad habits, not necessary consequences of human population.

Every epoch has its challenges. As with those who have gone before, we will be defined and judged by the creativity and diligence with which we craft our response.

If we start with an addiction to maintaining a status quo which gives so much to so few, we should expect a century of despair for the many, and violence for all. Human beings need structure to bridge the gap between mortality and hope. Structure means practical solutions to the issues we face. At the root of any redefinition is the ability to value what gives meaning to life.

The New Village Green is a testament that life endures, even flourishes. It is a compilation of reports from crossroads as new as the internet, old as the paths that lead to community gardens. They stretch from the smallest transactions of micro-enterprise lending in Bangladesh to the struggle for corporate accountability and sustainability in the board rooms of North America, Europe and Asia.

The ties that bind us to each other are either strengthened or weakened by the choices we make as individual and as societies. Do we know the factors that support community, enhance civility, and achieve sustainability? Read this book and find out.

Paul Freundlich is currently Chair, The Stakeholder Council,
The Global Reporting Initiative. He is Founder and President
Emeritus of Co-op America. His novel, Deus ex Machina: What Does Time
Mean to a Pig? *(The Public Press, 2005) explores the possibilities of time travel.*

But, Why Garlic?

Stephen Morris

When it came time to choose a visual symbol for *The New Village Green*, we scarcely hesitated before choosing garlic. Here are a few reasons why:

Garlic is the first green you see in the spring. Even while the crocuses are rubbing their eyes, garlic is pushing its way skyward through the mulch that kept it warm through the winter. Garlic is delightfully quirky. You plant in the fall, harvest in mid-summer, and enjoy all year long.

Garlic is a model of efficiency. The young, green shoots are edible, as are the corkscrew "scapes" that the plant shoots out as it reaches maturity. At a recent workshop I learned that the root tendrils from freshly picked garlic are highly prized by knowledgeable chefs.

You can cook garlic nearly every way, from the frying pan to the grill. The classic start to nearly everything I cook is garlic cooked to translucent perfection in olive oil. You would be amazed what you can elevate on the culinary scale with this bodacious beginning.

Garlic has powerful, slightly mysterious medicinal qualities. On one hand it boosts the immune system, and yet it is also a pest deterrent both in the garden as well as on the body. Eat raw garlic and you will not have to worry much about mosquito bites. Or vampires.

But you may not have to worry about being kissed, either. Garlic, especially eaten raw, produces notoriously malodorous breath that is undetectable by other garlic eaters. Ironically, the clove's sulphurous compounds are released only when it is crushed.

Human beings are the only species in the natural world that eats garlic. That tells you something, but I'm not sure what.

Garlic is a most sensuous creation. Its shape evokes the graceful curves of the female anatomy, and it is covered by layers of delicate skin that peel away like filmy negligee. Ooo-la-la.

And finally, garlic is not afraid to be controversial. Throughout history cultures have either violently opposed it (Victorian England) or ardently embraced it (Native Americans).

We know which side we are on.

You'll find garlic lore and legend in tasty factoids throughout the world of *The New Village Green*. It's our vegetable of default. Why have white space when you can learn something new about one of nature's most intriguing creations ... garlic! Garlic information was provided by Zel and Reuben Allen, publishers of *Vegetarians in Paradise*, a monthly internet magazine (vegparadise.com).

foreword
The New Village People

Frances Moore Lappé is the author of fifteen books, including the 1971 best-seller, *Diet for a Small Planet*. A graduate of Earlham College and past recipient of the Rachel Carson Award from the National Nutritional Foods Association, her most recent work, *Democracy's Edge: Choosing to Save our Country by Bringing Democracy to Life* completes a trilogy which includes the 30th anniversary sequel to *Diet,* and *Hope's Edge*, co-written with her daughter Anna.

Currently Lappé and her daughter Anna lead the Small Planet Institute, based in Cambridge, Massachusetts. The Institute's purpose is to help define, articulate, and further an historic transition: a worldwide shift from the dominant, failing notion of democracy as a set of fixed institutions toward democracy as a way of life, a culture in which the values of inclusion, fairness and mutual accountability infuse all dimensions of public life.

foreword
The New Village Library

The New Village Green is a collecting place for ideas, and ideas are most concisely and eloquently formalized in books. The Village Library is where we highlight some of our favorite books.

Diet for a Small Planet (20th Anniversary Edition). Ballantine Books, 1992

Hope's Edge: The Next Diet for a Small Planet (20th Anniversary Edition). Tarcher, 2003

Democracy's Edge: Choosing to Save our Country by Bringing Democracy to Life. Jossey-Bass, 2005.

1 THE GAIA HYPOTHESIS

"Although nothing we do will destroy life on Earth, we could change the environment to a point where civilization is threatened. Sometime in this or the next century we may see this happen because of climate change and a rise in the level of the sea. If we go on burning fossil fuel at the present rate it is probable that all of the cities of the world now at sea level will be flooded.**"**

— James Lovelock

The penny dropped for atmospheric scientist James Lovelock in the mid-1960s upon viewing the first pictures of the planet Earth taken from outer space. The Earth is not an orb of inert minerals inhabited by a few living organisms. The Earth is a living organism with all its components connected through a bewildering but awe-inspiring series of interwebbed connections.

The Gaia Theory, articulated in a series of books and articles by Lovelock over the next four decades, often in collaboration with widely respected biologist Lynn Margulis, is either the breakthrough perception of our time or, as critic Massimo Pigliucci describes it in *The Skeptical Inquirer*, "a hopeless mix of pseudoscience, bad science, and mysticism."

The hypothesis, named for the Greek goddess of Earth, was new enough and dramatic enough that even Lovelock admits that for the first ten years after the penny dropped he could not explain it. Over time and through repeated iterations of articulation, however, it has evolved into a theory, still controversial, but credible enough to frame important debates such as the one currently raging over global warming.

The relevance of Gaia is this: If the Earth is a living organism, then it will behave as one and will seek to maintain stasis or balance. As expressed by Lovelock, "The Earth is a self-regulating system made up from the totality of organisms, the surface rocks, the ocean and the atmosphere tightly coupled as an evolving system." Accordingly, the planet will "regulate surface conditions so as always to be as favorable as possible for contemporary life."

Space exploration has been minimal in the forty-odd years since Lovelock's initial observation, but Gaia Theory has migrated from the lunatic fringe to the borderline mainstream. Half a century ... that's about right as a time frame for a revolutionary new idea to gain acceptance. As we learn more about "what man hath wrought" in his creation of the circumstances that have led to the creation of the condition known as global warming, the only certainty is that the answer for "un-wroughting," if it is even possible (Lovelock himself thinks we are beyond the limits), will come from a deeper understanding of Gaia.

James Ephraim Lovelock was born July 26, 1919 in Letchworth Garden City, England, and studied chemistry at the University of Manchester and medicine at the London School of Hygiene and Tropical Medicine. A lifelong inventor, Lovelock has created and developed many scientific instruments, some of which have been adopted by NASA in its program of planetary exploration. It was while working for NASA that Lovelock developed the Gaia Hypothesis.

Lovelock developed sensitive instruments for the analysis of extraterrestrial atmospheres and planetary surfaces for NASA's Viking program that visited Mars in the late 1970s, motivated in part by the wish to determine whether Mars supported life. During work towards this program, Lovelock became interested in the composition of the Martian atmosphere, reasoning that many life forms on Mars would be obliged to make use of it (and thus alter it). However, the atmosphere was found to be in a stable condition close to its chemical equilibrium, with very little oxygen, methane, or hydrogen, but with an overwhelming abundance of carbon dioxide.

To Lovelock, the stark contrast between the Martian atmosphere and the chemically dynamic mixture of our Earth's biosphere was strongly indicative of the absence of life on the planet. However, when they were finally launched to Mars, the Viking probes still searched for life there.

Lovelock invented the Electron Capture Detector, which ultimately assisted in discoveries about the persistence of CFCs and their role in stratospheric ozone depletion. He is also credited with invention of the microwave oven.

Lovelock was elected a Fellow of the Royal Society in 1974, and in 1990 was awarded the first Dr A.H. Heineken Prize for the Environment by the Royal Netherlands Academy of Arts and Sciences. An independent scientist, inventor, and author, Lovelock works out of a barn-turned-laboratory in Cornwall. In 2003 he was appointed a Companion of Honour (CH) by Queen Elizabeth II.

Zoe Weil is the author of *The Power and Promise of Humane Education* and *Above All, Be Kind: Raising a Humane Child in Challenging Times*. This is an excerpt.

Above All, Be Kind
by Zoe Weil

Mahatma Gandhi was once asked by a reporter, "What is your message?" He answered, "My life is my message." When I first heard about this response, I was struck by its truth and universality. I realized that my life was my message, too, and that nothing I said mattered very much if I wasn't making sure that my life reflected my values. Gandhi had been a hero of mine for many years. His courage, self-discipline, and compassion had always been profoundly inspirational to me, yet the simple words "My life is my message" have become more significant to me as a guide for humane living than any of his heroic acts or compelling speeches. These five words are also terribly humbling. When I make an inhumane choice or treat someone with disrespect, I hear the echo of Gandhi's words and realize that my life is not always the message I want it to be.

Expanding Humane Values To Include Everyone

Below are some choices that we each make that can have an impact not only on ourselves and our children but also on others outside of our family:

- Choices about what our family wears
- Choices about what our family eats
- Choices about what kinds of entertainments we choose
- Choices about our vehicle(s)
- Choices about our homes, furniture, remodeling, and household repairs
- Choices about toys
- Choices about personal care and cleaning products

Hearing that these choices affect others, however, doesn't really help us make kinder decisions. In order to make humane choices, we need knowledge that most of us just don't have. We simply can't tell whether any given production process caused harm to someone far away from us unless we have information that is not generally offered to us on product labels. For example, unless a product label clearly states that during the production process, no sweatshop labor was used, no animals were caused to suffer, and no environmental pollution took place, we cannot know who or what might have been harmed. It's beyond the scope of this book, however, to provide the detailed information each of us would need to make the most compassionate choices. Instead, this chapter will teach you how to use the Four Elements described in Chapter 2 as a method to assess any choice.

Steps To Using The Four Elements

1. GATHER INFORMATION. In order to use the Four Elements yourself, consider the list of choices introduced above (under Expanding Humane Values to Include Everyone, page 57). Do you have a feeling that some of your choices in these different categories could be kinder? Are there areas where you sense that a little more information would help you make more compassionate decisions? Have you heard or seen anything that calls into question any particular choices? Has reading any of the "Did you know?" boxes made you aware of the effects of a choice that you hadn't thought about before? If your answer to any of these questions is "yes," then you already know some of what you need to learn. In addition to more information about the issues raised in the boxes, the Resources at the end of this book also offer reading suggestions, names of organizations, and web addresses. As you recognize areas where you could use more information, you'll probably be able to find a resource to help get you started.

2. THINK CRITICALLY. As you gather information, make sure to expose yourself to a variety of points of view in order to think critically and deeply. You can endeavor to obtain knowledge from reliable sources so that you are confident that your opinions are based on accurate and trustworthy information. Learning about different perspectives and struggling to sort through conflicting opinions will help you to become ever wiser.

3. USE THE THREE RS. The three Rs can be the guiding principles in your process of choice-making. By nurturing your reverence, you will be ever more prepared to respect others and take responsibility for your choices. As you seriously consider the effects of your choices, you will find that your reverence (for loved ones, for yourself, for people worldwide, for the Earth, and for other species) often inspires you to make more respectful and responsible decisions. Getting outdoors into nature, reading a biography about an inspiring historical figure, attending religious services, gathering with people whose company supports and nourishes you, creating rituals around meaningful holidays or events, or even making a habit of spending a few minutes simply watching your sleeping children can all nurture your reverence and deepen your respect for and sense of responsibility towards all that you love. But you need not rely solely upon reverence to determine whether or not you will be respectful and responsible. You can also rely upon your commitment to values of justice and fairness to help you make the most respectful and responsible decisions.

4. MAKE POSITIVE CHOICES. After you have considered the information you've gathered and used the three Rs as your guide, you can ask yourself, "What choice will be kindest?" While none of us will always make the most humane choices, good decisions will flow naturally from the first three elements. Although we will inevitably fail to live up to our own deepest values all the time, the best way to consistently make kind choices is to stay mindful. Choosing to be humane means lifting up the veil of denial each time it falls between our most enduring wish to do good and our most eager efforts to avoid fear or struggle. It is when we are willing to look at the destruction we have caused and continue to cause that we can choose to restore and repair. Sometimes the competing impulses may be too strong to outweigh your desire to be more humane, but the more you pause and consider your choices, the more often you will choose the one that is ultimately the most kind. As your choices change, your life will become ever more the message you want it to be.

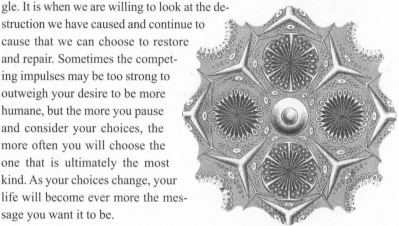

Calcareous sponge

Some love it — some hate it! Countless disciples praise its merits, while its denigrators reject it in disgust. Poor, innocent garlic has been the victim of a love/hate relationship throughout history.

While one person wrinkles his nose up at the mere thought of consuming an offensive smelling food like garlic, others praise its mystical healing powers. Henri Leclerc, a French writer who publicly scorned the herb, referred to garlic as *rose puante*, French for stinking rose, in a 1918 magazine article. In support of garlic, the ancient Egyptian medical papyri, *Codex Elsers*, dated about 1500 BCE, contained 22 formulas for medicinal remedies prescribing garlic as a cure for heart disease, worms, and tumors. The Egyptian remedies may have actually originated as early as 3500 BCE, before written forms existed.

Sine Quammen Non

David Roberts interviews David Quammen

Though we do not, alas, live in the kind of world where science writers become celebrities, David Quammen has developed an unusually devoted fan base. As a young man he aspired to write fiction, and that sensibility remains evident in science writing that reads like literature – humane, absorbing, occasionally thrilling. His "Natural Acts" column for *Outside* magazine, which ran from 1981 to 1995, yielded two National Magazine Awards and a Guggenheim Fellowship, and more awards awaited the series of critically and popularly lauded full-length books that came after.

The latest focus of Quammen's careful attention is Charles Darwin, father of modern biology and source of an idea so radical its implications are still only imperfectly understood: evolution by natural selection. Rather than the extensively covered journey aboard the Beagle, Quammen's *The Reluctant Mr. Darwin* tracks the naturalist's life through the 20 years afterward – 20 years when he kept his explosive idea under wraps, pondering when and how to release it to the world.

Since Quammen passed through town as we were putting together *Grist*'s God & the Environment series, I chose to push him into areas of religious, philosophical, and sociological speculation. The soft-spoken writer answered carefully.

QUESTION: *What do you think environmentalists have to learn from Darwinian evolution?*

ANSWER: If environmentalists are responsible for leading the fight to preserve species, to stave off the sixth great extinction, to prevent habitats from being chopped up into tiny pieces that can't support viable populations, then they need to understand how evolution functions – the importance of variation within populations, the amount of time it takes to create biological diversity, the necessity of habitat diversity to create species. Anybody who's arguing with the general public and politicians about things going extinct needs to understand where biological diversity, complexity, and adaptation come from, and how slow the process is, and how many of the things we're doing on this planet prevent further evolution, further speciation, from ever happening.

Is there a problem with someone who does not believe in evolution for religious reasons joining the environmental movement?

No. We need all the allies we can get. I don't think we can afford to say, oh, we don't want you guys helping to save this batch of habitat or stop this dam because you don't believe in evolution. If they believe that every species was created instantaneously, from scratch, in its current form, by a busy, interventionist God, and they believe that therefore it's wrong for humans to eliminate any of those God-made species, then let's set our differences aside, at least for the sake of political tactics, and work with them. Leave the arguing about where those species come from for later.

But if they say, the price for working with you is that we want intelligent design taught in science curricula, then it's a deal breaker. Nope, sorry. That cannot come into the science curricula of our public schools, because it's not science. Teach it in comparative religion, along with Buddhism, Christianity, Islam, Zoroastrianism, and the belief that the Earth is supported on four big elephants that stand on the back of a giant turtle.

A religious environmentalist might say, you have science on your side, but what I have is a reason to prevent species loss: God has imbued all creatures with value and given me dominion over them. From your perspective, there's just a meaningless pageant of one change after another. Why does any of it matter?

That is a wise question for them to ask. Why should we care? It's a question I've been dealing with since I published an earlier book, *The Song of the Dodo*, about extinctions.

People who instinctively care about these things have to realize that the question doesn't have any obvious or easy answer. Our first incentive to prevent those extinctions is an instinctive, irrational one: we care about these things ourselves. We find inherent value in them. But you can't transfer that value to other people. It's not necessarily persuasive.

You have to think carefully, and craft arguments realistically, as to what is lost if we lose biological diversity on the planet. Part of the argument is anthropocentric: it comes back to harm us physically. We lose ecosystem services essential to the health of the human population. We lose the possibilities of applications for medical and other utilitarian purposes.

But we have to realize that those arguments only go so far, and some of them are double-edged. If we're going to save such-and-such tree in the rainforest mainly because it produces some sort of medicine for humans, fine for now, but what happens when they discover a way to synthesize that medicine in the laboratory much more cheaply than they can grow it in the Amazon? You lose that argument abruptly.

Having realized the limitations on pragmatic arguments, we have to go beyond that, immediately and routinely, and argue that one of the main reasons we shouldn't eliminate half the biological diversity on this planet is that the universe will be a whole lot uglier, more boring, and more lonely. That's not as much a tangible argument, but we need to make it tangible.

Darwin himself famously lost faith over the years. Was it your sense that his discoveries and thoughts on biology drove the loss of faith? How much of a relation do you think there was?

I think it was two things, closely related.

He was very rational, careful, orderly thinker. He discovered the older he got, the more he wanted his convictions to be grounded in observable evidence. You could say he was a materialist by disposition. As he got older, that disposition put him in conflict with a lot of conventional beliefs. Specifically, there was this question of where diversity comes from, and the closer he looked at it, the more he realized there was a very logical, economical explanation that involved only physical causes. It satisfied him very much and conflicted completely with the conventional explanation. So that pushed him away from conventional religion.

Then there was the death of his father, followed by the death of his daughter, Annie. The second in particular completely soured him on the notion that the universe was ruled by a God who determined all things, who had all power, and preferred the good, yet would allow for irrational, inexplicable evil such as the suffering of innocents. That was more on the emotional side than the intellectual side.

Those two things converged, and he was done with Christianity.

Do you think that evolution is incompatible with Christianity?

Evolution? No. Darwinian evolution? Yes.

Darwin believed the variations within populations that natural selection works on are undirected – essentially random. Not random in the sense that they have no causes; random in the sense that whatever causes them – and he didn't know – is independent of adaptive needs.

Random variations worked on by natural selection – I think that's incompatible with the idea of evolution guided by God. It's not incompatible with the idea of the existence of God. It's not incompatible with the idea that God created the universe and set it in motion. But I think it is incompatible with the idea embraced by theistic evolutionists that God used evolution as a way of accomplishing His design. The design part is completely contradictory to the random variation part.

I also think [Darwinian evolution] is incompatible with the idea that, as humans evolved from other primates, at a certain point God reached down and went "Bing!" and put in an immortal soul which has capacities and responsibilities completely different from what you might find in a chimpanzee.

But I know that not everybody sees it that way, even some people who've thought about it pretty carefully.

What do you think about the popular notion that physical evolution of humankind has been overtaken by intellectual or spiritual evolution, or mimetic evolution, or cultural evolution, or what have you?

That's mostly true. Most evolution now is cultural evolution, for humans. But I doubt that it's completely true – it's almost impossible that it be completely true. Whenever you have excess reproduction and differential survival, you have changes of gene frequency in populations, and therefore you have evolution.

I would say, at risk of saying something that has me apologizing like the Pope or the president of Harvard, that evolution must be occurring, and that the way to detect the direction of it would be to look at the people who have the greatest reproductive success. Who on this planet has the greatest reproductive success? It probably is not educated people in North America, who tend to limit their reproduction to 2.1 kids. It's probably people in the tropics who have little access to education, little access to family planning techniques and information, and who are in some cases still having six and eight kids. That's reproductive success.

So, it might be that evolution is still occurring among the human species, and making the human species incrementally better capable of living in impoverished conditions in the tropics. Maybe we're gradually acquiring some increased resistance to malaria. Maybe we're gradually acquiring some sort of increased resistance to all sorts of intestinal parasites you're afflicted with if you don't have access to clean water. People who live under those circumstances and still have nine kids, of whom six survive, are the reproductively successful individuals of our global population.

[Physical] evolution is happening – with the understanding that evolution doesn't make a particular species better or smarter, necessarily, just better attuned to whatever circumstances it's living in. That's my guess.

Polls still show that half of Americans, more than half in some polls, reject evolution. Do you ever see that changing?

It's an American thing. Actually, it's an American and a Turkish thing. There's an article just published in *New Scientist* that assembled poll data from 34 countries – 32 European countries plus the US and Japan. They were ranked from one to 34 in terms of acceptance of evolution. Number one was Iceland, then Denmark, France, Germany, Sweden, Japan, Britain ... 33 was US, 34 was Turkey. Latvia, Bulgaria, Romania – much more acceptance of evolution than in the US or in Turkey. And Turkey has an Islamist creationist movement of some force.

What do you make of that? Why the US?

We're a country that was founded by religious cranks. Maybe that's part of it.

But even they were less religious than we are now.

The Jeffersonian founding fathers were less religious, but the group that came before them – the Jamestown wave, the Mayflower wave – they were religious cranks.

That's only a half-serious answer, at most. I don't know. It's mysterious. There was a lot of resistance in this country to Darwinian ideas when they first came out, and then some biologists got on board. There was another wave of resistance around the time of the Scopes trial, and then it settled down. Then there was another wave of resistance in the late 60s with old-fashioned creationism, and that was essentially turned back by legal decisions like *Edwards v. Aguillard*, in the Supreme Court. Then came intelligent design.

There's a political element, too, no?

Yeah, it's part of a political agenda of the Christian right to undermine the teaching of evolution – to undermine, therefore, a leftist, materialist, godless, merely science-based drift into social relativism. It's all connected. It's as much a political movement as a scientific movement.

It's also something else too – part of the American character, if there is such a thing – and that is an eagerness to tell the experts, "Well, no. Screw you."

David Quammen's writings have appeared in *National Geographic, Outside, Harper's, Rolling Stone*, and *The New York Times Book Review*. Born in Cincinnati, he was drawn to Montana in the early 1970s by the trout fishing. He studied literature at Yale and as a Rhodes Scholar at Oxford, concentrating on the works of William Faulkner.

Nudibranch

David Roberts is staff writer for *Grist*.
Reprinted by permission from *Grist* (www.grist.org). For more environmental news and commentary sign up for *Grist*'s free email, www.grist.org/signup/.

Before the era of pharmaceuticals, beginning in the late 1800s, foods and herbs were the common health remedies. Herbalists through the ages compiled texts listing numerous plant foods and herbs they prescribed even for matters of life and death. People understood the value of garlic and its cousins in maintaining their vigor and curing their ills.

Jessica Prentice is a professional chef and a passionate home cook who seeks to help us find ways to feed ourselves that are satisfying and health-supportive on all levels: delicious, environmentally responsible, and grounded in the nourishing traditions of our forebears.

New Corn Moon
August moondark kitchen notes
by Jessica Prentice

Happy Corn Moon! [In August] we move into the lunar cycle known as The Corn Moon in the old Celtic calendar. It is the time of year when grain is ripening in the fields, readying for harvest. Throughout much of the United States the plant *zea mays* is being harvested and Americans are enjoying plenty of their beloved sweet corn.

I have been able to witness this abundance of corn in many states as I've been traveling. I've eaten ears of it raw out in cornfields near Madison, Wisconsin and the Twin Cities in Minnesota. I've demo'd one of my corn-rich seasonal recipes – calabacitas – more times than I can count: at farm festivals, in farmers' markets, in food co-op teaching kitchens, and even on television. And I'm not done yet! I'm squeezing the most I possibly can out of this corn season. . .

Many people across America are looking at corn a bit more critically this year than they have before – thanks to Michael Pollan turning his probing journalistic eye onto the plant in his popular new book, *The Omnivore's Dilemma*. Of course it's not the plant itself that he is critical of, it is our relationship to it in our modern society. It is a story that badly needed to be told.

I have to admit that in the first few months after the release of *The Omnivore's Dilemma*, I developed a mild case of adolescent resentment against the book. Our books came out within a few weeks of each other's, and his was instantly on the New York Times Bestseller List. What this meant was that – as my publisher put it – Pollan's book "sucked up all the oxygen" around food issues for a number of months. His was the book that everyone who was interested in food and sustainability was reading; excerpts from it were the cover stories in all the alternative magazines; and he was the person everyone in the media wanted to interview about food.

In the long run this explosion of interest is a really great thing – for all of us who care about transforming the food system and even for the rest of us writers who have something important to say about it. The American consciousness is being raised once again about the many failures of our current approach to feeding ourselves. And hopefully, people will want to continue to educate themselves about how they can make choices that will support the transformation that needs to happen, and will pick up one of the many other wonderful books that are out there on the subject – including mine!

But for the past few months of traveling around promoting MY book, I have to admit that there were times when if one more person asked me – as I was trying to get them excited about *Full Moon Feast* – whether I had heard of a book called, perhaps "the carnivore's dilemma" or "the omnivore's delight" or a writer named – maybe – "Michael Pollard," I thought I would scream. The scream would go something like this: YES OF COURSE I HAVE – I'VE HEARD ABOUT NOTHING ELSE FOR MONTHS!!!!! CAN WE PLEASE TALK ABOUT MY BOOK FOR JUST ONE TEENY TINY MINUTE?

But most of that resentment melted away as I began to actually read Pollan's book. It is a wonderful and important work of journalism that gets down to the nitty-gritty of the food issues that we're struggling with in this society. Except for the issue of traditional fats, I agree with Pollan on just about everything. And I have learned a great deal that is new to me, and gained fresh insights into many aspects of the food system that I thought I knew well, including corn. Pollan shines a sharp spotlight on a food system that masquerades as a diverse horn of plenty, and reveals an insidious monoculture instead.

It is a monoculture of corn.

Corn seems such a sweet, innocent and appealing symbol of American agrarian life. Steaming hot, dripping with butter, corn on the cob promises pleasure, and something beyond pleasure too – a sense of well-being and right-relation, a connectedness to the earth and the season and the history of this continent and its peoples.

How strange that something so redolent of everything I do believe in should also reek of everything that drives me crazy about the state of food in America. How ironic that this most promiscuous of plants, which cross pollinates readily and easily to produce an endless array of variations in color and sweetness and starch should be reduced to a few bioengineered hybrids planted in monocultural fields.

Pollan points out that the government-subsidized glut of conventional corn has made its way into nearly every processed food we eat in America. It is the basis for sodas, cereals, and even for the milk, eggs, and meat products we eat – which come from animals fed a diet made up largely of the excess cheap corn we grow in the Midwest. Pollan discusses isotope tests done on Americans to see what plants are at the bottom of the food chain we consume. The tests look at the proportion of carbons in our flesh, and carbon 13 (C-13) is an indicator of a preponderance of corn. Pollan points out that the people of Mexico have long identified themselves with corn:

Descendents of the Maya living in Mexico still sometimes refer to themselves as "the corn people." The phrase is not intended as metaphor. Rather, it's meant to acknowledge their abiding dependence on this miraculous grass, the staple of their diet for almost nine thousand years. Forty percent of the calories a Mexican eats in a day comes directly from corn, most of it in the form of tortillas. So when a Mexican says "I am maize" or "corn walking," it is simply a statement of fact: The very substance of the Mexican's body is to a considerable extent a manifestation of this plant.

Very interestingly, the isotope tests tell a different story:

One would expect to find a comparatively high proportion of carbon 13 in the flesh of people whose staple food of choice is corn – Mexicans, most famously. Americans eat much more wheat than corn – 114 pounds of wheat flour per person per year, compared to 11 pounds of corn flour. . . But carbon 13 doesn't lie, and researchers who have compared the isotopes in the flesh or hair of North Americans to those in the same tissues of Mexicans report that it is now we in the North who are the true people of corn. "When you look at the isotope ratios," Todd Dawson, a Berkeley biologist who's done this sort of research, told me, "we North Americans look like corn chips with legs." Compared to us, Mexicans today consume a far more varied carbon diet: the animals they eat still eat grass (until recently, Mexicans regarded feeding corn to livestock as a sacrilege): much of their protein comes from legumes; and they still sweeten their beverages with cane sugar.

So that's us: processed corn, walking.

Ever since reading that, I can't seem to get the phrase out of my head: "processed corn, walking."

I don't necessarily believe that human beings need to eat a varied diet, despite the fact that this is virtually a sacrosanct concept in nutritional circles. A look at healthy traditional diets will show that the diet was often limited to a few staple foods – especially in Northern climes that supported a smaller array of plants and animals. Many pastoralist peoples consumed half of their daily calories or more in the form of dairy products alone.

But when you look at the plants that were at the bottom of the food chain in these limited traditional diets (which is what you do in an isotope test) you begin to see how nature's biodiversity is at the base of even a very limited traditional diet. Pasturelands are not a monoculture at all, but an incredible polyculture of grasses, clovers, weeds, herbs and other plants. Traditionally, hay for winter animal feed was simply the dried cut form of this same diverse polyculture. Similarly, the plant life of the oceans that was at the bottom of the food chain for peoples who depended largely on seafoods for sustenance was also made up of an amazing array of different species. And hunters who depended on buffalo or other game were also ultimately drawing their food from an extensive polyculture of wild plants that wild grazers and browsers feasted on.

So even if traditional diets don't support the notion that humans need to "eat a variety," I believe they absolutely do show that our diets should still be built on biodiversity, and not based to any great extent on any one plant species. How strange that the American diet, which seems on the surface to be so incredibly varied, is just hybrid corn dressed up to look like a thousand different foods; and that a traditional diet such as the Norse one, which looks like milk and meat and then more milk and meat, would actually be made up of incredible biodiversity at root.

I love unexpected and surprising revelations like that. Another one that may be new to many people who read Pollan's book is that grazing pastures in a well-managed system actually increases the biodiversity of plant life in those grasslands. The relationship between grazers and pastures is a synergistic one – as cattle, bison, or other animals browse the grasses they allow sunlight to reach a greater variety of species, thereby encouraging them to thrive – not to mention fertilizing them with their manure. Without grazers, pastures can tend to be dominated by a few more aggressive species, or can become depleted of nutrients.

I love the idea that biodiversity is an essential truth in the way that nature works. It is science's way of saying: "It takes all kinds." I find that the older I get, the more I cherish and value diversity – the wonderful diversity of human cultures on planet Earth (what ethnobotanist Wade Davis calls "the ethnosphere"), the limitless, still uncharted biodiversity of plant and animal life in nature ("the biosphere"), and of course all the different ways life is expressed through each individual organism.

I spent some time recently with a woman who has worked for the Kinsey Institute in Indiana, where the legacy of American sex researcher Dr. Alfred Kinsey is being kept alive. She reminded me that Kinsey was – by training – a biologist, and that his work on sexuality came out of his understanding that life expresses itself through variation and diversity. He knew that our sexual and gender identities couldn't be adequately represented in the oppressive monoculture that was 1950s America – a monoculture that despite Kinsey's very important work and the sexual revolution – is still very much with us today. Our notions of sexuality and gender are still pretty binary: a person is either male or female, straight or gay.

But I don't think life on Earth can be adequately expressed in these simple dualisms, and I think it is crucial that we begin to deepen our appreciation for diversity and its importance for life on earth. It will help us understand what is so tragic about being "processed corn, walking"; it will help us appreciate what is so miraculous about well-managed pasture grazing; it will help us to preserve the wisdom and gifts of the vanishing indigenous cultures of the world; it will help us appreciate a diversity of writers' voices on an issue as important as food; it will help us see beyond our prejudices about race, gender, and sexual orientation.

On the Corn Moon, I give great thanks for variety – it is not only the spice of life, it is the very nature of life.

Ammonite

Lynn Margulis is a biologist and Professor at the University of Massachusetts Amherst. She is best known for her theory on the origin of eukaryotic organelles, now generally accepted but initially heavily rejected. Weathering constant criticism of her ideas for decades, Margulis is famous for her clarity and tenacity.

The Germs of Life
by Lynn Margulis and Emily Case

Watch TV for an hour. Flip through a mainstream magazine. Peruse personal hygiene or cleaning products in a store. You'll feel the need to defend yourself with antibacterial soaps and cleaning agents, even antimicrobial pillows and socks. Fear of bacteria has reached a feverish pitch recently, thanks in large part to the work of ever-industrious advertisers.

In our efforts to eliminate these "germs" we have had devastating effects – not on the bacteria, but on ourselves.

The bacteria that now pose the greatest threats to humans are products of our own making. The evolution of pests and pathogens resistant to human poisons has a long, well-documented history. Hospitals, where antibacterial drugs, soaps, and cleaners are used in volume, are hotbeds of antibiotic-resistant strains of bacteria. Farmers feed livestock excessive amounts of antibiotics, thereby selecting for bacteria that are resistant to those medicines – versions of which are also used for humans.

But our xenophobia also blinds us to a more fundamental insight: the health of our environment, and our bodies, depends on bacterial communities. Indeed, they are responsible, as ancestors, for our very existence.

If Life had a yearbook, bacteria would win all of the awards, especially "most likely to succeed." A bacterium is an organism made up of one or more small prokaryotic cells, those that have DNA genes but lack nuclei and chromosomes. Bacteria inhabit the farthest reaches of the biosphere. They live in the hottest, coldest, deepest, saltiest, and most acidic environments. They are the most ancient life-form, having lived on Earth for at least 3.8 billion years, over 80 percent of its history. By contrast, humans have occupied a narrow range of environmental conditions – and for only about 0.003 percent of the Earth's existence. If we even made it into the yearbook, the caption would have read "photo not available."

Earth's environment is in large part the product of bacterial metabolism. Bacterial nitrogen fixation enriches the soil at no cost to us. And the photosynthesis that excretes oxygen and makes food for all life is carried out by the blue-green bacteria called cyanobacteria – both the free-living kind and those that became chloroplasts in the cells of algae and plants. These are just two of bacteria's life-sustaining processes, invented at least 2 billion years ago. We should view them as the wisdom of the ancients.

Even disease-causing bacteria – exceedingly rare despite the fear-mongering of marketers – play a part in ecological health. Anthrax spores, for example, float in the dust of over-eaten and sun-exposed fields, enter the lungs and blood of vulnerable or weak grazers, and kill them. Fields recover their vegetation. The grazers' food supply is spared, the stability of the ecosystem restored.

Bacteria also sustain us on a very local, intimate scale. They produce necessary vitamins inside our guts. Babies rely on milk, food, and finger-sucking to populate their intestines with bacteria essential for healthy digestion. And microbial communities thrive in the external orifices (mouth, ears, anus, vagina) of mammals, in ways that enhance metabolism, block opportunistic infection, ensure stable digestive patterns, maintain healthy immune systems, and accelerate healing after injury. When these communities are depleted, as might occur from the use of antibacterial soap, mouthwash, or douching, certain potentially pathogenic fungi – like Candida or vaginal yeast disorders – can begin to grow profusely on our dead and dying cells. Self-centered antiseptic paranoia, not the bacteria, is our enemy here.

But in our ignorance, we also miss a larger lesson. Bacteria offer us evidence that health depends on community, and independence is an ecological impossibility. Whenever we treat isolated medical symptoms or live socially or physically isolated lives, we ignore warnings from our more successful planetmates.

Bacteria in their natural environments live in well-structured communities based on reciprocity. As one type excretes acid, sugar, or oxygen, its wastes become food or gas for others. And these communities are ecologically sensitive. Bacteria change form and metabolism in response to environmental cues like dryness or heat. Many multicellular bacteria (such as those made of long filaments of cells) revert to single cells in the laboratory. But in the richness of their normal habitat, from pond water to tongues, they transform back into their long chains.

The bacterial propensity to live in ecological communities has also left its mark in the cells of all larger life. Protoctists (like algae or ciliates) and fungi (like yeasts or molds) – not to mention plants and animals – are all nucleated-cell organisms; their cells contain nuclei that divide by mitosis, a complex dance of chromosomes. As research from our lab and others has proved, nucleated-cell organisms could not have evolved without the multimillion-year-old permanent mergers of specific bacteria. Cellular respiration, for example, the process that releases energy from food, occurs in the cell's mitochondria. Mitochondria were once independent bacteria that attacked, or were engulfed by, an early protist.

More recently, some of us have studied what we think is another historic incorporation of bacteria. This one involves the wily bacteria known as spirochetes, including one that we suspect is an ancestor of all of us nucleated-cell organisms. By new molecular biology techniques we expect to prove that an ancient spirochete fused with another very different bacterium, and that the result was that certain free-swimming spirochetes contributed remnants of their lithe, snaky bodies to become moving components of cells. These parts include the familiar waving hairs called cilia, and the tubules of the mitotic spindle, which moves chromosomes so that cells divide equally.

But an even later consequence of the hypothetical merger evidently extends to sensory tissues. In mammals, the cells of the tongue's taste buds, the inner-ear cells required for hearing, and light-sensitive cells in the retina of the eye all have traceable, peculiar features in common. Even cells of the semicircular "canal-balance organ," the stimulus-receiver that tells us whether we are on our feet or upside down, share the detailed features we interpret as clues to their origin.

The salient feature is that these cells have the hairlike cilia, which sense stimuli like light, touch, or sound. It is widely accepted that these cilia, all composed of skinny tubules arranged in a distinct pattern, evolved from a common ancestor, whose identity remains unknown. Our evidence indicates that it was the ancient spirochete: that in the complex ecology of bacterial communities, the merger happened; and that ultimately out of that merger our sensory apparatus evolved, giving us the basis of our awareness – and by extension our consciousness.

In the symbiotic associations that have persisted, co-habitation ultimately succeeded. Our nucleated-cell ancestors evolved because they could swim, breathe oxygen, eat whole bacteria, and merge. Their success was predicated on an attraction to sugars and each other, struggle, fusion, eventual incorporation, and integration by compromise. Our sensibilities come directly from the world of bacteria. Like all life, we thrive in communities. It's natural that people who have strong social relations prove healthier and longer-lived.

Humans have nonetheless found no shortage of ways to foul communities, cause extinctions, and threaten our own existence in the process. But bacteria wouldn't miss us. They have run the planet for most of its history, and our rush to indiscriminately kill them only reveals our own naïveté. The bacteria, with their complex history and virtuoso performances in energy and food recycling, will easily endure our assault. But our own survival depends on a revolution in human attitudes toward – and ability to learn from – our microbial ancestors.

Trilobite

This article originally appeared in *Orion* and is reprinted by permission. Lynn Margulis, the article's principal author, would like to acknowledge the many people who made the article possible. In addition to coauthor Emily Case, she extends special thanks to Russell Powell of *New England Watershed Magazine* and Celeste Asikainen and Michael Dolan of the Margulis lab.

How Insects Hunker Down for Winter

by Madeline Bodin

Imagine a day in late autumn. The landscape is painted in a palette of grays and browns. You've watched the geese fly south. You know that bears, bats, and woodchucks will soon hibernate.

But where are the insects? Sometimes it seems they disappear with the first chill wind. But insects don't just disappear. They prepare for winter through the fall, and some through the summer, too, just as other animals do.

Maybe because they are so small, or maybe because we are so relieved that they'll soon be gone, insects' preparations for winter usually escape our notice.

Monarch butterflies may be one exception. Monarch butterflies are the insect world's best-known migrants. Their 3,000-mile migration to the Transvolcanic Mountains of Mexico is an epic journey. (Just think what you could do with their frequent-flier miles.)

The Monarch butterflies that flit about in late summer and autumn make the journey from here to Mexico, spend the winter, and in the spring make the first leg of the journey back north. Upon reaching Texas, however, these adults lay eggs and die, leaving the rest of the return trip to subsequent generations. The trip is still considered a true migration because it's a 'round-trip' that all monarchs take part in.

But monarchs are not the only butterflies that travel to escape the cold. The painted lady migration is not as dramatic as the monarch migration, because it does not occur every year and not all painted ladies migrate. Botanists believe that cyclical variations in climate, such as El Nino, may be related to the butterflies' cyclical urge to head south for the winter.

Green darner dragonflies do something similar. Most dragonflies, even most green darners, spend the winter as nymphs (an immature life phase) underwater. But some adult green darner dragonflies head south when strong winds blow from the north. Because it's not organized like the Monarch's and not all individuals take part, the green darner exodus is not considered a true migration.

Mourning cloak butterflies stay close to home, overwintering as adults in the cracks of bark on trees. That's why you may see a mourning cloak butterfly flitting over spring's muddy roads, long before any other butterflies are around. They aren't part of a new generation – they're the remainder of last year's.

Viceroy butterflies, those famous mimicking butterflies that look just like monarchs, don't migrate but rather spend the winter here as caterpillars. In the fall, these caterpillars find a good willow or poplar leaf. The tiny caterpillar rolls itself up in the leaf, binding it to a twig with a strand of silk.

Despite these exceptions, most butterflies – and in fact most insects – spend the winter as eggs. A new year's bugs generally hatch from eggs laid by adult insects the previous summer or autumn. In general, it's a far simpler task for eggs to survive the freezings and thawings of winter then it is for fully formed adults.

But it's the adults that provide the more interesting story. Take the honeybee, the long-term planner of the insect world. Honeybees lay in extra supplies of honey all summer to be used for survival over the winter. The colony stays together in the hive over the winter, with individual bees dining on the stored honey and using that energy to keep warm by shivering.

Our native bumblebees (honeybees are an introduced species) and paper wasps use another tactic to get through our hard winters. In these species, only the queen over-winters. Bumblebee queens spend the winter underground, and paper wasp queens under bits of cracked bark (or in your attic).

Come spring, they emerge, build nests, and lay eggs of sterile workers. In late summer, they lay eggs that turn into fertile males (the first males of the year) and fertile females, who mate and continue the cycle.

These males are members of the "short, happy lives" club, not uncommon in the insect world. They live a few weeks, at most. Their mates are interested in only one thing from them, and it's not mowing the lawn.

Ladybugs, which are beetles, and cluster flies are two more insects that overwinter as adults. These two get our attention because they often try to overwinter in our houses, substituting the chinks in our wooden shelters for the bark cracks they would have used back in their natural surroundings. (Both cluster flies and house-dwelling ladybugs are not native to New Hampshire and Vermont.)

As you look around the gray and brown landscape, the insects aren't really gone. Sure, some have flown south. But there are insect eggs and pupae on twigs, under bark, and under the ground. Larvae are wrapped in leaves or safe underwater. Adults are hidden in sheltered places – under bark, underground, and even in our houses – waiting for spring.

Madeline Bodin is a writer who lives in Andover, Vermont.
Butterfly illustration and insect (previous pages) by
Adelaide Tyrol.

Egyptian tombs may have the oldest visible records of garlic's existence in burial chambers in El Mahasna. Archeologists discovered clay sculptures of garlic bulbs dating about 3700 BCE in one tomb, while paintings of garlic were found in another tomb dating about 3200 BCE.

Egypt's youngest pharaoh, Tutankhamen (1350 BCE), was sent on his journey into the afterlife accompanied with garlic, considered the protector of the soul and guardian of his riches in the afterlife. Archeologists found garlic remnants when poring through many items found in the pyramid. According to a translated papyrus, Ramses II had abundant quantities of garlic sent to the great temples. The Egyptians buried their dead with food offerings that frequently included garlic so their relatives would have sustenance on their journey into the afterlife. Sometimes garlic was employed in the process of mummification.

chapter 1 : The Gaia Hypothesis

Chellis Glendinning lives in the village of Chimayó, New Mexico, where she works for cultural preservation and environmental justice. She is the author of five books, including *My Name Is Chellis and I'm in Recovery from Western Civilization* and *Chiva: A Village Takes on the Global Heroin Trade*.

Off Map Nuggets
by Chellis Glendinning

How to construct a stick/corn/pebble map. We begin with discomfort. It is a discomfort born of having our heads shot through with messy bullet holes in the seventh grade, enhanced by decades of watching television. We do not know the truth. But when the truth is finally revealed, when the voices of the colonized penetrate to our hearts, the discomfort does not subside. It grows. We are transported to a world so fraught with contradiction it is as if we are being pierced by a medieval sword trap.

We are hardly alone. The hallmark of the native experience is the juxtaposition of conflicting worlds. Two languages. Two ways of thinking. Two stories of origin. Two feelings for land. Two legal systems. Two notion of what is human. At the 1993 International Testimonials on the Violation of Indigenous Sovereignty Rights, two political strategy workshops go on at once: one on hard organizing to gain support for sovereignty struggles within the United Nations; the other, equally serious, on creating a kind of parallel-universe indigenous-based United Nations that, no matter the successes or failures of the first effort, gives legitimacy to a reality that is believed but not embodied.

Two worlds. The empire and the conquered. And you and I, here within the empire, after centuries and generations of the certainty of our maps: it is time to reside at the border between worlds that do not mesh.

How to construct a stick/corn/stone map. Gather willow. The borderlands we are charting make no sense at all. And look: the colonized are crossing without us, creating maps we cannot even decipher. Twist husks. Weave them into patterns. Hold everything you find close to your heart.

The border. (Truth and contradiction.) Look. Desert willow bends so easily. Shape it to reflect the currents of our lives and times. Strap corn husks like bandages around the points of connection. The map echoes the scale required: it is tangible; it is of the natural world. The map reveals the space: it is changing. What resides in the background is now bursting forward. (What is central) falls back. (Lies) recede. Things merge reconstitute coincide.

Our maps to the future seem dark and unformed, like a horse at nightfall. One thing we know: we do not want any more of this conquering. Each stone we place onto out handmade maps is a nugget pointing in the direction of our ambition. It is not a known place or destination; rather it is a quality we might take with us on the journey. HUMILITY. Some of the stones are minute boulders of molten rock. RESPECT. Some are flecked with silvery mica. HEALING. Some stones are colored pink and brown like trout in the stream. PASSION. Galaxies of granite, quartz, and turquoise. RESPONSIBILITY. Some are ridged with imprints of ancient shells, revealing that they are survivors of the epoch when the desert was ocean floor. SOVEREIGNTY. Shells and buckskin. The notion bores deeper than the justice it proposes for today's native peoples. It has a universal feel. The empire world cracks open, scatters, breaks up the rocks. How did people live before imperialism? SUSTAINABILITY. Look. Homelands lie beyond the straight-line borders and Latin-Long checkerboards of nation-states. The journey to them promises to sever us from empire's perceptions and dictates. Are we ready to disembark? Ready to move toward a terrain shaped by mountains, demarcated by watersheds, populated by animals and trees, reachable only with clear sight and deep caring?

The journey home severs us from empire's constructions of kings and suction pumps, of linear perspective and kilobits per second microwave. We make our own maps – maps not of parchment or cyberspace, but of twigs and corn husks, of shells and buckskin, of our bodies lying against the reverberations of history. Maps not of destinations, but of directions and currents, of visions and relationships. We place small stones on these maps to remind us of the strengths and awarenesses we must bring to the trek. Look at them carefully, study them, memorize. Take a full breath. Now: leave all the maps behind.

Excerpted from Chellis Glendinning, *Off the Map: An Expeditiuon Deep into Empire and the Global Economy* (New Society, 1999, 2002)

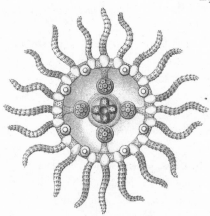

Hydroid polyp

The Gaia Hypothesis:
The New Village People

❝ John Muir said 'If you try to pick one thing out by itself, you find that it's hitched to everything else in the universe.' This sums up the relationship between humans and the environment. John Muir also was the inspiration and impetus behind the National Parks Movement, which has served as a lasting legacy that brings people into contact with nature.

"The Book of Genesis places humans apart from the natural world. The story of the creation where humans would have 'dominion over the fish of the sea, and over the fowl of the air and over the cattle and over all the earth and over every creeping thing that creepeth upon the earth' certainly puts humans in a hierarchical relationship with the environment."

— Elizabeth Courtney
Executive Director, Vermont Natural Resources Council

❝ Different people draw different conclusions from the same events. I've been a pacifist all of my adult life, but it is only in recent years that I have seen clearly the futility of war and violence as a tool of advancing anything but self-destruction. Perhaps it is a function of age, but witnessing the repetition of mistakes (such as seeing Vietnam reprised in Iraq) has crystalized the importance of pacifism for me."

— Spencer Putnam
Executive Director, Vermont Businesses for Social Responsibility

❝ The concept of Earth as spaceship was given substance by the iconic first photo of Earth from space. We have never since been able to think of our relationship to Earth in quite the same way."

— David C. Korten
Author, The Great Turning: From Empire to Earth Community

❝One of the most important ideas to shape the relationship between humans and the environment is the notion of interdependence and interconnections. This 'systems thinking' approach describing our connections to the natural world has been expressed in landmark works, events and developments including: Rachel Carson's *Silent Spring* (1962), the first Earth Day in the US (1970), the World Commission on Environment and Development's *Brundtland Report* (1987), the Montreal Protocol on *Substances that Deplete the Ozone Layer* (1987), the Earth Summits in Rio de Janeiro and Johannesburg (1992, 2002) and the Kyoto Protocol to the United Nations *Framework Convention on Climate Change* (2005)."

— Andres Edwards
Author, The Sustainability Revolution *and Founder, EduTracks*

❝ Lovelock's & Margulis's Gaia Hypothesis got it profoundly right. The atmosphere is a key equilibrium regulator for a living planet and, while humans are still a minor influence compared to other facets of the body of earth, they have the capacity to tamper with atmospheric chemistry without knowing what they are doing. We are just beginning to understand what we have done, and it is entirely possible we are coming to this understanding about half a century too late. Honey, We Killed the Planet."

— Albert Bates
Author, Climate in Crisis: The Greenhouse Effect *and* The Post-Petroleum Survival Guide and Cookbook: Recipes for Changing Times.

" Each and every creature is — not has a relationship to, but is nature — and this, despite a recent history of alienation and domination, includes humans. As Wendell Berry so cogently puts it: we pass through the environment and the environment passes through us. The salmon feeds the bears, the bears feed the forest, the forest feeds the salmon. The Whole is a miracle beyond understanding."

— *Chellis Glendinning*
Author, Off the Map: An expedition deep into Empire and the Global Economy

" Jim Lovelock's Gaia Hypothesis helped us see the Earth as an integrated system which supports life, for the moment, but has no particular investment in humankind.

— *John Elkington*
Author, Cannibals With Forks: The Triple Bottom Line of 21st Century Business

" James Lovelock's Gaia Hypothesis has provided a crucial way of understanding the earth as a living, self-regulating being that gives a scientific and intellectual substructure to environmentalism and shows all who will think about it the only way humans can successfully live on the only living planet in the known universe."

— *Kirkpatrick Sale*
Author, Dwellers in the Land: The Bioregional Vision, *and* The Green Revolution: The American Environmental Movement, 1962-1992.

❝ The most important book is the Bible. Having a true belief and an intimate association with the Bible keeps us all honest. It is a lack of honesty that has contributed to the environmental mess we're in. We are also guilty of naivete. It has been easy to shortchange the environment through the good years, not even knowing we were doing something wrong. Now that problems with weather/economy/health/lifestyles are cropping up, however, average folks are becoming environmentally responsible — used to be just the 'kooks' who carried their own basket into the grocery store and refused bags — now common people are beginning to do it. The idea of environmental accountability is gaining momentum, and that's such a positive thing!"

— Burr Morse
Seventh generation farmer and author of Sweet Days and Beyond:
The Morse Family — Eight Generations of Maple Sugaring

The Gaia Hypothesis:
New Village Library

Sand County Almanac: Outdoor Essays and Reflections, by Aldo Leopold. *Ballantine Books, 1986.*

Sex, Economy, Freedom & Community: Eight Essays, by Wendell Berry. *Pantheon, 1993.*

The Unsettling of America: Culture and Agriculture, by Wendell Berry. *Sierra Club Books, 1986.*

The Collected Poems of Wendell Berry, 1957-1982, by Wendell Berry. *North Point Press, 1987.*

The Wild Muir: Twenty-Two of John Muir's Greatest Adventures, by John Muir, Lee Stetson, and Fiona Key. *Yosemite Association, 1994.*

The Sustainability Revolution: Portrait of a Paradigm Shift, by Andres Edwards. *New Society Publishers, 2005.*

Post-Petroleum Survival Guide and Cookbook: Recipes for Changing Times, by Albert Bates. *New Society Publishers, 2006.*

Human Scale, by Kirkpatrick Sale. *Coward, McCann & Geoghegan, 1980.*

Dwellers in the Land: The Bioregional Vision, by Kirkpatrick Sale. *New Society Publishers, 1991.*

The Great Turning: From Empire to Earth Community, by David Korten. *Berett-Koehler, 2006.*

When Corporations Rule the World, by David Korten. *Kumarian Press, 1996.*

Cannibals with Forks: The Triple Bottom Line of 21st Century Business, by John Elkington. *New Society Publishers, 1998.*

My Name Is Chellis and I'm in Recovery from Western Civilization, by Chellis Glendinning. *Shambhala, 1994.*

The Bible

2 SILENT SPRING

Siphonophore

" *The more clearly we can focus our attention on the wonders and realities of the universe around us, the less taste we shall have for destruction."*

— Rachel Carson

The Roaring Twenties were followed by the Great Depression of the 1930s. Then came the decade of The Greatest Generation, followed by the decade when Everything Went Right, and inevitably, the 1960s when Everything Went Wrong.

The wake up call was delivered by a marine biologist from Pennsylvania to whom fell the task of telling a trusting generation that our institutional faith was dangerously misplaced. That such a message would originate with a non-rabble rousing, non-ax grinding lover of nature is as unexpected as it was dramatic. And beyond ironic is the personal price that Rachel Carson paid. She was diagnosed with breast cancer midway through the writing of Silent Spring and died just two years after its publication.

Institutional distrust is so prevalent today (Did someone say "weapons of mass destruction?"), it can be difficult to recreate the reservoir of faith that existed at the time. We had prevailed in the Great War and our lads returned to unprecedented prosperity. Two terms of a placid presidency under Ike gave way to the excitement of Camelot. We survived the Cuban Missile Crisis, but the jury is still out on whether we have survived Silent Spring.

The publication of *Silent Spring* caused an uproar from the entrenched establishment of chemical companies and regulatory agencies. Science and technology had become synonymous with progress during the era when Everything Went Right. Suddenly the miracle chemicals with the unpronounceable names were no longer the beacons of modernity and prosperity, but rather the threats to life as we knew it.

Rachel Carson singlehandedly delivered a body blow to America ... hopefully, just in time.

Rachel Louise Carson was born May 27, 1907 on a small family farm near Springdale, Pennsylvania. As a child, she learned about ponds, fields, and forests from her mother. She went to college to study English and creative writing, but switched her major to marine biology. Her talent with words helped her to "make animals in the woods or waters, where they live, as alive to others as they are to me." She graduated magna cum laude from the Pennsylvania College for Women, today known as Chatham College, in 1929, then, despite depression era hardships, continued her studies in zoology and genetics at the Johns Hopkins University, earning a master's degree in zoology in 1932.

Carson taught zoology at Johns Hopkins and at the University of Maryland for several years while continuing to work towards her doctoral degree. When family cares made continued studies impossible, she accepted a part-time position at the US Bureau of Fisheries as a science writer working on radio scripts. She next faced and overcame resistance to the then-radical idea of a woman sitting for the Civil Service exam, and outscored all other applicants on the exam. In 1936 she became only the second woman to be hired by the Bureau of Fisheries for a full-time, professional position, as a junior aquatic biologist.

Starting in the mid-1940s, Carson became concerned about the indiscriminate use of newly invented pesticides, especially DDT. "The more I learned about the use of pesticides, the more appalled I became," she later wrote. "What I discovered was that everything which meant most to me as a naturalist was being threatened, and that nothing I could do would be more important." She was captivated by environmental connectedness: although a pesticide is aimed at eliminating one organism, its effects are felt throughout the food chain, and what is intended to snuff an insect ends up poisoning larger animals and humans.

The four-year task of writing *Silent Spring* began with a letter from a close friend of Carson's who owned a bird sanctuary that had been sprayed unmercifully by the government. Could Carson use her influence to begin an investigation into pesticide use? Expecting governmental opposition, Carson considered raising the issue in a popular magazine instead, but publishers were (surprise!) uninterested. Eventually the project became the book we know as *Silent Spring*.

Silent Spring focused generally on the environment, with pesticides receiving Carson's particular attention. The book became known as "Carson's Crusade," and she worked on it until her death from lung cancer on April 14, 1964. *Silent Spring* is often credited with having launched the global environmental movement, and had an immense effect in the United States, where it spurred a reversal in national pesticide policy. Appearing on a CBS documentary about *Silent Spring* shortly before her death, Carson remarked, "Man's attitude toward nature is today critically important simply because we have now acquired a fateful power to alter and destroy nature. But man is a part of nature, and his war against nature is inevitably a war against himself…[We are] challenged as mankind has never been challenged before to prove our maturity and our mastery, not of nature, but of ourselves."

Next Year in the Garden
Famous Last Words
by Stephen Morris

Part I–Spring

Next year in the garden I won't plant my seeds too early just because I am excited by a warm day in April. I will wear a long sleeve shirt while pruning roses, raspberries, and blackberries. I will open seed packets the right way so that they reseal. I won't just rip off the tops, then wonder why my pockets are filled with spilled seed.

Next year in the garden I will read the instructions before planting the seeds. That is, I will read the instructions IF I remember my reading glasses. Gardening is yet one more activity that now requires those damn things.

Next year in the garden I won't read the newspapers as I lay down the mulch, and I will take off my muddy boots before coming into the kitchen.

I won't shout "Ignition!" when I see the first green dots of germination. I won't pump my fist and say "Yes!" when green shoots of garlic poke through the hay. I will take it in stride, with the right stuff of a master gardener.

Next year in the garden I will keep detailed records of what I do, when, and where.

I won't mark planted rows with little sticks and kid myself that I will remember what I planted.

And I won't plant too many zucchini, or too few. I promise.

Part II–Summer

Next year in the garden I won't wander out after showering and changing clothes to admire my work and bend down to pluck just one errant weed, because I've learned that one good weed deserves another.

I won't work with my shirt off, even though it feels so good, because I know the sun is bad for me. I will always put on sun screen (SPF 45) and wear a wide-brimmed hat.

I will make myself smile by singing "Inch by inch, row by row...", and not once will I think about the Dow Jones Industrial Average. I will, however, wonder who the Red Sox will use as a fifth starter and marvel at the ability of David Ortiz to deliver in the clutch.

chapter 2 : Silent Spring

Next year in the garden I will do successive plantings so that I always have tender lettuce. I won't say "What the heck" and empty the rest of the packet.

I won't plant peas in August that don't have a prayer of bearing fruit before the frost. Next year in the garden I won't curse potato bugs, but will accept my responsibility for the pests I attract. I will outwit potato bugs by not planting potatoes. Next year, that is.

I will de-sucker the tomatoes religiously, and I will build those groovy bent-wood trellises I saw in the gardening magazine. I will say a prayer when I eat the first red fruit.

I won't let the rogue squash grow, thinking it might turn out to be the elusive "great pumpkin."

Next year in the garden, at least once, I will strip off all my clothes, lie spread-eagled in the dirt and say "Take me, God, I'm yours!" Then I will take an outdoor shower, scrubbing every nook and cranny, and feel like the luckiest man on the face of the earth.

Part III–Fall

Next year in the garden, as I pull weeds, I won't think that I coined the phrase "Nature abhors a vacuum." (Who did coin that phrase, if not me?)

I won't wonder why I planted mustard greens.

I will wear a long-sleeve shirt while pruning the roses. Did I already say that?

I won't start the chipper-shredder "just to see if it will start," then put through a sunflower stalk "just to see what happens," especially when I am just killing time before we go out to dinner.

Next year I won't bore visitors with extensive garden tours, filled with eloquent soliloquies on the virtues of compost. I won't describe myself as the "poor man's Eliot Coleman."

I will pick the chard before it becomes tough and stringy.

I won't stand speechless before a ten foot sunflower and marvel at the memory of pressing a single seed into the soil with my thumb. I won't laugh out loud when I see three blue jays hanging upside down on the foot-wide seed pods, possessed by gluttony.

I won't be disappointed when the Sox fall by the wayside, because I know there is always next year.

Next year in the garden, I will cover at the hint of frost.

I will plant my bulbs and garlic before the ground freezes, but I won't cover them with mulch until the ground is hard and critter-proof.

I won't pretend not to be disappointed when my garlic and cherry tomatoes fail to score ribbons at the Tunbridge World's Fair.

Next year in the garden I won't break into Joni Mitchell's "Urge for Going" when I see a chevron overhead.

Part IV—Winter

Next year in the garden I won't get delusional when I see this year's seeds on sale. I won't buy enough to feed all of central Vermont and I won't think I'm a rich man as I flip through the colorful packets in January. I won't question why I bought two types of turnips. I hate turnip.

I won't delude myself into thinking I can grow seven varieties of pepper from seed.

I won't buy seeds for inedible greens with exotic Japanese names.

I will store my squash properly, so they don't rot.

I will give gifts of garlic and elderberry wine as if I am bestowing frankincense and myrrh (even though the elderberry wine sucks). I won't take it personally when I see how cheap garlic is at Costco.

I won't check the mail for the first seed catalog the day after Christmas.

I will think good thoughts when we eat last summer's pesto.

Next year in the garden I won't think I am part of life's great cycle just because I pee on the frozen compost.

Stephen Morris is Editor of *Green Living Journal*. His most recent writings and many chestnuts may be found at greenlivingjournal.com . His latest thoughts about the New Village Green may always be found at the book's website, ThePublicPress.com/green

Pennatulacean (Sea pen)

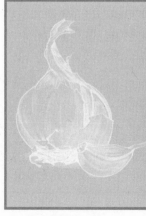

The Sumerians, using clay tablets, created the first written forms called cuneiform. The first written mention of garlic may have appeared about 2600 BCE when the Sumerians described the staples of their diet that included the herb along with grains, legumes, some root vegetables, leafy greens like lettuce and mustard, cucumbers, and a variety of fish. The Sumerians also used garlic for healing as noted in the medical texts of King Ashurbanipal's library dating 688 to 826 BCE.

chapter 2 : Silent Spring

Bob Ramlow lives in northern Wisconsin, where the winters bite. He is a founder and a director of the Midwest Renewable Energy Association (MREA) and author of *Solar Water Heating: A Comprehensive Guide to Solar Water and Space Heating Systems*.

Conservation and the Economics of Solar Water Heating

by Bob Ramlow with Benjamin Nusz

Whatever brought you to this point, whether it was the realization that we are trashing our environment or the simple need to lower your living expenses, now you are here and you want to do something. But what to do first? The answer is simple: start by conserving the energy you use to heat water. Three general principles that are easy to follow will also save you money: reduce losses, increase efficiency, and reduce consumption.

To start, examine your heating system from top to bottom and look for places where heat might leak out. Heat losses in the system end up wasting the energy you just used to heat your water. Many can be reduced by just a little bit of cheap insulation. For instance, insulate all of your hot pipes. If you are working on a new construction, insulating the hot pipes is easy. Even if you don't have access to all your pipes, insulating the ones you can get at will make a noticeable difference. You should also insulate your water heater. A tank-type water heater heats a whole batch of water. As this water sits there waiting for use, it slowly cools down. The more you insulate it, the better it will retain its heat. Heat losses can also come from leaks. A faucet that leaks 30 drops of water a minute will waste almost 100 gallons a month. Fix leaky faucets promptly.

Next, try to increase the efficiency of everything in your home that uses hot water, for instance, the washing machine and the dishwasher. Upgrading these appliances to more energy efficient models will significantly reduce the amount of energy consumed. A front-loading washing machine uses half the hot water of a standard top-loading model. This results in around 10-20 gallons of hot water saved for each load you do. You can save thousands of gallons of hot water a year.

Finally, you can conserve energy by simply using less. Much can be done without a significant change in your daily habits. For instance, when washing dishes in the sink by hand, don't let the water run while rinsing. Fill one sink with wash water and the other with rinse water. Soak pots and pans instead of letting the water run while you scrape them clean, and if you are using a dishwasher, only wash full loads. Use cold water with the garbage disposal. Cold water solidifies grease, allowing the disposal to get rid of it more effectively. You can take short showers instead of baths. You should first install a low-flow showerhead. Most standard showerheads use three to four gallons per minute. Even if you take a relatively brief 5 minute shower, you can end up consuming 20 gallons of hot water. Low-flow showerheads will use half of that. A family of four can save well over 1,000 gallons a month. If you are particularly attached to your showerhead, your can install a flow restrictor that will reduce the number of gallons per minute that it uses. For only a couple of dollars, you can reduce your load substantially.

Reducing losses, increasing efficiency, and reducing consumption: these are the first steps. What should be stressed more than quick fixes, though, is the notion of conscious consumption. We have forgotten the financial and environmental costs of hot water. If everyone recognized that whenever they turned on the hot water faucet they were using up energy produced by nonrenewable sources, this would reduce energy consumption more than any other measure.

People often say to me, "Bob, I have done a lot of energy conservation and now I am ready to invest in a renewable energy system. What should I do next?"

Today, homeowners and business people can choose from a wide range of renewable energy technologies. Popular options include photovoltaic (solar electric) systems, wind electric systems, and solar water heaters. In almost every case, a solar water heating system is the best place to start. It provides a higher return on your investment than any other renewable energy system. A solar water heater works 12 months a year providing hot water to your home or business with little or no additional costs, thus offsetting your previous bill for heating water with conventional energy sources. Depending on your particular situation, the savings in conventional fuel can pay for the cost of the solar water heating system in as little as three years. Most often the payback is around five to ten years — still a great investment, even without taking into account the ecological benefits of not burning all that fossil fuel.

In fact, I think it's time to let you in on a little secret. Solar water heaters don't cost anything. They're FREE! I know it may sound absurd, but it's true. Now I'm not recommending that you run over to the nearest solar distributor and just take a system. Don't do that. I'm just asking you to take a step back and think about solar in a different way. With a little change in perspective, you will see that in the end solar water heaters have a net cost of zero dollars.

> During archeological excavation of the palace of Knossos on the Greek Island of Crete, workers found evidence of garlic dating from 1850 to 1400 BCE. Early Greek military leaders employed garlic to embolden their warriors at the outset of battle. Perhaps, breathing on their enemies helped to ensure victory. While some athletes of today resort to dangerous remedies like ephedra as a stimulant, the early Greek Olympic athletes chewed on garlic to ensure a boost in performance.

Kirkpatrick Sale is an author, technology critic, self-proclaimed neo-luddite and tax resister. He is the Director of the Middlebury Institute for the study of separatism,secession, and self-determination.

Agriculture: Civilization's "Great Mistake"
by Kirkpatrick Sale

From about 12,000 to about 8,000 years ago, agriculture became the established way of life for the great majority of the world's people – and when I say "way of life" I mean that in the fullest sense. Agriculture was not simply a way of getting food, satisfying one basic human need. Agriculture cemented in the human mind the psychology by which people understood their world: it was we who chose what seeds to plant and where, what forests to cut down, what weeds to pull, what fields to fire, what waters to divert, in short what species were to live and die, and when and how. Agriculture was a superb demonstration that humans could control nature (or believe they could); that humans could literally domesticate nature and place it under regular and systematic human will and design.

Hunting had certainly had its impact on local ecosystems, especially hunting to extinction as had happened all over the world in the preceding few millennia, but for the most part and the longest time it was no more harmful to nature as a whole than any other species' predation. Now, with deforestation, dams and irrigation, soil exhaustion, extensive settlements, and all that goes with agriculture, almost all natural systems were disrupted and degraded. We were declaring war not just on a species but a world.

That portentous attitude was surely behind the thinking that led to the next round of domestication: of fellow creatures. Like the planting and harvesting of grains, this seems to have begun in the Fertile Crescent, which had four of the easiest mammalian species to domesticate – goat, pig, sheep, and cow – out of the only 14 species that have ever allowed themselves to fall under human control. Whatever possessed humans to think of and carry through such a process is lost in the pre-historical mists, but we can assume that once they had fenced in wheat fields for convenient food (and protection from being eaten by other species) it was not that much of a leap to try to fence in animals (or at least to control herds) for convenient food. Thus the domestication of animals – "enslavement" might be a more appropriate word – joined that of plants.

Agriculture had numerous consequences, mostly deleterious, which is why a sober academic like Jared Diamond, a physiologist at the UCLA School of Medicine who has studied it extensively, could call agriculture "the worst mistake in the history of the human race."

Perhaps the first important consequence was an increase in population numbers and densities. Farming and herding allow a significantly higher yield per acre of land than hunting and foraging, and wheat and barley in particular are highly productive, so larger populations could be supported – 100 times greater than hunting societies – and larger populations are what farmers always want anyway, given the laboriousness of their job. This was apparently achieved in most places by women giving birth to more children during their reproductive years, birth intervals being much shorter for farm families that can wean infants on to milk and gruel and not have to extend female lactation (and hence infertility) for years as hunting families must. In a very short period of time clan sites became villages, villages proliferated, and some of them grew into small, densely packed cities, of 1,000 (Jericho) and even 5,000 people (Catal Huyuk).

But think of what this means. Sedentary communities of more than 50 people are living as no one had ever lived before: they would need to create all sorts of new political, economic, cultural, and social institutions and policies to handle complexities at those scales. Gone the ancient rules of reciprocity, for no goat shepherd is going to give his hungry neighbors one of his animals for dinner, as was regularly done in hunting bands when the men came in with a catch, or he would soon be impoverished. Gone too the life of limited possessions imposed on mobile hunting societies, for now with a sedentary population, one could have all the possessions one could accumulate, from goats to grindstones and animals to acres, and the more the better.

Population accumulations and densities had other consequences. Diseases, many from the domesticated animal populations now living in close proximity to humans for the first time, had fertile territory in which to spread, and communicable "crowd diseases" flourished (measles, smallpox, and tuberculosis from cattle, for example, flu and pertussis from pigs, plus plague and cholera) that would have died out in the small populations of hunter-gatherers. It is little wonder that human life spans quite rapidly grew shorter – hunter-gatherer women on average reached the age of 40, men 50 or even 60, but agriculturalist longevity was in general 10 years shorter.

Another apparent effect of crowding was a decrease in body size, because when populations expanded to the limit of their food-growing, as farming settlements inevitably do, then, as the British Museum's Christopher Stringer explains, "humans therefore had to drop in either number or size, and evolved the latter course." Average body height of the *Sapiens* hunters was about 6 feet, of the women maybe 5 feet 5 inches, but as early as 5,000 years ago the average height of agriculturalists was 5 feet 3 inches for men and 5 feet for women. Even more alarming was a decrease in brain size, of 8 to 10 percent, after the beginning of agriculture, perhaps as a result of the tediousness and repetitiveness of farming and herding as well as a response to the social overload of larger settlements, and possibly also because the continual concentration and information-processing of the hunter in the wild was no longer necessary.

Food surpluses proved another feature of agricultural societies because of the productivity of their concentrated fields, and this, coupled with better techniques for storage of grain and its protection from rot and rodents, allowed farmers in good harvest years to contribute their surplus grains to a communal grain supply. This in turn fed the development of two characteristics that were carried over from late-on hunting societies – division of labor and hierarchy – but now in just a few millennia came to have an increasingly decisive economic and social role in the life of agriculturalists.

Because of surpluses there could be full-time artisans and potters who would be supported from the communal granary, full-time shamans, full-time laborers for dams and irrigation ditches, full-time guards to protect the village from predators human and otherwise, full-time accountants to regulate the collection, storage, and distribution of grain – and full-time rulers, the high-status chieftains who would have had to try to bring order to such a complicated society and see that all these tasks were efficiently done. The hierarchy that had been resorted to in the hunter-gatherer world at times of stress now evolved into a full-blown stratified "class society."

And here's the kicker: in the end, agriculture always failed. It was an environmental assault on the Earth that was almost never sustainable for much more than a few centuries without disruption and devastation: in the long history of empires dependent on agriculture and irrigation (Babylonia, Sumeria, Assyria, Carthage, Mesopotamia, Egypt, Inca, Aztec) we may read the story over and over again, of the exhaustion and salinization of the land, the destruction of forests, the overgrazing of fields, the compaction of soils, the extinction of wild animals, the silting and salting of rivers, the alteration of climate, erosion, desertification – and, as agriculture and its attendant systems began to fail, the revolt of the underclasses, or the collapse of the imperial systems, or the invasion of outsiders, or often all three. Nature always ended up having her revenge: of all the places where agriculture started, only one, central China, remains a productive agricultural area today; the rest are deserts or jungles.

As the story of agriculture makes clear, the domination of the Earth can come only at a price, and as we can tell today, the price may well be the despoliation of the Earth and the destruction of human systems, perhaps the decimation of the species itself.

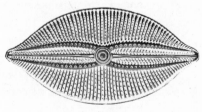

Diatom

The Truthdig Interview: Michael Pollan

interviewed by Blair Golson

I t became obvious to journalist Michael Pollan in the summer of 2002 that America had a national eating disorder.

That July, *The New York Times Magazine* published an article titled "What if It's All Been a Big Fat Lie?" which reported that a growing number of respected nutritional researchers were beginning to conclude that perhaps Dr. Robert Atkins had been right all along: Carbohydrates, not fats, were the cause of America's obesity problem.

Almost overnight, in Pollan's estimation, bakeries went out of business, dinner rolls in New York restaurants went the way of the pterodactyl, and pasta became regarded as a toxin.

"These foods were wonderful staples of human life for thousands of years," Pollan told Truthdig, "and suddenly we've decided that they're evil. Any culture that could change its diet on a dime like that is suffering from an eating disorder, as far as I can see."

Pollan was well placed to make such an observation. The previous year, he had published a critically acclaimed, best-selling book called *The Botany of Desire*, an examination of humans' relationships to plants, and how plants shape human societies as much as we shape them. His writings on the natural world and food stretch back to the late 1980s. Early in his career, he was an editor at *Harper's* magazine, and since 1995 he has been a contributing editor at *The New York Times Magazine*. Over the years he won a gaggle of writing awards and fellowships from environmental, food, and journalistic organizations, in addition to publishing two other books, on gardening and architecture.

So when Atkins-mania achieved terminal velocity in the summer of 2002, Pollan started to wonder whether it wasn't time to ask some fundamental questions about a country so apparently susceptible to the whims of a fad diet. Pulling together the threads of stories he had written in the past decade on topics ranging from the ethics of vegetarianism to the dangers of over-reliance on corn, Pollan set off on a journey to answer a deceptively sophisticated question: "What should we have for dinner?"

The Omnivore's Dilemma

The search for an answer found expression in Pollan's just-published book *The Omnivore's Dilemma*. The title refers to the quandary faced by animals like humans (and rats and cockroaches) that, in order to stay alive, must choose from the bewildering array of edible and non-edible substances. We can eat a lot, but what should we eat?

The subtitle of his book is "A Natural History of Four Meals," which is Pollan's way of describing his exploration of four types of food that eventually terminate in some kind of human meal: food that he himself grew and hunted; organic or "alternative" food (found at farmer's markets); industrial-organic foods (much of the stock at Whole Foods); and industrial, or processed, food (the snack or cereal aisles at Safeway).

Through this series of "food detective stories," the author found things to cheer and things to fear about the ethical, biological, and ecological ramifications of the American way of eating.

Truthdig managing editor Blair Golson recently spoke with Pollan from his home in Northern California, where he is the Knight Professor of Journalism at UC Berkeley's Graduate School of Journalism. He discussed how the omnivore's dilemma had returned in the unlikeliest of places; the truth about so-called "free range" chickens; and how in the world food manufacturers can get away with labels that read: "This product may contain one or more of the following...."

QUESTION: *The omnivore's dilemma is typically associated with animals in the wild that have to choose between food that will either nurture or kill them. What's the relevance of the term to modern human society?*

ANSWER: Out in nature, if you're a creature looking for something to eat, you might see some attractive looking red berries and think to yourself, "I wonder if I can eat those without getting sick? And what about those mushrooms?" Well, the same thing is happening in the supermarket. There are many tasty things, some of which can kill you. Trans fats, for example, or all the sugar we're eating.

So we're back where we were once upon a time, trying to navigate a treacherous food landscape – full of attractive things, but some of which are liable to shorten our lives.

Is that what prompted you to write the book?

It was a gathering sense that Americans – myself included – had gotten deeply confused and worried about what they were eating and unsure where to turn. To read the newspaper over the last couple of years is to read one story after another that makes you wonder if the way you've been eating all these years is such a good idea – for yourself or the planet or the animals.

Just reading the coverage of mad cow disease was an incredible educational experience. For example, we read that you've got to stop feeding cows to cows. It's like, "What? We've been feeding cows to cows?" And we've got to tighten up those rules about feeding chicken litter to cows. "We've been feeding chicken crap to cows?" If you read those stories, it made me realize that the system by which we're producing our food is not one I feel very good about participating in.

So I began looking into the food chain and alternatives to the main industrial food chain – doing what I think of as a series of food detective stories, and much of what I learned in these detective stories was astonishing to me, and forced me to re-approach the way I shop for food and go about eating it.

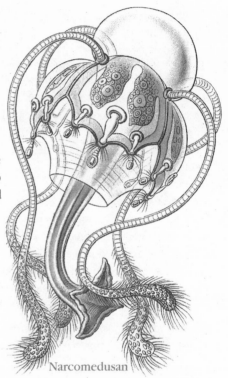

Narcomedusan

Michael Pollan is a professor of journalism at the University of California, Berkeley, where he is also the director of the Knight Program in Science and Environmental Journalism and author of *The Omnivore's Dilemma: A Natural History of Four Meals.*

The Greek citizenry, especially the aristocracy, firmly rejected garlic and found its smell repugnant. Anyone smelling of garlic was considered vulgar and was prevented from entering the temples. However, in Aristophanes' play *Wives at the Feast of Thesmophores*, the women who were cheating on their husbands found garlic the perfect cover-up for a night of indulgence. Contrasting the negative Greek attitudes, Aristotle listed garlic among the foods he considered aphrodisiacs.

— Garlic snippets are by Zel and Reuben Allen, *Vegetarians in Paradise*, a monthly internet magazine (vegparadise.com)

Paul Scheckel is an energy efficiency specialist in Vermont, and the author of *The Home Energy Diet: How to Save Money by Making Your House Energy Smart.*

The Home Energy Diet
by Paul Scheckel

Just as science continues to prove the health benefits of a proper diet, new forces are motivating us to save energy: dwindling and unpredictable fossil fuel supply, desire for security, stresses on personal and national economies, and pressures on social and natural environments. Energy efficiency is the first step towards a sustainable energy supply and lower pollution levels. Reduced resource consumption at home offers you greater independence, flexibility, and security along with lower energy bills, and will make your house a more comfortable place to live. I can't promise you this will be a painless process, but it will be worth your efforts, and you will feel better as you go along. Location, amenities, price, schools, and possibly utility costs generally make it to the top of the prospective homebuyer's list. When you bought or rented your home, did you ask about how the heat and hot water worked before you moved in? Was the furnace ductwork checked for costly leaks? Did you have the ventilation system tested to see if it actually moved air? How was the previous occupant's health?

Why are these things important? Energy-related problems are often masked as comfort issues. You may feel cold, dry, stuffy, or even sick inside your home. Indoor air quality is becoming a cause for concern as homes are being built more tight with better construction practices designed to be more energy efficient. Most of us spend up to 90 percent of our time indoors, yet are more aware of outdoor air pollution than of poor indoor air quality. How do you address these issues? We will examine how the systems in your home can work with and against each other to alter your home environment.

If I had to choose only one message to rise like cream to the top of my milk bottle full of advice, it would be that energy efficiency is an investment, not a hardship. The cheapest kilowatt is one you don't have to buy, a concept called negawatts. Studies show that the cost of buying efficiency is about half the cost of buying energy. Purchasing a product that uses less energy than another similar product has significant, long-term impacts on your energy consumption and costs. The price you pay to buy a new refrigerator, light bulb, or furnace is a small percentage of the price you will pay to operate it over its lifetime. Many of us look to banks or the stock market for retirement funds, but efficiency improvements offer cost-effective, tax-free returns that are greater than many traditional investments. Compound these returns by re-investing energy cost savings and you can begin building your energy savings account today. As energy prices rise, your savings increase.

* * *

We ask a great deal from our homes. They need to shelter us in comfort in addition to providing heat, light, hot water, and all the modern conveniences and entertainments. And we expect all of this to happen economically over a long period of time — without an owner's manual! You probably know more about the operation of your car or VCR than about how your house operates. In fact, we don't really think in terms of the operation of our homes at all. We buy a house for price, square footage, location, and amenities. We optimistically assume that the builder and the building codes have taken care of everything else and that the house will work. Builders and building owners rarely envision the house as a whole, as a living organism with multiple, interdependent systems and functions, much like our own bodies. Very often, heating systems are installed almost as an afterthought, and indoor air quality is largely ignored. What you can't see in a house sometimes matters more than what you can see. I'll show you the inside of your walls later in this book.

Home Energy Fuels

Look at the largest area of energy consumption: electricity losses. These losses are due to inefficiency! Electric companies burn fuel to generate electricity. Losses in power generation, transmission, and distribution mean that three units of fuel energy burned at the power plant give you only one unit of energy at the outlet in the wall. This power system (the grid) is only about 30 percent efficient at delivering power to your home. And the problem gets worse inside our homes. The appliances we use are not very efficient either. An incandescent light bulb is only about ten percent efficient at converting electrical energy into light energy – the remaining 90 percent is lost as waste heat. When electricity generation, transmission, and distribution losses are added in, the overall efficiency of the same light bulb at converting the primary energy from the power plant to the actual light that you use in your home has dwindled to just three percent.

One way of addressing the inefficiency of power transmission and distribution is through what power companies call "distributed generation." Distributed generation is where electricity is fed into power lines by small, scattered power plants such as wind mills, solar electric arrays on roof tops, small-scale hydro power, methane captured at farms or landfills, or fossil fuel powered turbines. The energy from these decentralized power sources tends to be used on-site by whoever is producing it, with the excess going out onto the grid for everyone else. Energy security analysts think distributed generation is preferable because reducing the demand on a single, central power plant makes widespread power interruptions less likely.

Another way to increase power plant efficiency is by way of co-generation (cogen) also known as combined heat and power (CHP). Co-generation means producing useful energy for more than one use from the same fuel source. For example, power plants generate enormous amounts of heat. Most of that heat boils water into high-pressure steam, which spins a turbine to produce electricity. Energy is lost in the process via low grade heat left in the water after the steam has passed through the turbine. If that heat energy is captured it can be used to heat the power plant, or even neighboring buildings in the town. Your car is an excellent example of a co-generation power plant. It uses a single fuel source – gasoline – to produce mechanical power, electrical power, heat, and air conditioning. That still doesn't make the car very efficient – only about 25 percent under ideal conditions. A huge amount of waste heat comes off the engine.

Excerpted from Paul Scheckel's book, *Home Energy Diet.* An online
interview with Scheckel can be found at
thepublicpress.com/page/index.php?e=PHED10

Brittle star

Like the Greeks, the early Roman nobility did not embrace garlic in their own diets but considered the herb worthy only of being fed to the laborers and slaves, to give them strength and vigor. Any man smelling of garlic was considered of low breeding. Horace, Roman lyric poet and satirist (65 to 8 BCE), said of garlic in his *Epodes*, it is "more poisonous than hemlock." Yet, Julius Caesar, Roman general, politician, and writer (100 to 44 BCE) was said to indulge his love of garlic without hesitation.

Magical Flocks of Birds

by Carrie Chandler

Birds wheel through the air en masse, swooping and diving as a flock but never hitting one another. It's not because they have magical powers, although that was one suggestion made in the mid-nineteenth century. So how do they do it? And why?

Contrary to popular belief, birds do not simply follow the leader. Each bird in a flock makes its own decisions about how to maneuver in flight, and these decisions are guided by three natural inclinations that all flocking birds share. First, a bird always tries to maintain a minimum distance between itself and every bird immediately surrounding it. By doing this, the bird usually ensures that it does not collide with a fellow avian traveler.

Countering this tendency towards repulsion is the second key inclination – cohesion. An individual bird within a flock is always trying to move toward the average position of its fellow flyers. The net result of these two inclinations is a continuing effort to be as close as possible to the neighboring birds without coming too close.

The third inclination is the flocking instinct itself. This inclination drives each individual bird to keep track of the average heading and general speed of the entire flock. Without this tendency, splinter groups of birds would constantly be breaking away.

In order to remain with the flock, each individual bird constantly responds to these three inclinations. Following the cues of the surrounding birds, an individual moves in order to maintain a balance between distance and cohesiveness without leaving the flock.

A bird is inclined to stay with the flock to take advantage of the many evolutionary benefits that it provides. First, flocks allow birds to draft behind one another, greatly increasing their efficiency. Drafting allows large groups to travel a greater distance than solo flyers: a flock of geese flies 70 percent further than a lone goose. Riding in the wake also helps birds that are less strong and less competent fliers remain with the flock.

A second benefit of flocking is protection in numbers, and that means preservation of the gene pool. If a hawk is circling and swooping into a flock of European starlings, it can be overwhelmed by the sheer number of birds to choose from and be unable to focus effectively on a single bird. In addition, a large group of birds is more likely to see a predator and take evasive action in time.

But the most important benefit of flocking comes during migration. Not all birds in a flock will have migrated before, and others might only have a vague idea of where they need to go. With multiple birds combining their memories and senses of direction, the whole flock is more likely to end up where it needs to be.

Essential to all three reasons for flocking is acute vision. The size of a bird's eye in relationship to its head is a testament to its importance. Human eyes make up 1 percent of the mass of the human head, but the eyes of European starlings, those fanatic flockers, make up 15 percent of the mass of a starling head. Without keen vision, a bird would not be able to fly, much less maintain its three-dimensional position in a flock of other birds, each constantly adjusting its own three-dimensional position.

Eye position is a key factor in the effectiveness of bird vision. Flocking birds have monocular vision, meaning their eyes are located on the sides of their heads. This allows some birds (depending on how far back their eyes are placed) to see up to 300 degrees without turning their head. Although this compromises depth perception, it allows them to see the bird flying next door much more easily. Since each decision in flight is made based on neighboring birds, this serves a flocking bird much better than eyes located on the front of the head.

Monocular vision does mean, however, that flocking birds are not as effective at being predators. Depth perception – a critical skill for a predatory bird trying to gauge the distance to its prey – requires binocular vision, with eye placement at the front of the head. Though hawks and other predators will fly together during migration in order to draft, they do so more as loose groups than as tightly spaced flocks.

Birds flocking in a cloudless, blue, autumn sky may seem like magic, but it's really a combination of vision, instinct, and skill. It's the ease with which birds combine these three things that makes bird flight appear magical.

Siphonophore

Carrie Chandler works with Northern Woodlands magazine in Corinth, Vermont. To respond to this article or suggest a future topic, contact the New Hampshire Charitable Foundation's Wellborn Ecology Fund: wef@nhcf.org.

Silent Spring:
The New Village People

66 Rachel Carson's *Silent Spring* had a profound influence. It helped us understand just how dramatically humans could influence the environment through the application of pesticides. This book was a wakeup call that gave birth to the environmental movement."
— *Dan Chiras*
Author, The Homeowner's Guide to Renewable Energy

66 Rachel Carson has done more than anyone to influence our relationship with nature, since it was *Silent Spring* that created the modern environmental movement and brought ecological consciousness to a wide public, particularly in the United States."

— *Kirkpatrick Sale*
Director, Middlebury Institute

66 Rachel Carson led us to see that what goes around comes around."
— *Christopher Plant*
Publisher, New Society Publishers

66 Rachel Carson was the first to effectively communicate the message that we are poisoning ourselves in the name of progress. She broke a sacred silence to make the case that what we have defined as progress is, in fact, a path to collective suicide."

— *David C. Korten*
Author, The Great Turning: From Empire to Earth Community

"Rachel Carson's *Silent Spring*, in conjunction with all the yeasty things and activism that produced the first Earth Day, started everything. I can remember late night discussions in which we taught each other what we were reading and hearing and learning. This intellectual nurturing was replicated hundreds of times across the country. And we can't discount the hard slogging of people like David Brower who led significant numbers of our generation to an ecological world view."

— Nancy Jack Todd
Editor, Annals of Earth.

"Rachel Carson awakened the people of the developed nations of the Earth to what was going on with their planet.

The idea that is doing the most damage to the environment (and the social order) around the world is the American interpretation of Milton Friedman's essay in which he firmly declared that the business of business is business. That has become the guiding principal for US multinational corporations, and they have used their enormous wealth and power to persuade the US government to make it our policy for the global economy. The resulting damage is immeasurable."

— Stuart Auchincloss
Environmental lawyer
Board member, Sierra Club and CERES

"As a work of art Rachel Carson's *Silent Spring* contains the power to move people to action. No matter how brilliant our attempts to inform, it is our ability to inspire that makes the difference."

— Joe Uehlein
Musician
CERES Advisory Board, Union of Concerned Scientists

"George Perkins Marsh's *Man and Nature* contains the memorable and telling description of man as 'everywhere a disturbing agent.'"

— Bill Mares
Author, Bees Besieged: One Beekeeper's Journey to Understanding

" To understand our present situation, we have to look back to the Neolith — which is really just 300-something generations ago. At that time, the ground was laid with the survival means and resulting experience/mindset that have ultimately devolved into this end-stage empire/capitalism/mass society/global megamachine. It began with the wrenching of human from nature, which occurred through agriculture and animal domestication. For all the ingenuity and bravery that probably went into launching these new modes of being, they have subsequently metasticized into the unfortunate social problems that plague us today — out-of-control population expansion, political exploitation, dominance, violence, the rat race, economic inequity, sexism, racism, systemic war — as well as psychological problems like traumatic stress, anxiety, and schizophrenia that so perfectly mirror the psychic splitting, scattering, and dissociation of the original separation of human from the natural world."

— *Chellis Glendinning*
Author, Off the Map *and* Chiva

" Rachel Carson's *Silent Spring* was, in terms of both content and timing, one of the most important books ever. The very idea that we had this power was mind-bending. To the Earth's everlasting sorrow, though, what should have been a wakeup call and the inspiration for a completely different course of action is in danger of becoming no more than an 'I told you so!'"

— *Ingrid Witvoet*
Managing Editor, New Society Publishers

"

Rachel Carson's *Silent Spring* woke up many of us 50-somethings and 60-somethings who went on to create Earth Day, the EPA, and the green companies that are leading a clean-tech revolution in the marketplace."

— *Kevin Danaher*
Cofounder, Global Exchange
Co-Executive Producer, Green Festivals
Executive Director, Global Citizen Center

Silent Spring:
The New Village Library

Silent Spring, by Rachel Carson. Penguin Books, 1970.

The Sea Around Us, by Rachel Carson. Signet, 1954.

The Edge of the Sea, by Rachel Carson. Signet, 1955.

The Sense of Wonder, by Rachel Carson. Harper & Row, 1965.

For Earth's Sake: The Life and Times of David Brower, by David Brower. Gibbs Smith, 1990.

Man and Nature, by George Perkins Marsh. Capen and Lyon, 1833. U of Washington Press, 2003.

George Perkins Marsh: Prophet of Conservation, by David Lowenthal. U of Washington Press, 2000.

Bees Besieged: One Beekeeper's Bittersweet journey to Understanding, by Bill Mares. A.I. Root Company, 2005.

3 THE LIMITS TO GROWTH

Periphylla

❝*The world works a little better any time we manage to make the invisible visible, embed real costs into prices, and impose the consequences of decision-making upon those who make the decisions.***❞**

— Donella Meadows

While the Nearings built a stone house, rock by rock, on the coast of Maine, and while Pete Townsend (of The Who) hit Abbie Hoffman with his guitar when the latter attempted to commandeer the microphone at Woodstock, something very different was happening in the hallowed halls of MIT (The Massachusetts Institute of Technology). Some young people — "turks" by one description, "nerds" by another — were getting very excited by the results they were seeing from computer models comparing known natural resources with consumption rates.

The computer was predicting cataclysmic events occurring in the finite future, such things as running out of oil. Holy %&##!! And we thought we had enough problems with Watergate and the Vietnam War.

The publication of *The Limits to Growth* drew more fire than the Tet Offensive. Not only was the information coming from a machine, but the messengers were snotty-nosed kids wearing pocket protectors. The intellectual debate quickly became ugly.

Three things made this book revolutionary:

1. It was the first popular application of systems thinking. The models that the young scientists had developed were non-linear, and more closely replicated the interconnectedness that characterizes real life. The synaptic jump that James Lovelock had experienced when first seeing the earth from space had not been duplicated, but at least it was approximated in binary code.

2. The real-life implications were dire. Business-as-usual was no longer an option if the human species expected to sustain itself into the future. We would have to change our patterns of unbridled consumption.

3. The book challenged the biblical notion that "Man has dominion" over the natural world. The entrenched power elite, i.e., those with dominion, were going to resist this challenge with all available weapons.

The challenges to the message of *Limits* continue to this day, even though the projections of the original book have been refined, verified, and reported in the publication of two updates of the original book using vastly improved models and more powerful computers.

Donella Meadows, the principal author and spokesperson for the *Limits* team, grew weary of the intellectual fallout that dogged her. Increasingly, she found pleasure in her life from music and performing the homesteading chores in the cohousing community she helped to found, Cobb Hill, in rural Vermont. Wearing rubber mucking boots and raking the straw from the animals' stalls, she finally became a complete global citizen.

Donella (Dana) Meadows was born on March 13, 1941 in Elgin, Illinois, and died on February 20, 2001, in New Hampshire.

She was educated in science, earning a B.A. in chemistry from Carleton College in 1963 and a Ph.D. in biophysics from Harvard University in 1968. She taught at Dartmouth College for 29 years and, beginning in 1972, was on the MIT team that produced the global computer model "World3" that provided the basis for the book, *Limits to Growth*.

Limits to Growth (1972) used computer modeling to predict the consequences of a rapidly growing world population and finite resource supplies. Authors Donella H. Meadows, Dennis L. Meadows, Jørgen Randers, and William W. Behrens III used the World3 model to simulate the consequence of interactions between the Earth's and human systems. The book was updated in 2004 as *Limits to Growth: The 30-Year Update*. One key idea that the book discusses is that if the rate of resource use is increasing, the amount of reserves cannot be calculated by simply taking the current known reserves and dividing by the current yearly usage, as is typically done to obtain a static index; experience shows that growth tends to be exponential.

Meadows, working with the tools of systems analysis, proposed a list of ways to change a system running amok.

Starting with the observation that there are levers, or places within a complex system (such as a firm, a city, an economy, a living being, an ecosystem, an ecoregion) where a "small shift in one thing can produce big changes in everything," she suggested that we should study these shifts, where they are and how to make them. She believed that most people instinctively know where these points are, but, due to perverse feedback mechanisms, tend to adjust them in the wrong direction.

"The concept of 'systems thinking' is the most important idea that is/will redefine the way we think about the relationship between humans and the environment. It forces us to think differently, in a less fragmented way. It helps ensure that our thinking is 'whole' and wholistic. While I'm not sure that I would attribute the idea to anyone person, Peter Senge has done more than just about any one else to popularize the idea."

— Jeffrey Hollender
President & Chief Inspired Protagonist, Seventh Generation
Author, Naturally Clean: The Seventh Generation Guide
to Safe and Healthy Non-Toxic Cleaning

Dana Meadows' 12 leverage points for intervening in a system
(in increasing order of effectiveness)

12. Constants, parameters, numbers (such as subsidies, taxes, standards)
11. The size of buffers and other stabilizing stocks, relative to their flows
10. The structure of material stocks and flows (such as transport network, population age structures)
9. The length of delays, relative to the rate of system changes
8. The strength of negative feedback loops, relative to the effect they are trying to correct against
7. The gain around driving positive feedback loops
6. The structure of information flow (who does and does not have access to what kinds of information)
5. The rules of the system (such as incentives, punishments, constraints)
4. The power to add, change, evolve, or self-organize system structure
3. The goal of the system
2. The mindset or paradigm that the system — its goals, structure, rules, delays, parameters — arises out of
1. The power to transcend paradigms

sustainabilityinstitute.org/pubs/Leverage_Points.pdf

Salt Spring Island, between Vancouver Island and mainland British Columbia, is a magnet for innovative thinkers. If money is the root of all evil, why not re-invent it, only nicer?

The Birth of a Currency
by the Salt Spring Island Coalition

The concept of Salt Spring Island Dollars was the result of roundtable discussions of the Sustainable Salt Spring Island Coalition.

In the fall of 2000, the group was looking at different island nations around the world (Isle of Man, Jersey, Cayman Islands, etc.) examining how their governments and economies functioned.

One of the common factors of these islands was that they each had their own local currency.

Two questions arose – would it be possible to establish a local currency for Salt Spring, and if so, how could it benefit the community?

The Problems

Further research examined a wide range of "alternative" currencies (e.g., Toronto Dollars, LETS and Hours systems). It appeared that none of the alternative currencies had achieved "near universal acceptance."

The primary limiting factor identified was that none of the local currencies were 100% redeemable into their national currency, and, as a result, the majority of merchants were hesitant or unwilling to accept a currency unless it could "pay the bills."

Next was the question of how a currency goes into circulation and receives and/or maintains any value to the holder.

It also appeared that, in most cases, operation of local currencies were segregated from local financial institutions.

The Solutions

Having identified these problems, it was decided any solutions must address all of these concerns.

Several brainstorming sessions later, an idea surfaced that provided an answer directly and indirectly, to all of the major problems. It was suggested that if our currency had a two-year expiry date, any bills that had not been redeemed by the expiry date (e.g., collected, left the island, lost, etc.) would represent a "profit."

By creating a profit, to cover costs, it would be possible to have the currency go into circulation through a one-to-one exchange with the Canadian dollar.

This meant it could be backed 100% by the Canadian dollar. To our knowledge this had never been done by any local currency, anywhere in the world.

Limited Editions

Next came the idea to have limited editions of Salt Spring Island art featured on the back. This would help to make the bills collectible, after the expiry date.

It was soon pointed out that with a year-round population of 10,000, an annual tourist flow of over 200,000, and tens of thousands of currency collectors around the world, the potential income from an edition of 20,000 of each bill was significant.

It was then decided to form a not-for-profit society, the Salt Spring Island Monetary Foundation, to facilitate the process of returning the proceeds of the venture back to the community.

Mission Statement

Thus, on July 17, 2001, the SS IMF was registered with the Province of British Columbia. Its mission statement is as follows:

"The purposes of the Society are to design, issue and maintain a local currency for Salt Spring Island with the goal of raising funds for worthwhile community projects while promoting local commerce and goodwill."

Following the formation of the IMF, major institutions (Island Savings Credit Union, CIBC, Bank of Montreal, Canada Post, SSI Chamber of Commerce, etc.) on the Island were approached with the concept. With these institutions lending their support to this community initiative, it came to pass that Salt Spring Dollars are now available and accepted on Salt Spring on the same basis as the national currency.

The Salt Spring Island Dollars were introduced to the Island on September 15, 2001, at Salt Spring's largest annual gathering, the Farmers' Institute Fall Fair.

Evolution of the Solution

As we approached the first expiry date, the Board of Directors discussed the successes and challenges of the future. During these discussions, it was brought forward that the expiry date was causing some concern with members of the community.

It was decided that our role in the community would be either to offer loans, at no interest, to worthwhile community projects, co-invest with those groups, or invest on our own.

The reason we did this was to ensure we did not deplete the assets which back the Salt Spring Dollars in circulation.

As a result, we decided to eliminate all expiry dates from the bills and to move towards an asset-based currency.

Although the currency is now backed mainly by Canadian dollars, it has always been our intention to back it with solid community investment. This will maintain the assets while, at the same time, benefiting the community long term.

The Next Step – Silver

In the spring of 2006, we began planning our first silver coin edition. Recognizing the long standing history of currencies backed by precious metals, we felt this was a natural progression for a local currency.

Salt Spring Island coins and paper currancy are now available online.

For more information about Salt Spring Island
Monetary Foundation visit
www.saltspringdollars.com
For the latest updates on this and other stories,
visit this book's companion website:
ThePublicPress.com/green

Larry Saltzman and Linda Buzzell-Saltzman are Fellows at For the Future (www.forthefuture.org), a sustainability think tank based in Santa Barbara.

Eight Things You Need to Know about the Shaky US Economy
by Larry Saltzman and Linda Buzzell-Saltzman

On the macro level, we may be concerned about the negative impacts of globalization and so-called "free trade." We may also be uncomfortable with the kind of planet-destroying capitalism that has sprung up under the giant international corporations. But there is more – much more – we need to understand about how economics is impacting our personal and collective lives and the health of our planet.

The economic consequences of globalization and late stage hyper-capitalism are reaching a crisis point that will be felt by most of us in the next few years "up close and personal" – probably even before we feel the immediate results of Peak Oil or global warming. Even if we are doing everything we can to live a low-impact, sustainable lifestyle, we need to understand what's happening in the US and world economies.

The Big Picture

We have lived most of our lives in a growth economy, and our society has been getting rich off the consumption of cheap fossil fuel. That "free ride" up to peak is just about over and a number of disturbing economic trends are appearing that spell big trouble for oil-dependent economies and for the average US citizen. The era of endless "economic growth" is coming to an end. The Energy Descent economy has begun.

So let's examine eight worrisome economic trends. They are interconnected and when stirred together create a nasty brew…

1. Private Debt

Annual income twenty pounds, annual expenditure nineteen and six, result happiness. Annual income twenty pounds, annual expenditure twenty pounds ought and six, result misery.
— Charles Dickens, *David Copperfield*

America has forgotten Charles Dickens' famous words of wisdom. We are collectively trying to buy happiness by going on the greatest credit binge in the history of humanity.

Here are a few of the shocking facts:

The Federal Reserve reports that Americans collectively owe $2,164 trillion, of which $804 billion is credit card or other revolving debt. By 2001, Americans were paying $50 billion a year in finance charges to service their debt, and that number has since climbed higher. The average American owes $8,562 on their credit card(s) and will need ten years to pay that amount off at the minimum payment. At that point, they will have paid out over $16,000 or almost double the amount they originally borrowed.

These levels of personal debt are virtually enslaving Americans, forcing many of us to work harder and harder, for longer hours, at often meaningless corporate jobs in order to pay off our obligations. And bankruptcy laws have recently been toughened to make it even more difficult to escape the impact of serious personal debt, often caused by huge medical bills as well as our own intemperance.

2. The Real Estate Bubble

Thanks to low interest rates, Americans have been on a real estate binge, buying any property at any imaginable price in the belief that real estate will appreciate forever. Interest-only loans, variable interest loans, balloon payments, and low- or no-down payment arrangements have become the norm in the usually conservative world of home loans. The result is that as interest rates continue their inevitable ride upwards, many recent home buyers are going to see their home payments rise beyond their ability to pay. And as home prices begin to fall, and perhaps collapse, some home owners are going to experience negative amortization. That means that every month, instead of the equity on your home increasing, it will decrease and the total amount you owe will increase.

As real estate prices soften, which is already happening on the South Coast and elsewhere, foreclosures may rise as people go "upside down" on their loans, owing more on their mortgage than their properties are currently worth. Banks, stuck with unwanted properties, may begin to sell them at fire-sale prices, further depressing the price of real estate.

Any fall in real estate values is especially worrisome, as some Americans have been using their home equity as a kind of last-resort personal bank, taking out second mortgages to pay off credit card balances, remodel, buy cars or take expensive vacations. Others have used their equity to pay monthly or extraordinary bills, masking the fact that it's getting harder and harder for many Americans to retain a middle-class lifestyle in the era of outsourced jobs and flattened incomes.

3. Our Savings Rate

The citizens of the United States can now boast having a negative savings rate. We remove more money every month from our collective piggy banks than we put in. The average baby boomer will retire with a net worth of $23,000. The parents of baby boomers left their children far better off than the baby boomers are going to leave their children. Perhaps we can partly blame boomers' extravagance, consumerism, and sense of entitlement. But we also have to look at changes in the US economy that have allowed those at the top to earn more and more while paying less and less tax, while the middle and working classes are being squeezed with job losses and the export of much of our manufacturing.

4. The Bond Bubble

This is a slightly more obscure problem, but worth understanding. As interest rates have been increasing on short term debt, the interest rates on long-term debt have remained stubbornly low – probably because of foreign investment in US Treasury Bonds and the fact that US currency has been until recently the preferred currency to accept payment in. Recently a 90-day Treasury bill paid approximately the same interest rate as a ten-year bond. As interest rates keep rising, the value of bonds may plummet, causing many people to lose a lot of money in supposedly safe and secure US Treasury Bonds.

Bonds are confusing to most people. High interest rates mean that the price of existing lower-yielding bonds falls. Why buy an existing bond paying 5% when you can get a new bond paying 6%? Much of this US debt is of course held by foreign countries, most notably China. If foreign countries ever panic and begin dumping U.S. Treasury Bonds, we will see interest rates rise dramatically and we will be very lucky to escape a full-blown depression.

5. Government Debt

Whatever happened to old-fashioned conservative fiscal responsibility? Thanks to George Bush and his imbecilic economic policies, we have now become the nation with both the largest personal debt and the largest government debt. Our military policies are hugely expensive as well as immoral and stupid. And as the effects of Peak Oil and Energy Descent begin to be felt, we will have little wealth available to invest in new solutions.

If we are lucky enough to elect one of the hapless Democratic candidates for President and this person turns out to be a Franklin Roosevelt disguised as a centrist Democrat, he or she will have none of the maneuvering room, which Roosevelt had, to get us out of the economic depression that we may face in the not too distant future. Roosevelt was able to keep the much smaller federal budget of that era in balance while spending on programs to jump-start the economy. Today's Bush economics will leave a great deal of our federal budget servicing the debt the fiscally irresponsible Republicans have run up.

6. Inflation and Higher Prices

By lowering interest rates to near zero to encourage false and unsustainable economic growth, the Federal Reserve under recently retired Chairman Alan Greenspan set the stage for inflationary pressure in the economy. Virtually non-existent interest rates not only fueled the current real estate bubble, but made borrowing in general too cheap and easy. This conned millions of Americans into a borrowing binge that has left us deep in debt to the banking industry. If we cannot pay those debts, the banks themselves may also falter.

7. Loss of True Productivity

What does the US actually produce these days? Our financial services sector is now far larger than our manufacturing base. In other words, the business of the US is moving money around. And what happens to this truly unproductive economy when the shaky American dollar falters or exorbitant fossil fuel prices make it impossible to import what we need?

8. The Shaky US Dollar

A currency has to be based on something of true value. But the US dollar is increasingly dependent on its status as the world's default currency rather than the underlying worth of America's productivity. So what would happen if oil producers, for example, decide they'd rather be paid in euros than dollars?

Add it all up...

So what do these eight interconnected trends add up to? An unsustainable situation, a house of cards waiting for a tiny breeze – another spike in oil prices caused by a natural or terrorist supply glitch; a sneeze from our major creditor, China; a major oil producer requesting payment in euros; another bad hurricane season – to start the downward cascade.

How You Can Survive and Thrive in Spite of these Trends
The solutions at the individual level are clear.

1. Stay out of debt, and if you are in debt get out ASAP. If you don't pay your credit cards off in full every month, get rid of them and use a debit card.

    Even if you aren't in credit card debt, consider getting rid of your cards anyway as a political act. Credit cards have tricked and deluded Americans into feeling richer than we actually are. They start arriving in the mail while we are in college so we get hooked young. Then these plastic handcuffs enslave many of us, creating an illusion of wealth and disguising the fact that our salaries have stagnated and fallen. This has benefited politicians and banks, not ordinary people. Credit cards lock us into the world of materialism, consumerism, and greed, and keep us like hamsters in a treadmill, running to keep up, going nowhere. If you think of debt as an addiction, the credit card companies are the pushers.

2. Find work that has a future in an Energy Descent economy in which "economic growth" is a relic of the pre-Peak past.

3. Learn to take your pleasures from simple and sustainable living. Live at or below your means and save for the future, even if you can sock away only a few bucks a month. Let friends, family, and spiritual pursuits replace consumerism and greed. The Voluntary Simplicity movement has done a great job of showing us how to enjoy a rich and satisfying lifestyle without excessive materialism. And Permaculture offers the practical tools for sustainable living that increase our real prosperity and the true wealth of the earth rather than squandering it on the impossible nightmare of endless economic growth at the cost of environmental and social destruction.

This piece has been reprinted with permission from HopeDance: Radical Solutions Inspiring Hope. You can reach them at www.hopedance.org

Chad Heeter grew up eating fossil fuels in Lee's Summit, Missouri. He's a freelance writer, documentary filmmaker, and a former high-school science teacher.

My Saudi Arabian Breakfast
by Chad Heeter

Please join me for breakfast. It's time to fuel up again.

On the table in my small Berkeley apartment this particular morning is a healthy looking little meal – a bowl of imported McCann's Irish oatmeal topped with Cascadian Farms organic frozen raspberries, and a cup of Peet's Fair Trade Blend coffee. Like most of us, I prepare my breakfast at home and the ingredients for this one probably cost me about $1.25. (If I went to a café in downtown Berkeley, I'd likely have to add another $6.00, plus tip for the same.)

My breakfast fuels me up with about 400 calories, and it satisfies me. So, for just over a buck and half an hour spent reading the morning paper in my own kitchen, I'm energized for the next few hours. But before I put spoon to cereal, what if I consider this bowl of oatmeal porridge (to which I've just added a little butter, milk, and a shake of salt) from a different perspective. Say, a Saudi Arabian one.

Then, what you'd be likely to see – what's really there, just hidden from our view (not to say our taste buds) – is about four ounces of crude oil. Throw in those luscious red raspberries and that cup of java (another three ounces of crude), and don't forget those modest additions of butter, milk, and salt (another ounce), and you've got a tiny bit of the Middle East right here in my kitchen.

Now, let's drill a little deeper into this breakfast. Just where does this tiny gusher of oil actually come from? (We'll let this oil represent all fossil fuels in my breakfast, including natural gas and coal.)

Nearly 20% of this oil went into growing my raspberries on Chilean farms many thousands of miles away, those oats in the fields of County Kildare, Ireland, and that specially raised coffee in Guatemala – think tractors as well as petroleum-based fertilizers and pesticides.

The next 40% of my breakfast fossil-fuel equation is burned up between the fields and the grocery store in processing, packaging, and shipping. Take that box of McCann's oatmeal. On it is an inviting image of pure, healthy goodness – a bowl of porridge, topped by two peach slices. Scattered around the bowl are a handful of raw oats, what look to be four acorns, and three fresh raspberries. Those raw oats are actually a reminder that the flakes require a few steps twixt field and box. In fact, a visit to McCann's website illustrates each step in the cleaning, steaming, hulling, cutting, and rolling that turns the raw oats into edible flakes. Those five essential steps require significant energy costs.

Next, my oat flakes go into a plastic bag (made from oil), which is in turn inserted into an energy-intensive, pressed wood-pulp, printed paper box. Only then does my "breakfast" leave Ireland and travel over 5,000 fuel-gorging, CO_2-emitting miles by ship and truck to my grocery store in California.

Coming from another hemisphere, my raspberries take an even longer fossil-fueled journey to my neighborhood. Though packaged in a plastic bag labeled Cascadian Farms (which perhaps hints at a birthplace in the good old Cascade mountains of northwest Washington), the small print on the back, stamped "A Product of Chile," tells all – and what it speaks of is a 5,800-mile journey to Northern California.

If you've been adding up percentages along the way, perhaps you've noticed that a few tablespoons of crude oil in my bowl have not been accounted for. That final 40% of the fossil fuel in my breakfast is used up by the simple acts of keeping food fresh and then preparing it. In home kitchens and restaurants, the chilling in refrigerators and the cooking on stoves using electricity or natural gas gobbles up more energy than you might imagine. For decades, scientists have calculated how much fossil fuel goes into our food by measuring the amount of energy consumed in growing, packing, shipping, consuming, and finally disposing of it. The "caloric input" of fossil fuel is then compared to the energy available in the edible product, the "caloric output."

What they've discovered is astonishing. According to researchers at the University of Michigan's Center for Sustainable Agriculture, an average of over seven calories of fossil fuel is burned up for every calorie of energy we get from our food. This means that in eating my 400-calorie breakfast, I will, in effect, have "consumed" 2,800 calories of fossil-fuel energy. (Some researchers claim the ratio to be as high as ten to one.)

But this is only an average. My cup of coffee gives me only a few calories of energy, but to process just one pound of coffee requires over 8,000 calories of fossil-fuel energy – the equivalent energy found in nearly a quart of crude oil, 30 cubic feet of natural gas, or around two and a half pounds of coal.

So how do you gauge how much oil went into your food? First check out how far it traveled. The farther it traveled, the more oil it required. Next, gauge how much processing went into the food. A fresh apple is not processed, but Kellogg's Apple Jacks cereal requires enormous amounts of energy to process. The more processed the food, the more oil it required. Then consider how much packaging is wrapped around your food. Buy fresh vegetables instead of canned, and buy bulk beans, grains, and flour if you want to reduce that packaging.

By now, you're thinking that you're in the clear, because you eat strictly organically grown foods. When it comes to fossil-fuel calculations though, the manner in which food's grown is where differences stop. Whether conventionally grown or organically grown, a raspberry is shipped, packed, and chilled the same way.

Yes, there are some savings from growing organically, but possibly only of a slight nature. According to a study by David Pimentel at Cornell University, 30% of fossil-fuel expenditure on farms growing conventional (non-organic) crops is found in chemical fertilizer. This 30% is not consumed on organic farms, but only if the manure used as fertilizer is produced in very close proximity to the farm. Manure is a heavy, bulky product. If farms have to truck bulk manure for any distance over a few miles, the savings are eaten up in diesel-fuel consumption, according to Pimentel. One source of manure for organic farmers in California is the chicken producer Foster Farms. Organic farmers in Monterey County, for example, will have to truck tons of Foster's manure from their main plant in Livingston, California to fields over one hundred miles away.

So the next time we're at the grocer, do we now have to ask not only where and how this product was grown, but how far its manure was shipped? Well, if you're in New York City picking out a California-grown tomato that was fertilized with organic compost made from kelp shipped from Nova Scotia, maybe it's not such a bad question. But should we give up on organic? If you're buying organic raspberries from Chile each week, then yes. The fuel cost is too great, as is the production of the greenhouse gases along with it. Buying locally grown foods should be the first priority when it comes to saving fossil fuel.

But if there were really truth in packaging, on the back of my oatmeal box where it now tells me how many calories I get from each serving, it would also tell me how many calories of fossil fuels went into this product. On a scale from one to five – with one being non-processed, locally grown products and five being processed, packaged imports – we could quickly average the numbers in our shopping cart to get a sense of the ecological footprint of our diet. From this we would gain a truer sense of the miles-per-gallon in our food.

What appeared to be a simple, healthy meal of oatmeal, berries, and coffee looks different now. I thought I was essentially driving a Toyota Prius hybrid – by having a very fuel-efficient breakfast, but by the end of the week I've still eaten the equivalent of over two quarts of Valvoline. From the perspective of fossil-fuel consumption, I now look at my breakfast as a waste of precious resources. And what about the mornings that I head to Denny's for a Grand-Slam breakfast: eggs, pancakes, bacon, sausage? On those mornings – forget about fuel efficiency – I'm driving a Hummer.

What I eat for breakfast connects me to the planet, deep into its past with the fossilized remains of plants and animals which are now fuel, as well as into its future, when these non-renewable resources will likely be in scant supply. Maybe these thoughts are too grand to be having over breakfast, but I'm not the only one on the planet eating this morning. My meal traveled thousands of miles around the world to reach my plate. But then there's the rise of perhaps 600 million middle-class Indians and Chinese. They're already demanding the convenience of packaged meals and the taste of foreign flavors. What happens when middle-class families in India or China decide they want their Irish oats for breakfast, topped by organic raspberries from Chile? They'll dip more and more into the planet's communal oil well. And someday soon, we'll all suck it dry.

from: TomDispatch.com

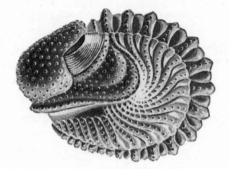

Trilobite

Bill McKibben was the first to write about climate change in language we could all understand. (There is much more about Bill in chapter 4.)

How Close to Catastrophe?
by Bill McKibben

James Lovelock is among the planet's most interesting and productive scientists. His invention of an electron capture device that was able to detect tiny amounts of chemicals enabled other scientists both to understand the dangers of DDT to the eggshells of birds and to figure out the ways in which chlorofluorocarbons (CFCs) were eroding the ozone layer. He's best known, though, not for a gadget but for a metaphor: the idea that the earth might usefully be considered as a single organism (for which he used the name of the Greek earth goddess Gaia), struggling to keep itself stable.

In fact, his so-called Gaia hypothesis was at first less clear than that – "hardly anyone, and that included me for the first ten years after the concept was born, seems to know what Gaia is," he has written. But the hypothesis has turned into a theory, still not fully accepted by other scientists but not scorned either. It holds that the Earth is "a self-regulating system made up from the totality of organisms, the surface rocks, the ocean, and the atmosphere tightly coupled as an evolving system" and striving to "regulate surface conditions so as always to be as favorable as possible for contemporary life."

Putting aside questions of planetary consciousness and will (beloved as they were by an early wave of New Age Gaia acolytes), the theory may help us understand how the earth has managed to remain hospitable for life over billions of years even as the sun, because of its own stellar evolution, has become significantly hotter. Through a series of processes involving, among others, ice ages, ocean algae, and weathering rock, the earth has managed to keep the amount of heat-trapping carbon dioxide in the atmosphere — and hence the temperature — at a relatively stable level.

This homeostasis is now being disrupted by our brief binge of fossil fuel consumption, which has released a huge amount of carbon dioxide into the atmosphere. Indeed, at one point Lovelock predicts – more gloomily than any other competent observer I am aware of – that we have already pushed the planet over the brink, and that we will soon see remarkably rapid rises in temperature, well beyond those envisioned in most of the computer models now in use – themselves quite dire. He argues that because the earth is already struggling to keep itself cool, our extra increment of heat is particularly dangerous, and he predicts that we will soon see the confluence of several phenomena: the death of ocean algae in ever-warmer ocean waters, reducing the rate at which these small plants can remove carbon from the atmosphere; the death of tropical forests as a result of higher temperatures and the higher rates of evaporation they cause; sharp changes in the earth's "albedo," or reflectivity, as white ice that reflects sunlight back out into space is replaced with the absorptive blue of seawater or the dark green of high-latitude boreal forests; and the release of large amounts of methane, itself a greenhouse gas, held in ice crystals in the frozen north or beneath the sea.

Some or all of these processes will be enough, Lovelock estimates, to tip the earth into a catastrophically hotter state, perhaps eight degrees centigrade warmer in temperate regions like ours, over the course of a very few decades, and that heat in turn will make life as we know it nearly impossible in many places. Indeed, in the photo section of Lovelock's book there is one picture of a red desert captioned simply "Mars now – and what the earth will look like eventually." Human beings, a hardy species, will not perish entirely, he says; in interviews during his book tour, Lovelock has predicted that about 200 million people, or about one thirtieth of the current world population, will survive if competent leaders make a new home for us near the present-day Arctic. There may also be other survivable spots, like the British Isles, though he notes that rising sea levels will render them more an archipelago. In any event, he predicts that "teeming billions" will perish.

Lovelock, who is in his eighties, concedes that this is a gloomier forecast than those of scientists more actively engaged in peer-reviewed climatology; it is, in a sense, a visceral feeling. It should be approached somewhat skeptically, for Lovelock has been (as he has always forthrightly admitted) wrong before in his immediate reactions. Though he invented the machine that helped us understand the dangers of CFCs, he also blithely dismissed those dangers, arguing that they couldn't do enough damage to matter. The American chemists Sherry Rowland and Mario Molina ignored his assurances and performed the groundbreaking work on the depletion of the ozone layer that won them the Nobel Prize. (And won for the planet an international agreement on the reduction of CFCs that allowed the earth a chance to repair the ozone hole before it opened so wide as to annihilate much of life through excess ultraviolet radiation.) Lovelock has also failed to identify any clear causal mechanism for his sudden heating hypothesis, explaining that he differs with more conventional forecasts mostly because he thinks they have underestimated both the extent of the self-reinforcing cycles that are causing temperatures to rise and the vulnerability of the planet, which he sees as severely stressed and close to losing equilibrium. It also must be said that parts of his short book read a little oddly – there are digressions into, say, the safety of nitrates in food that don't serve much purpose and raise questions about the rigor of the entire enterprise.

That said, there are very few people on earth – maybe none – with the same kind of intuitive feel for how it behaves as a whole. Lovelock's flashes of insight about Gaia illuminate many of the interconnections between systems that more pedestrian scientists have slowly been trying to identify. Moreover, for the past twenty years, the period during which greenhouse science emerged, most of the effects of heating on the physical world have in fact been more dire than originally predicted. The regular reader of *Science* and *Nature* is treated to an almost weekly load of apocalyptic data, virtually all of it showing results at the very upper end of the ranges predicted by climate models, or beyond them altogether. Compared with the original models of a few years ago, ice is melting faster; forest soils are giving up more carbon as they warm; storms are increasing much more quickly in number and size. As I'm writing these words, news comes across the bottom of my computer screen that a new study shows methane leaking from Siberian permafrost at five times the predicted rate, which is seriously bad news since methane is an even more potent greenhouse gas than CO_2.

In this fast-changing scientific puzzle, the Intergovernmental Panel on Climate Change (IPCC), which has given the world valuable guidance for a decade, stands the risk of being outrun by new data. The panel is supposed to issue a new report in the coming year summarizing the findings made by climate scientists since its last report. But it's unlikely that its somewhat unwieldy procedures will allow it to incorporate fears such as Lovelock's adequately, or even to address fully the far more mainstream predictions issued during the last twelve months by James Hansen of NASA, the planet's top climatologist.[1]

Hansen is not quite as gloomy as Lovelock. Although he recently stated that the Earth is very close to the hottest it has been in a million years, he said that we still have until 2015 to reverse the flow of carbon into the atmosphere before we cross a threshold and create a "different planet." When Hansen gave this warning in December 2005 we had ten years to change course, but soon we'll have only eight years, and since nothing has happened in the intervening time to suggest that we're gearing up for an all-out effort to reduce greenhouse gas emissions, the divergence between Hansen and Lovelock may be academic. (Somehow it's small comfort to be rooting for the guy who says you've got a decade.)

What's amazing is that even Al Gore's fine and frightening film *An Inconvenient Truth* now lags behind the scientific cutting edge on this issue – the science is moving fast. It's true that the world is beginning slowly to awaken to the idea that global warming may be a real problem, and legislatures (though not ours) are starting to nibble at it. But very few understand with any real depth that a wave large enough to break civilization is forming, and that the only real question is whether we can do anything at all to weaken its force.

It's to the question of solutions to mitigate the effects of global warming that Lovelock eventually turns, which is odd since in other places he insists that it's too late to do much. His prescriptions are strongly worded and provocative – he thinks that renewable energy and energy conservation will come too slowly to ward off damage, and that an enormous program of building nuclear reactors is our best, indeed our only, real option. "We cannot turn off our energy-intensive, fossil-fuel-powered civilization without crashing," he writes. "We need the soft landing of a powered descent." That power can't come from wind or solar energy soon enough.

Even now, when the bell has started tolling to mark our ending, we still talk of sustainable development and renewable energy as if these feeble offerings would be accepted by Gaia as an appropriate and affordable sacrifice.

Instead, "new nuclear building should be started immediately."

With his extravagant rhetoric, Lovelock does us a favor – it is true that we should be at least as scared of a new coal plant as of a new nuclear station. The latter carries certain obvious risks (which Lovelock argues convincingly loom larger than perhaps they should in our imaginations), while the coal plants come with the absolute guarantee that their emissions will unhinge the planet's physical systems. Every potential source of non-carbon energy should be examined fairly to see what role it might have in avoiding a disastrous future. But Lovelock also undermines his own argument with what amounts to special pleading. He is a foe of wind power because, as he says, he doesn't want his Devon countryside overrun with windmills, placing him in the same camp as Cape Cod vacationers resistant to wind farms offshore in Nantucket Sound or Vermonters reluctant to see some of their high ridgelines dotted with towering turbines. "Perhaps we are NIMBYs," he writes, referring to the abbreviation for the phrase "Not In My Back Yard," but

> we see those urban politicians [pushing wind power] as like some unthinking physicians who have forgotten their Hippocratic Oath and are trying to keep alive a dying civilization by useless and inappropriate chemotherapy when there is no hope of cure and the treatment renders the last stages of life unbearable.

This is an understandable aversion, but it would need to rest, as Lovelock admits, on something more than aesthetics, and in this case the foundation is all but nonexistent. He quotes a couple of disillusioned Danes to the effect that wind power hasn't been a panacea in Denmark, and says that Britain would need 54,000 big wind turbines to meet its needs, as if that huge number simply ends the argument. (The lack of adequate notes in this book makes checking sources laborious.) But in fact the Germans are adding 2,000 windmills annually, and nearing 20,000 total. Some object to the sight of them scattered across the countryside, and others are enchanted. In any event, whatever one's opinion of wind power, it's not at all clear that a crash program of building atomic reactors makes sense. Most of the economic modeling I've seen indicates that if you took the money intended for building a reactor and invested it instead in an aggressive energy conservation project (one that provided subsidies to companies to modify their factories to reduce power use, for instance), the payoff in cutting back on carbon would be much larger. This doesn't end the argument, either – we will obviously need new energy sources, and the example of the French success with nuclear power (it generates three-quarters of their electricity) means it has to be included in the mix of possibilities, as Jim Hansen recently argued.[2] But Lovelock's argument against wind power is remarkably unpersuasive.

Much more deeply researched, and much more hopeful, data come from the investment banker Travis Bradford. MIT Press has just issued his first book, *Solar Revolution*, which argues at great length and in great detail that we will soon be turning to solar panels for our power, in part for environmental reasons but more because they will soon be producing power that's as cheap – and much easier to deploy – than any other source. This is a fairly astounding claim – the conventional wisdom among environmentalists is that solar energy lags behind wind power by a decade or more as a cost-effective source of electricity – but he makes the case in convincing fashion.

During the last decade (as Janet Sawin of the Worldwatch Institute has previously described), Japan has heavily subsidized the purchase of rooftop solar panels by home owners. The Japanese authorities began to do this, in part, because they wanted to meet the promises they made on their own soil at the Kyoto conference on global warming, but also, Bradford suggests, because they sensed that the industry could grow if it were encouraged by an initial investment. Within a few years, the subsidy had the desired effect – the volume of demand made both manufacturing and installation much more efficient, driving down the price. Today, the government subsidy has almost entirely disappeared, but demand continues to rise, for the panels now allow homeowners to produce their own power for the same price charged by the country's big utilities. Japan in some ways is a special case – blessed with few domestic energy sources, it has some of the world's most expensive electricity, making solar panels more competitive. On the other hand, it's not particularly sunny in Japan. In any event, Bradford says the Japanese demand for solar power (and now an equally large program in Germany) will be enough to drive the cost of producing solar panels steadily down. Even without huge technological breakthroughs, which he says are tantalizingly near, the current hardware can be made steadily cheaper. He predicts the industry will grow 20 to 30 percent annually for the next forty years, which is akin to what happened with the last silicon-based revolution, the computer chip. No surprise, too, about who will own that industry – almost all the solar-panel plants are now in Japan and Germany.

You can see signs of this change already. When I was in Tibet this summer, I repeatedly stumbled across the yak-skin tents of nomadic herders living in some of the most remote (and lofty) valleys in the world. They depended on yak dung, which they burned to cook food and heat their tents, and also often on a small solar panel hanging off one side of the tent, powering a lightbulb and perhaps a radio inside. Every small town had a shop selling solar panels for a price roughly equivalent to that of a single sheep. Solar power obviously makes sense in such places, where there's probably never going to be an electric line. But it also increasingly makes sense in suburban developments, where new technologies like solar roof tiles are reducing the cost of outfitting a house to use solar power; in any event, the cost of such tiles would be a small part of the government-subsidized mortgage. These systems are usually tied into the existing grid – when the sun is shining, my Vermont rooftop functions as a small power plant, sending power down the line. At night, I buy electricity like everyone else; in the sunny months of the year, the power the house uses and the power it generates are about the same. All this would make more economic sense, of course, if the destructive environmental costs of burning, say, cheap coal were reflected in the price of the resulting electricity. That seems almost certain to happen once George W. Bush leaves office. All plausible presidential candidates for both parties are committed to imposing some limits on the use of coal. It's already the rule in the rest of the developed world. But the testimony of Lovelock, Hansen, and the rest of organized science makes it very clear that it would be a wise investment, indeed the wisest possible investment, to spend large sums of government money to hasten this transition to solar power. Where should it come from? One obvious candidate is the Pentagon budget, now devoted to defending us against dangers considerably less threatening than climate change.

But even the widespread adoption of solar power would not put an end to the threat of global warming. The economic transition that our predicament demands is larger and more wrenching even than that. Some scientists have estimated that it would take an immediate 70 percent reduction in fossil fuel burning simply to stabilize climate change at its current planet-melting level. And that reduction is made much harder by the fact that it is needed at just the moment that China and India have begun to burn serious quantities of fossil fuel as their economies grow. Not, of course, American quantities – each of us uses on average eight times the energy that a Chinese citizen does – but relatively serious quantities nonetheless.

Kelly Sims Gallagher, one of the savviest early analysts of climate policy, has devoted the last few years to understanding the Chinese energy transition. Now the director of the Energy Technology Innovation Project at Harvard's Kennedy School, she has just published a fascinating account of the rise of the Chinese auto industry. Her research makes it clear that neither American industry nor the American government did much of anything to point the Chinese away from our addiction to gas-guzzling technology; indeed, Detroit (and the Europeans and Japanese to a lesser extent) was happy to use decades-old designs and processes. "Even though cleaner alternatives existed in the United States, relatively dirty automotive technologies were transferred to China," she writes. One result is the smog that is choking Chinese cities; another is the invisible but growing cloud of greenhouse gases, which come from tailpipes but even more from the coal-fired utilities springing up across China. In retrospect, historians are likely to conclude that the biggest environmental failure of the Bush administration was not that it did nothing to reduce the use of fossil fuels in America, but that it did nothing to help or pressure China to transform its own economy at a time when such intervention might have been decisive.

It is precisely this question – how we might radically transform our daily lives – that is addressed by the cheerful proprietors of the WorldChanging Web site in their new book of the same name. This is one of the most professional and interesting Web sites that you could possibly bookmark on your browser; almost every day they describe a new technology or technique for environmentalists. Their book, a compilation of their work over the last few years, is nothing less than *The Whole Earth Catalog*, that hippie bible, retooled for the iPod generation. There are short features on a thousand cool ideas: slow food, urban farming, hydrogen cars, messenger bags made from recycled truck tarps, pop-apart cell phones, and plyboo (i.e., plywood made from fast-growing bamboo). There are many hundreds of how-to guides (how to etch your own circuit board, how to break in your hybrid car so as to maximize mileage, how to organize a "smart mob," a brief gathering of strangers in a public place). WorldChanging can tell you whom to text-message from your phone in order to advocate for international debt relief, and how to build an iPod speaker from an old tin of Altoids mints. It's a compendium of everything a younger generation of environmental activists has to offer: creativity, digital dexterity, networking ability, an Internet-era optimism about the future, and a deep concern about not only green issues but related questions of human rights, poverty, and social justice. The book's pragmatism is refreshing: "We can do this" is the constant message, and there are enough examples to leave little doubt that sheer cleverness is not what we're lacking as we approach our uncertain future. "We need, in the next twenty-five years or so, to do something never before done. We need to consciously redesign the entire material basis of our civilization," Alex Steffen writes in his editor's introduction,

> If we face an unprecedented planetary crisis, we also find ourselves in a moment of innovation unlike any that has come before.... We live in an era when the number of people working to make the world better is exploding.

He's right.

If there's one flaw in the WorldChanging method, I think it might be a general distrust of the idea that government could help make things happen. There's a Silicon Valley air to the WorldChanging enterprise – over the years it's been closely connected with *Wired* magazine, the bible of the digerati and a publication almost as paranoid about government interference and regulation as *The Wall Street Journal*. Like Internet entrepreneurs, they distrust both government intentions and abilities – bureaucrats tend, after all, to come from the ranks of those neither bold nor smart enough to innovate. A libertarian streak shines through: "When we redesign our personal lives in such a way that we're doing the right thing and having a hell of a good time," Steffen writes, "we act as one-person beacons to the idea that green can be bright, that worldchanging can be lifechanging." I'm sympathetic to this strain of thinking; I believe we're going to need more local and more nimble decision-making in the future to build strong, survivable communities. But it also makes it a little harder to be as optimistic as you'd like to be when reading these pages, which are filled with good ideas that, chances are, won't come to all that much without the support of government and a system of incentives for investment.

You can see a close-up of some of that futility in the new book *Design Like You Give a Damn* from the nonprofit Architecture for Humanity,[3] a book that is lovely in every sense of the word. The group started by sponsoring a competition for new shelters for refugees, and the range of replacements that people thought up for canvas tents makes clear just how much talent is currently going to waste designing McMansions. There are inflatable hemp bubbles and cardboard outhouses and dozens of other designs and prototypes for the world's poorest people and biggest disasters. As time went on, the group also collected photos and plans for attractive buildings around the world: health clinics that generate their own power, schools cheap enough for communities to construct. Still, there's something sad about the entire project – most of these designs have never been carried out, because the architects lacked the political savvy or influence to get them adopted by relief agencies or national governments. When there's a disaster, relief agencies still haul out the canvas tents.

There's another way of saying what is missing here. Almost every idea that might bring us a better future would be made much easier if the cost of fossil fuel was higher – if there was some kind of a tax on carbon emissions that made the price of coal and oil and gas reflect its true environmental cost. (Gore, in an important speech at New York University last month, proposed scrapping all payroll taxes and replacing them with a levy on carbon.) If that day came – and it's the day at least envisioned by efforts like the Kyoto Treaty – then everything from solar panels to windmills to safe nuclear reactors (if they can be built) would spread much more easily: the invisible hand would be free to do more interesting work than it's accomplishing at the moment. Perhaps it would actually begin to operate with the speed necessary to head off Lovelock's nightmares. But that will only happen if local, national, and international officials can come together to make it happen, which in turn requires political action. The recent election-driven decision by California governor Arnold Schwarzenegger to embrace a comprehensive set of climate-change measures shows that such political action is possible; on the other side of the continent, a Labor Day march across Vermont helped to persuade even the most right-wing of the state's federal candidates to endorse an ambitious program against global warming. The march's final rally drew a thousand people, which makes it possibly the largest global warming protest in the country's history. That's a pathetic fact, but it goes to show how few people are actually needed to begin working toward real change.

The technology we need most badly is the technology of community – the knowledge about how to cooperate to get things done. Our sense of community is in disrepair at least in part because the prosperity that flowed from cheap fossil fuel has allowed us all to become extremely individualized, even hyperindividualized, in ways that, as we only now begin to understand, represent a truly Faustian bargain. We Americans haven't needed our neighbors for anything important, and hence neighborliness – local solidarity – has disappeared. Our problem now is that there is no way forward, at least if we're serious about preventing the worst ecological nightmares, that doesn't involve working to-gether politically to make changes deep enough and rapid enough to matter. A carbon tax would be a very good place to start.

Notes

1. See Jim Hansen, "The Threat to the Planet," *The New York Review*, July 13, 2006.

2. "'The Threat to the Planet': An Exchange," *The New York Review*, September 21, 2006.

3. A short essay of mine, which describes the Brazil-ian city of Curitiba and its efforts to integrate design and architecture into citywide planning and development, is appended to the end of the book.

Siphonophore

In spite of all the rejection garlic endured by the early Greeks and Romans, the herb did have its place as a revered medicinal remedy. Hip-pocrates, along with later ancient physicians such as Galen and Dioscorides, considered gar-lic a panacea for a host of ailments from diges-tive discomforts and intestinal infections to high blood pressure, senility, and impotence. However, Hippocrates did warn that garlic "caused flatulence, a feeling of warmth on the chest and a heavy sensation in the head; it excites anxiety and in-creases any pain which may be present. Nevertheless, it has the good quality that it increases the secretion of urine."

The New Village People

❝America's current most significant cultural event is NASCAR — any culture which can celebrate the mindless consumption of a finite resource in driving around a track like Skinner rats deserves to be dependent upon Middle East oil and all that flows from that fact."

— Bill Mares
Teacher in Burlington, Vermont and author of Bees Besieged
and other books

❝The Industrial Revolution is the most important cultural event to shape our current world view. We broke into Nature's safe deposit box of fossil carbon, turning it into a wider range of fuels, and potentially destabilizing the global climate in the process."

— John Elkington
Author, Cannibals With Forks: The Triple Bottom
Line of 21st Century Business

❝The world unhinging before our eyes is a huge cultural event that is shaping our current world view. In my case, I've seen Vermont winters go from 'lion to pussycat' in a mere 25 years! We used to get winters propelled by frigid temperatures and huge amounts of snow, starting in November. These days the salt truck is much more needed than the snowplow and our maple

seasons have become a complete 'nail-chewer'—gotta have freezin' nights for sugarin' to happen. Maple sugarmakers are truly the 'canaries in the mineshaft' when it comes to global warming."

— Burr Morse
Seventh generation farmer and author, Sweet Days and Beyond: The Morse
Family — Eight Generations of Maple Sugaring

Bill McKibben's Book List

The Revenge of Gaia: Earth's Climate Crisis and the Fate of Humanity, by James Lovelock. Basic Books, 2006.

China Shifts Gears: Automakers, Oil, Pollution, and Development, by Kelly Sims Gallagher. MIT Press, 2006.

Solar Revolution: The Economic Transformation of the Global Energy Industry, by Travis Bradford. MIT Press, 2006.

WorldChanging: A User's Guide for the 21st Century, by Alex Steffen, ed. Harry N. Abrams, 2006.

Design Like You Give a Damn: Architectural Responses to Humanitarian Crises, by Architecture for Humanity, eds. Thames & Hudson Ltd.

The Limits to Growth
The New Village Library

Beyond the Limits: Confronting Global Collapse, Envisioning a Sustainable Future, by Donella Meadows & Jorgen Randers. Chelsea Green, 1992.

The Fifth Discipline: The Art & Practice of the Learning Organization, by Peter Senge. Currency, 1994.

Cannibals with Forks: The Triple Bottom Line of 21st Century Business, by John Elkington. New Society Publishers, 1998.

4 THE END OF NATURE

66 *...An idea, a relationship, can go extinct, just like an animal or a plant. The idea in this case is 'nature,' the separate and wild province, the world apart from man to which he adapted, under whose rules he was born and died. In the past, we spoiled and polluted parts of that nature, inflicted environmental 'damage.' But that was like stabbing a man with toothpicks: though it hurt, annoyed, degraded, it did not touch vital organs, block the path of lymph or blood. We never thought that we had wrecked nature. Deep down, we never really thought we could: it was too big and too old; its forces – the wind, the rain, the sun – were too strong, too elemental. But, quite by accident, it turned out that the carbon dioxide and other gases we were producing in our pursuit of a better life... could alter the power of the sun, could increase its heat. And that increase could change the patterns of moisture and dryness, breed storms in new places, breed deserts...We have produced the carbon dioxide – we are ending nature."*

— Bill McKibben

Bill McKibben is a regular guy. I say that because we inhabit the same small state. If you move in similar spheres you cross paths with people enough that they become human scale. Vermont's politicians are that way. You see them frequently enough that you begin thinking "If I called that person, I bet he'd answer. If I sent that person a note, I bet they would reply."

McKibben is also a regular guy because he does ordinary things. He takes people on walks to raise awareness of global warming. He goes cross-country skiing. He eats local food for a few months. He watches a year of cable TV, then compares it to a day on a mountaintop. But then he writes about the ordinary things in extraordinary ways.

In person McKibben (just call him "Bill") is modest and affable. He's a man of faith, but doesn't preach. He's got a great sense of humor, but he is saying some of the scariest things you will ever hear. He's saying we may have done the unthinkable. We may have killed nature.

It's easy to be dismissive of Lovelock. He's the guru of New Age cultists and a lot of what he says sounds like the ramblings of a mad genius. And Rachel Carson's quiet voice can be lost in the din. And as for those MIT kids and their computers ... they're just a little too smart for their own good.

But McKibben ... Bill ... is hard to ignore. He's mature, articulate, and open-minded.

He says we're in trouble and we better start doing something about it. We'd best listen.

> **"**I believe that Bill McKibben will prove to be an even more significant contributor to a positive relationship between humans and the environment if we follow the evolution of his thinking from *The End of Nature* to his upcoming book on living close to the land."
>
> — *Elizabeth Courtney*
> *Executive Director*
> *Vermont Natural Resources Council*

Bill McKibben grew up in suburban Lexington, Massachusetts. At Harvard he was president of the *Harvard Crimson* newspaper. Upon graduation he became a staff writer at the *New Yorker* magazine, and wrote much of the "Talk of the Town" column from 1982 to early 1987. When longtime editor William Shawn was forced out, McKibben quit and moved to the Adirondacks.

McKibben's first book, *The End of Nature* (1989) is regarded as the first book for a general audience about climate change, and has been printed in more than 20 languages. McKibben is a frequent contributor to various magazines with varying environmental credentials, and has written several more books, including *Hope, Human and Wild* (1995), *Maybe One: A Case for Smaller Families* (1998), and *Enough* (2003). In late summer 2006 he helped lead a five-day walk across Vermont to demand action on global warming that some newspaper accounts called the largest demonstration to date in America about climate change.

> ❝ The time has come to move beyond 'growth' as the paramount economic ideal and begin pursuing prosperity in a more local direction, with cities, suburbs, and regions producing more of their own food, generating more of their own energy, and even creating more of their own culture and entertainment. This concept is already blossoming around the world with striking results, from the burgeoning economies of India and China to the more mature societies of Europe and New England. For those who worry about environmental threats, there are solutions to work through the worst of those problems; for those who wonder if there isn't something more to life than buying, I encourage you to consider your life as an individual and as a member of a larger community."
>
> www.billmckibben.com

Slow Food Movement Has Global Outreach

by Carol Ness

Americans who think of Slow Food as an elite supper club for snobby food purists would be stunned by the scene unfolding inside the former Olympic speed skating arena in Turin, Italy over the past four days.

Senegalese cereal farmers in purple satin and matching headdresses trade packaging tips with Peruvian potato growers in traditional red embroidered garb. Goat cheese makers and Hmong long-bean growers from California find common ground with their Italian and Eastern European counterparts. Israeli and Palestinian farmers, along with Iraqi and American food producers, share space and the excited chat that food never fails to stimulate.

This is Terra Madre, a gathering that is the Olympics of the international movement to deindustrialize food production. That means putting taste back at the heart of food, saving heirloom fruits, vegetables and animals, keeping small farmers in business and in local communities, and pushing farming back on sound environmental ground.

Mingling with the farmers are prominent Bay Area names in the sustainable food movement – Chez Panisse founder Alice Waters and UC Berkeley journalism professor and *The Omnivore's Dilemma* author Michael Pollan, just to name a couple.

Invited to cook next door at the Salone del Gusto, the giant artisanal food fair that showcases some of Terra Madre producers, were hot Spanish chef Ferran Adria of El Bulli and renowned Piedmont chef Cesare Giaccone.

More than 5,000 small farmers and foodmakers from 130 countries, plus 1,000 chefs – including more than a dozen from the Bay Area – are in Turin to eat, network and build what Waters called "a global counterculture" in her address to the opening session.

It's the second such gathering organized by Slow Food International, which is based in the nearby town of Bra. The first Terra Madre, in 2004, generated an astounding force field around the ideas of Slow Food, which started 20 years ago as a way of saving inexpensive Italian restaurants serving tagliarini with butter and sage and other traditional foods from the wave of nouvelle cuisine that put salmon with dill on plates around the world.

Now, Slow Food has grown into an international movement, with 80,000 members in 50 countries, including 12,000 in the United States.

About 500 Americans were invited as delegates and observers, more than a quarter of them Californians, including a contingent of organic farmers from the

Capay Valley in Yolo County who are familiar faces at San Francisco's Ferry Plaza and Berkeley farmers' markets.

Health problems like obesity and diabetes, widening economic disparities across the world, and environmental issues like global warming show that the current system "defined by speed, abundance and waste" can no longer sustain itself, Slow Food founder Carlo Petrini told the conference.

The time is ripe, he said, to bring food economies back to their local roots.

For a group of Hmong, Latino and African American farmers from the Central Valley of California brought to Terra Madre with help from the Davis-based Community Alliance With Family Farmers, that meant connecting with farmers from around the world.

Ali Shabazz, an African American herb farmer from Fresno, helped a Tanzanian farmer who wanted technical advice on equipment. Va Moua, who says many of the Hmong farmers in the Central Valley use lots of fertilizer, talked to farmers who don't.

"Now we'll find out if we can do it naturally," he said.

The point, said Blong Lee, a representative of the Fresno County Economic Opportunities Commission, is to get Central Valley farmers thinking about ways they can distinguish themselves and their crops, and to get their products into the local economy instead of the global one.

At one point, the California farmers found themselves dubiously eyeing a plate of cured meat called capocolla from the southern Italian town of Martina Franca.

Its maker, Costantini Angelo, had ideas for the California farmers, most of whom grow just one crop, sell into the wholesale market, but fail to make enough to gain a real foothold in the Central Valley economy. Angelo feeds his pigs only acorns from his home region, so his meat has the unique taste of its soil. That's a value-added intangible that helps him sell directly to stores and obtain the price he wants.

Moua and Cindy Mai Xiong, farmers who grow jujube – a kind of fruit – on four acres near Fresno, touched the acorns and heard the advice – but they were distracted by their growling stomachs. This was their third day in Italy and amid all this beautiful Parmigiana Reggiano and prosciutto di Parma, they were starving.

"We went to a fancy restaurant last night," said Lee of the Fresno commission. "We tried to order pizza with pepperoni and they didn't have it, and lasagna and spaghetti and meatballs, but they didn't have it. It's not the type of Italian food we expected."

The chefs, meanwhile, reveled in the Italian Italian food. Incanto chef Cosentino ate his way through all the lardo – a cured meat made from pig fat – and prosciutto he could find, and sought esoteric ingredients like tuna heart.

Jackie Martine, chef-owner of the Seaweed Cafe in Bodega Bay, who tries to source all of her ingredients locally, made a connection with an African grower of vanilla beans – something she knows she can never find in Northern California – from whom she may buy directly. And from a Mauritanian's bottarga di mugine, a salted mullet roe, she was inspired to create a similar product using her native halibut roe "which is usually thrown away."

On a trip through a local farmers' market, though, she was stunned to see that most of the apples were Granny Smith, red delicious and golden delicious, the same ones that dominate American supermarkets. "It's the effect of globalization," she said.

San Franciscan Cosentino, who participated in a panel on meats, said he felt a divide between affluent chefs like himself and struggling farmers from poorer regions – a divide that Slow Food has yet to bridge.

"I complain because we can't get lungs," he said of federal laws that ban what for some is a delicacy. In contrast, a Kenyan livestock farmer on the same panel described how water shortages and power failures decimate his cattle before he can get them to slaughter, threatening his entire livelihood.

"There's this disconnect," Cosentino said of the enormous disparity in resources among participants in the conference.

In the United States, Slow Food leaders are well aware that there's a similar disconnect between the political ideals forged at Terra Madre and consumers' perceptions of Slow Food.

"The media still regards Slow Food as a dining club; they still don't perceive the political content," Michael Pollan told a meeting of the US delegation.

To try to bridge that gap, to take the ideas of Terra Madre home, Slow Food USA is planning an unprecedented gathering of regional artisanal food producers in San Francisco in May 2008, Waters said. The idea, dubbed Slow Food Nation, could be replicated all over the country, she added.

"It's clear there is a political movement growing around food," Pollan said. "And it's about a lot more than food – it's about health, the health of local economies, the energy crisis.

"People are ready to hear this movement. It seems the important work now is to show that San Francisco is at the center of this movement."

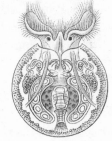

Rotiferan

Published on Monday, October 30, 2006
©2006 San Francisco *Chronicle*

Look Homeward, America
Review by Thomas Naylor

Bill Kauffman is an impeccably honest, witty, insightful observer of American politics and culture who is committed to that which is small, local, and nonviolent. Although he has been characterized as a populist, an agrarian libertarian, and a paleo conservative, Kauffman is above all his own man. With many political writers you can figure out who the good guys are and who the bad guys are just by looking at the title, of a piece. Not so with Kauffman. You've got to read the entire piece.

In *Look Homeward, America*, Kauffman introduces us to "the reactionary radicals, front-porch anarchists, and traditionalist rebels who give American culture and politics its pith, vim, and life." His book is a collection of skillfully crafted vignettes describing such American originals as Catholic Worker founder Dorothy Day, regionalist painter Grant Wood, farmer-writer Wendell Berry, maverick US senators Eugene McCarthy and Patrick Moynihan, President Millard Fillmore, labor leader Mother Jones, and backwoods Maine novelist Carolyn Chute. Kauffman accurately describes his work as larded with "memoir and personal asides the way my wife adds garlic to her cooking: liberally, unabashedly, with the conviction that flavor and spice make savor and nice." Kauffman knows his craft, and he knows it very well.

Some of Kauffman's descriptions are absolutely priceless. Take New York City, for example, which he calls "Vampire City." Others include "Nagasaki Harry, a.k.a. Harry Truman; Arkansas Senator William Fullbright, "a kind of Tory Confederate anti-imperialist;" Senator Patrick Moynihan, "a deft dipper in the pork barrel;" and New York Governor Nelson Rockefeller, "Rocky the irrepressible hi-ya-fella backslapper." One of Kauffman's favorites is "President of the World Bush, a deracinated preppie, a petulant boarding-school cheerleader." Kauffman's vocabulary and skill with the English language are without equal.

Millard Fillmore, who Kauffman described as an "underrated president," is one of the most interesting characters in *Look Homeward, America*. For his opposition to American imperialism, particularly in the Mexican War, "Fillmore ranks with the Quaker Herbert Hoover as the most pacifist president in our history."

Kauffman's vignette on obscure, Civil War era Ohio Democratic Congressman Clement L. Vallandigham is particularly revealing. Vallandigham was deported by Abraham Lincoln for his opposition to the Civil War. Lincoln's shabby treatment of "Valiant Val" was but one example of his imperial presidency which included invading the Confederate States without the consent of Congress, suspension of habeas corpus, imprisonment of thousands of Americans without trial, censoring all telegraph communications, closing opposition newspapers, nationalizing the railroads, and confiscating firearms. From whom the current imperial president learned most of his dirty tricks, there can be little doubt: Honest Abe.

Finally, there is Maine writer Carolyn Chute and her husband Michael, two of my favorite people. The award-winning author of *The Beans of Egypt*, Chute is also co-founder and secretary of the 450-member 2nd Maine Militia. She and Michael are ardent supporters of the constitutional right to bear arms. Michael is the local grave-yard man, who sports a spiffy two-foot-long black beard and a green-felt crusher hat.

Carolyn, a 60-year-old grandmother, often appears at militia meetings carrying her AK-47, wearing a camo jacket, a colorful kerchief, workboots, and military sunglasses. The 2nd Maine Militia (2MM) is similar to hundreds of small shooting clubs scattered throughout Switzerland. Above all, the 2MM is a diverse social organization consisting of working-class people from all over New England – Democrats, Republicans, Greens, lefties, libertarians, feminists, patriots, and anarchists. They all share a common distrust of Corporate America, the US government, and political correctness.

The battle cry of the 2MM could easily be, "Remember the 2nd Maine," which would be a not-so-subtle reminder of American imperialism in the Spanish American War, launched after the U.S.S. *Maine* was allegedly blown up by the Spanish.

Kauffman, a self-described American patriot, Jeffersonian decentralist, and fanatical localist, concludes his book with a chapter entitled, "Why I am Not Ashamed to be an American." He is currently writing a book on American secession movements. He may soon find it increasingly difficult to have it both ways.

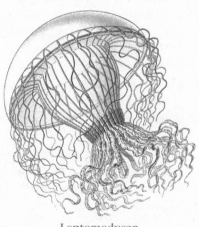

Leptomedusan

---

reprinted by permission. Published originally in *Vermont Commons*.

Thomas H. Naylor is Proffessor Emeritus of Economics, Duke University, and founder of the Second Vermont Republic.

Swami Calls for an Up-Wising
Wise Up, Everybody ... The Evolution Has Begun!
By Swami Beyondananda

For years now, we've been hearing "shift happens," and wondering when, where and how. Now finally, it looks as if the shift is about to hit the fan. This is good news for all those shift fans who've been wondering if the new age will arrive before old age does. Of course, if you're looking for signs in the news, you won't find them. At least, not yet. The news might as well be called the "olds," because the world still seems stuck in greedlock, ruled by fossilized fools fueled by fossil fuels. But I have been receiving encouraging intelligence reports that say indeed, humans are becoming more intelligent. Yes, people everywhere are wising up. And that's great, because we could sure use an up-wising!

The evolution has begun. But before we see changes in the old needy-greedy, we humans must change our consciousness – and the first step is becoming conscious of how unconscious we've been. As the saying goes, the truth shall upset you free, and last year saw lots of disillusionment. But what better to free us from the far more dangerous condition of illusionment? If we want to stop the abuse of power, the first step is to disabuse ourselves. So, here's some good news: Despite a massive media impropaganda machine that feeds the public "babblum" (strained bullshit made digestible for a simple child's mind), more and more Americans are reading between the lyins' and peering behind the Irony Curtain.

In 2005, Americans had to face the sad realization that the Bush Administration's "pro-life" stance appears to be limited to the unborn and the brain-dead. Despite being panned by critics everywhere, the Iraqi Horror Picture Show continued its run, as thousands and thousands of born fetuses – ours and theirs – lost their right to life. While we may or may not have saved face by staying there, we have most definitely lost ass. And we've been assured we'll be stuck in that morass until – well, until there's no more ass to lose. Meanwhile, more and more Americans reached another sad conclusion: We're not in Iraq to keep the peace, we're there to keep the pieces.

The signs of up-wising are everywhere. Even the most unpleasant stories are beginning to break through the soundless barrier and defy the President's "don't

chapter 4 : The End of Nature

ask, don't tell" policy: "You promise not to ask us what we're doing, and we promise not to tell you." Although we've been inundated with "fear-gnomes" and ominously warned we have to protect ourselves in this dogma-eat-dogma world, a majority of Americans are no longer comfortable with the notion that the only way to defeat the "evil-doers" in the world is to out evil-do them. Although our President has assured us that "we don't torture," it is now common knowledge that we simply send detainees to countries that do torture when we want them to "testify under oaf."

As for those progressives who've been whining that the President "never listens" to them, well it turns out he's been listening all along. And thanks to the so-called Patriot Act (which, I understand, is about to be renamed the Eternal Insecurity Act), it looks like he'll be able to listen in even more – all in the name of making us safe. But now even some Republicans are beginning to see that there's a difference between protection and the "protection racket." And with the recent revelations about Tom DeLay, Jack Abramoff and other gold collar criminals, some of the more devout conservatives have come to realize that the "family values" they voted for bear an uncanny resemblance to Soprano Family values.

If there was any warm feeling in 2005, chalk it up to climate change. Katrina hit, and in the government's response we saw a future when at last all Americans will be equal – where everyone regardless of race or creed will be treated like Black folks.

Alarming Policies Have Awakened Millions!

Fortunately this is the State of the Universe Address, and from a universal perspective, things are humming along quite nicely. It turns out that the Earth is the talk of the Universe these days. In fact, the odds-makers at the Intergalactic Enquirer say the odds are actually in our favor: "We're betting on the human race to reach critical mass before they get to critical massacre." And we could beat the odds, if we finally gave up our addiction to getting even and got odd instead. It stands to reason. If each of us used our unique oddness to improve the odds for everyone, there would be no need for getting even.

Yes, the up-wising has begun, and intergalactic observers are saying that we have none other than George W. Bush to thank. How is that, you may ask? Well, I am reminded of a story my guru Harry Cohen Baba used to tell. A well-known minister died and arrived at the Pearly Gates at the same time as a cab driver from New York. The cabbie was ushered in, but the clergyman was left waiting outside. After waiting and waiting and waiting, he finally called over the attending angel. "Excuse me, but I'm a renowned minister. How come you let that cab driver in, and I'm left waiting out here?"

"Well," the angel said, "when you preached, everyone slept. But when he drove, everyone prayed."

For millennia, spiritual teachers have been calling on us to go for the highest common denominator, but we've always seemed to end up with the lowest common dominator instead. And now, George W. Bush has done what preachers, teachers and other far-sighted visionaries have failed to do up until now: His policies have been so alarming, that he has awakened a slumbering body politic that slept through all previous alarms. Where others have failed, he has people all across the world praying, "God help us!" And instead of waiting for an intervention from above – after all, we cannot expect to be fed inravenously forever – people are beginning to help themselves, and even more importantly, help each other.

Sure, there are still plenty of Not-Sees out there who insist on not seeing that we humans are all in the same boat. The good news is, more and more Americans are getting that sinking feeling that there's only one Earthship, and ignoring a leak because it's "on the other side of the boat," is a mistake of titanic proportions.

We Are the Leaders We've Been Waiting For

America, the world's only super-power, doesn't need a revolution. We've already had one, thank you. What is needed now – and what has already begun – is the American Evolution where enough of us wake up and see that those two political parties have been partying on our dime, and we the people haven't been invited. Time to go beyond choosing the lesser of two weasels. If we want to evolve the dream of our Founding Fathers – instead of devolve into the nightmare of Big Brother – we must become the leaders we've been waiting for. I've said it before. The only force more powerful than a super-power is a Super-Duper Power – the power of the people plus the power of love. And anyone who doesn't believe we are a Super-Duper Power, well they have been super-duped!

It's true, many people still feel that the affairs of the world should be left to the bolder and badder among us. But look what that leaves us with: Are you satisfied choosing between Saddam Hussein and George Who's-Not-Sane? Now I know those "God, guns and guts" Old Testament Christians might have forgotten, but Jesus did say that the meek shall inherit the earth. In all undue immodesty, maybe it's time for us meek folks to boldly step forth and accept our inheritance.

For just as 2000 years ago Jesus stood up to a class that placed the rule of gold above the Golden Rule, today we face the modern version of the Pharisees – the Phallusees, I think they are called. They cynically cloak themselves in religious robes, but the only power they trust is the power of the stick. Well, there's another old saying: It doesn't matter how big your stick is, if you stick your stick where it doesn't belong, you're stuck.

Another sign of the up-wising and coming evolution is that people are growing dissatisfied with the positionality of "my side vs. your side," and are seeing the whole issue of sides from a new angle: Maybe we're all on the same side. For example, this argument between creationism and evolution is just another way for dueling dualities to steal our energy. I believe in both. I believe the Creator created us to evolve, otherwise Jesus would have said, "Now don't do a thing till I return." I have it on good authority that the Creator is pulling for us: "Come on, you children of God. Time to grow up and become adults of God instead."

Time to Overgrow the System From the Grassroots Up

The time for revolution and overthrowing has past. Now we need an evolution where we "overgrow" the current dysfunctional system from the grassroots up. You are probably familiar with the story of the Native American grandfather who tells his grandson that there are two wolves fighting inside all of us: The wolf of fear and anger, and the wolf of love and peace.

"Which wolf will win?" asks the young boy.

"Whichever one we feed," replies the grandfather.

And so when people ask me to predict what will happen, I tell them the only thing I can predict with certainty is the uncertainty of any prediction. The future's just too unpredictable these days. This is a Universe of infinite possibilities, so it all depends on which futures we invest in.

There is something far more empowerful than predictions, and that is Tell-A-Vision. If you're fed up with the current programming, my advice is turn off your TV and tell a vision instead. That way, we will have healing and functional visions to step into – and that beats what we've been stepping into. So I will tell my vision for 2006: This is the year of the American Evolution, where all those who prefer the Golden Rule to the rule of gold get past left and right, and come front and center.

I see Americans of all political stripes, plaids and polka dots (not to mention solids), choosing to face the music and dance together. Sure, we'll have to learn some new steps, but it's time for a new dance – A-Bun-Dance. That is where we get up off our assets, move our buns, and dance together in rhythm and flow. And what better way to turn the funk into function, and leave the junk at the junction?

I see us in a new reality show – Extreme Planetary Makeover – where everyone can play and everyone can win. Just think. Something more compelling than reality TV ... it's called reality!

I know, I know. Only a crazy person would dare to propose anything that sane. But maybe it's time to declare the current institutionalized insanity illegally insane, and set about building a sane asylum big enough for all six and a half billion of us. As my guru Harry Cohen Baba has said, "Life is like a good deli. Even if something isn't on the menu, if enough people order it they have to make it." So what kind of new world order are we ordering up? Do we feed the wolf of fear and buy into the "it's every man for himself" story? Or do we nourish the wolf of love and evolve into the "we're all in it together" story?

If we're going to be a Super-Duper Power, we have to be super-duper powerful in activating the power of love, and cultivating the power of joy. So laugh more. Why not? We all know there's something funny going on. The wall of lies cannot withstand the vibration of laughter. All seriousness aside, only a farce field that combines truth and laughter can bring down the Irony Curtain once and for all.

Release the old story – been there, done that – and speak the new story into the world. Dare to imagine what we could be doing if we weren't spending so much of our livelihood on weapons of deadlihood. Think about it ... think tanks where they think about something other than tanks. Young people living for their country instead of dying for it. Health and education fully funded, and the Air Force having to run a bake sale so they can buy a new bomber.

Can we change the course of history? Can we shift our karma into surpassing gear? I cannot say for sure, but if we choose to give up that old Dodge and trade it in for an Evolvo, that's a good first step. So ... let the Evolution begin. We don't have to wait until the first Big Shot is fired. If we create a powerful enough field, the Big Shots will end up firing themselves.

May the FARCE – as always – be with us.

Crab harboring Cerripedian

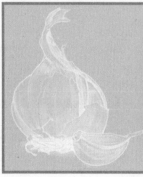

Dioscorides , who was chief physician to Nero's army, included garlic to remedy coughs and colds, expel intestinal worms, clear the arteries, eradicate skin rashes, and make bald mens' hair grow. His and Pliny's medicinal formulas were translated and used in Europe until the seventeenth century.

chapter 4 : The End of Nature

Float Like a Butterfly

Julia Butterfly Hill
interviewed by *Grist* Magazine

QUESTION: *What work do you do?*

ANSWER: I founded Circle of Life in 1999 while living in the branches of an over-1,000-year-old redwood to keep it from being cut down by MAXXAM-owned Pacific Lumber Company.

What does your organization do?

Circle of Life activates people through education, inspiration, and connection to live in a way that honors the diversity and interdependence of all life. We believe that you – yes, you – make the difference in the world.

What do you really do, on a day-to-day basis? What are you working on at the moment?

My days are filled with answering requests like this one from *Grist*. I also facilitate workshops, speak at events, fundraise for many organizations (including Circle of Life, which also needs funds to do the work we do), strategize with team members around programs and ideas, write forewords and endorsements for books for authors who publish in ecologically sound ways, make art that is auctioned for nonprofits, and have meetings with key movement leaders.

What long and winding road led you to your current position?

It actually was a road that led me to where I am now. Literally. I had a car wreck in August of 1996 when I was designated driver, driving my friend's car (she had been drinking), and we were hit from behind by a drunk driver. It took 10 months of physical and cognitive therapy to recover from the wreck, and during that time I realized I wanted to find a more powerful purpose for being here on this planet. After I was released from my last doctor, I went on a road trip with friends which led me to California, which led me to the redwoods, which led me to found Circle of Life, which led *Grist* to be able to have a way to contact me, which led to this moment of me answering these questions.

How many emails are currently in your inbox?

I do not use email – it takes all I have to just keep up with my life.

Where were you born? Where do you live now?

I was born in Mount Vernon, Missouri. I now am based in Oakland, California, and have been for the last four years.

Who is your environmental hero?

I have so many people I look to for inspiration and motivation including Gandhi, Mother Teresa, Amílcar Cabral, and Joan Baez. I am inspired continuously by all kinds of people, young and old, of all kinds of cultural and economic backgrounds, who are contributing to making our world a better place.

What are you reading these days?

Bury My Heart at Wounded Knee; *Prison Writings: My Life Is My Sun Dance* by Leonard Peltier; *The Lorax*; *Horton Hears a Who*; everything Rumi – just to name a few. I love to read.

What's your favorite meal?

Just about anything vegan! I am a joyous vegan, and an avid cook and un-cook. I love preparing food that is healthy for people, the planet, and animals, and tastes damn good.

What's your favorite place or ecosystem?

Of course, the redwood forests are some of the most beautiful and sacred to me. I also have a strong love for any place that is tropical with ocean and fruit trees. I love being on the beach in the middle of nowhere, baking in the sun and listening to the hypnotic ocean.

What's one thing the environmental movement is doing badly, and how could it be done better?

We are doing a sad job at un-learning and undoing racism and classism and sexism within ourselves, our organizations, and our movement. Also, as a whole, we are pretty profoundly lacking in integrity. We need to spend less time preaching and more time practicing.

If you could institute by fiat one environmental reform, what would it be?

We could learn a heck of a lot from many European countries, including making manufacturers responsible for the life of the products they make, taxing manufacturers and consumers on everything that falls under the term "disposable," and holding manufacturers responsible for paying for the end result of all their packaging.

Who was your favorite musical artist when you were 18? How about now?

My music tastes are actually still pretty much what they were when I was 18 only I have added more world music and conscious hip-hop like The Coup to my repertoire. I am very eclectic. Some of my favorite bands then and now include Sinead O'Connor, Tori Amos, Tool, Nine Inch Nails, Metallica, Sarah McLachlan, Bach, Beethoven, Mozart, and Tupac Amaru Shakur (2Pac), to name a few.

What's your favorite TV show? Movie?

TV kills your mind and your creativity.

Like my music tastes, my movie tastes are all over the place. My old-school all-time favorites are *The Princess Bride*, *The Secret of NIMH*, and *The Usual Suspects*. More recent favorites include the *Lord of the Rings* trilogy and *Whale Rider*.

What are you happy about right now?

This breath. And this one. And this one ... It is magic every time.

If you could have every reader do one thing, what would it be?

Siphonophore

Get rid of disposability consciousness – every paper bag, paper plate, paper napkin, plastic to-go container, and Styrofoam cup. I have walked on the earth that is connected to the thread at the other end of those horrific choices, and I am not being over-dramatic when I say disposables are weapons of mass destruction.

The End of Nature:
The New Village People

❝The most significant cultural event to shape our current world view was the extinction of less aggressive and more reflective human ancestral genetic lines, in part by violent conflict with our more aggressive ancestors (the *Quest For Fire* scenario), in part through natural cataclysm (notably the human genetic "bottleneck" 75,000 years ago), or, in the recent case of the Americas a mere 600 years ago, by sudden introduction of untoward pathogens auguring up to 95% genocide, along with nearly all the culture, science and art that had been accumulated by hundreds of millions of people. Sadly, this million-year morality play may prove merely a prequel to the great extinction event of the 21st century. That all of this is studiously absent from the curriculum taught to every schoolchild in the world would seem an illustrative demonstration of our Neanderthal gene lines."

— Albert Bates
Author, The Post-Petroleum Survival Guide and Cookbook

❝The No Nukes Concert and film, organized and produced by Danny Goldberg was as significant as any cultural event in our lifetimes. Again, the music, a form of art, reaches people in the soul and motivates, agitates and educates."

— Joe Uehlein
Musician

❝ The Ozone Hole. This appears to be a multi-lateral success story.
  Science says: "Hey, look out, there's a big problem up there. You can't see it but it can kill us all."
  Law makers and business say: "Yeah right, prove it."
  Science proves it.
  Law makers, business, and everyone else on the planet says: "So what are we supposed to do about it?"

Science says:"Do these things and hurry up about it"

Law makers and business say:"We can't do that, it will cost too much, nobody will buy our stuff and we'll be out of work. We need more study"

Science studies, reports back that the problem is getting worse. We have pictures and data to prove it. Science screams:"Do these things and hurry up about it!"

Law makers mandate and business grudgingly brings new products to the market.

The people are happy to spend a few bucks more for the privilege of not being fried by the sun.

This success story can carry over to the current global warming crisis we face. This will be a bigger challenge because it involves far greater levels of power and money in the form of petro-dollar warfare. But science has proven, and the greater part of the world agrees, that there is a problem. We await lawmakers and business to act in order to provide the people with choices that will lead to solutions. More pressure is needed. More courage, less oil."

— Paul Scheckel
Author, The Home Energy Diet

66 Over a number of years corporations have shifted from serving the public good to having the rights of citizens, without the corresponding responsibilities of citizenship. A turning point occurred in a US Supreme Court case *Santa Clara County* v. *Southern Pacific Railroad Company* (118 U.S. 394) when, almost as an aside, the opinion was stated that corporations were protected by the 14th Amendment to the Constitution. This allowed companies, which are able to amass enormous wealth by virtue of unlimited life, to gradually take over our political process."

— Stuart Auchincloss
Member, Woodstock Environmental Commission

66 The NGO Forum at the Rio Earth Summit in 1992 was the first time that many of us came to fully grasp the extent to which all humans share a deep consensus on core values that transcends boundaries of religion, language, culture, nationality, and race."

— David C. Korten
Author, The Great Turning

" Female suffrage and women getting the vote has happened gradually, one place at a time, over more than a century. This movement is one of the most positive elements in the evolution of human civilization. We are coming from a series of societies, throughout the world and throughout human history, in which physical power determined dominance. Where we are heading is toward civilizations in which outcomes are determined less by physical, political or economic power than by rules of fairness and justice, where compassionate concern for the needs of others will be the norm. Accompanying improvements in female suffrage have been related movements that promote the rights of prisoners, of the mentally ill, of animals, and of children. To be successful these movements depend on the willingness of those who have power to share or give up some portion of their power. We're a long way away from an ideal sharing between the weak and strong, but, in general, the human race seems to be moving in the right direction."

— Neva Goodwin
Co-director, Global Development And Environment
Institute, Tufts University

" It's hard to overstate the impact of Hurricane Katrina and the public response."

— Nancy Jack Todd
Editor, Annals of Earth *newsletter*

" Hurricane Katrina will be remembered as the most important turning point in the world's awareness and reaction to global warming."

— Jeffrey Hollender
President & Chief Inspired Protagonist,
Seventh Generation

" We can thank Herman Daly for the concept of full cost accounting, Buckminster Fuller for the power and possibility of thinking differently, and E.F. Schumacher as the father of the act locally/think globally movement."

— Jeffrey Hollender

chapter 4 : The End of Nature

" I've heard lots of criticism of Al Gore's film, *An Inconvenient Truth,* from inside the green movement, but we're already converted. The mainstream media coverage and my conversations with non-movement people have convinced me that it has done *so* much to bring them on board."

— *Nancy Jack Todd*
Author, A Safe and Sustainable World

" Our rampant and reckless despoiling of nature, which has increased rapidly in the last half-century, has now reached a crisis point where the future of life on the surface of the earth is highly problematic. The power and extent of modern industrial technology is taking our planet to catastrophe and will be averted only by the abolition of capitalism, industrialism, and human domination of the world's ecosytems."

— *Kirkpatrick Sale*

" The Culture of Fear, as practiced by our current leadership, has been pressing its hobnailed, weighty boot on the back of the world since the destruction of the Twin Towers on 9/11. The accompanying world view promotes a vision that is as petrifying as it is destructive. Fear cannot create — only hope can do that. Fear can only stifle and cause progress to die. Fear strangles hope, and hope is life. There must be some horribly incomprehensible reason why a privileged few choose a path that features plunder, expansion, destruction, chaos, corruption, and ultimately extinction. Only by refusing to follow this path, and choosing instead to live a real life will our species, and our kindred species on this planet, survive."

— *Dave Bonta*
President, BioQuantum
Vice President, The Vermont BioFuels Association

" The Precautionary Principle has made us aware not to invent, manufacture, or sell anything without conducting due diligence on the impact on future generations."

— *Christopher Plant*
New Society Publishers

❝ After Bill McKibben wrote *The End of Nature* and dug deeply into the bad news, he started a search for a more nuanced sense of the relationship between humans and the environment, which continues today, more than a decade later. His prolific, expansive, resonant examination of many issues not always considered to be 'environmental' — like reproduction, economy, and community — consistently raises the level of the whole conversation."

— John Abrams
President, South Mountain Company, Inc and Author, The Company We Keep: Reinventing Small Business for Community, People, and Place.

❝ Since The Industrial Revolution our world view has been shaped by the combustion engine. This brought us unimaginable mobility, but also dramatically altered life styles. It has created the separation of work and family, school and marketplace. It has brought us access to all corners of the world and beyond, a global economy and global climate change. The Industrial Revolution started something that we are now realizing can destroy the very life it made possible."

— Elizabeth Courtney

chapter 4 : The End of Nature

Hope, Human and Wild: True Stories of Living Lightly on the Earth, by Bill McKibben. Little, Brown & Co., 1995.

The Comforting Whirlwind: God, Job, and the Scale of Creation, by Bill McKibben. Cowley Publications, 2005.

Maybe One: a Case for Smaller Families, by Bill McKibben. Plume, 1999.

Long Distance: A Year of Living Strenuously, by Bill McKibben. Simon & Schuster, 2000.

Wandering Home: A Long Walk across America's most hopeful landscape: Vermont's Champlain Valley and New York's Adirondacks, by Bill McKibben. Crown, 2005.

Plan B 2.0: Rescuing a Planet Under Stress and a Civilization in Trouble, by Lester Brown. W.W. Norton & Co., 2006.

Earth in the Balance: Ecology and the Human Spirit, by Al Gore. Plume, 1993.

The Last Hours of Ancient Sunlight: The Fate of the World and What We Can Do Before It's Too Late, by Thom Hartmann. Three Rivers Press, 1998.

Beyond Growth: The Economics of Sustainable Development, by Herman Daly. Beacon Press, 1992.

Critical Path, by Buckminster Fuller. St. Martin's Press, 1981.

The Home Energy Diet: How to Save Money by Making Your House Energy Smart, by Paul Scheckel. New Society Publishers, 2005.

The Company We Keep: Reinventing Small Business for People, Community, and Place, by John Abrams. Chelsea Green, 2005.

5 ONE-STRAW REVOLUTION

If we throw mother nature out the window, she comes back in the door with a pitchfork."

— Masanobu Fukuoka

The most profound learning experience of my college career was reading Robert Ardrey's *African Genesis: A Personal Investigation into the Animal Origins and Nature of Man*, long since out of print, but available, used, on Amazon. Ardrey's contention that the human species is subject to the same influences and factors as all other species struck me...

Waitaminute ... is this guy saying we are animals?

Although we all profess to understand and believe this at some intellectual level, it took several years and a thorough reading of Ardrey's follow-up book *The Social Contract* for me to accept this principle at more of a gut level. But, once I did, so many other aspects of the human condition made sense.

Masanobu Fukuoka's *The One-Straw Revolution* is a similar work, easy to accept on a cerebral level, but difficult to incorporate on a meaningful basis. The world of farming is not about dominating nature (conventional), or being compatible with nature (organic), it is about being nature. My gardening partner who finds it easy to accept my abandonment of the rototiller in favor of the hand spade, cannot accept the principle of planting seeds on top of the ground. Something in her brain rebels at the rejection of 50,000 years of human agricultural heritage.

This is a revolution that begins with not a bang, but a whimper. Even within organic farming circles, when practitioners get together the talk gravitates towards equipment, pest control, and production efficiencies, the same subjects that interest conventional farmers.

The One Straw Revolution is not about conquering nature, but rather being nature. It's about rolling back the clock not to pre-insecticide days, not to pre-petroleum days, but rather to pre-agriculture days. It's not an easy concept for most of us to grasp.

> 66 When a decision is made to cope with the symptoms of a problem, it is generally assumed that the corrective measures will solve the problem itself. They seldom do. Engineers cannot seem to get this through their heads. These countermeasures are all based on too narrow a definition of what is wrong. Human measures and countermeasures proceed from limited scientific truth and judgment. A true solution can never come about in this way."
>
> — *Masanobu Fukuoka*

Masanobu Fukuoka was born February 2, 1913 to a farming family on the southern Japanese island of Shikoku. He trained as a microbiologist and began a career as a soil scientist specializing in plant pathology. By age 25, he began to doubt the wisdom of modern agricultural science, and eventually quit his job to return to his family's farm to grow organic mikans (clementines or satsumas). From that point on he devoted his life to developing his unique small scale organic farming system for no-till grain cultivation. This system does not require weeding, pesticide or fertilizer applications, or tilling.

Fukuoka bucks the trend to "organic farming," maintaining that organic farming and factory farming are both scientific, not natural. His books, *The One-Straw Revolution*, *The Road Back to Nature* and *The Natural Way Of Farming*, propose that farmers reproduce natural conditions as closely as possible. No plowing; seeds germinate quite happily on the surface if the right conditions are provided. Emphasis is placed on maintaining diversity. A ground cover of white clover grows under the grain plants to provide nitrogen. Weeds (and Daikons) are also considered part of the ecosystem, periodically cut and allowed to lie on the surface so the nutrients they contain are returned to the soil. Ducks are let into the grain plot, and specific insectivorous carp into the rice paddy at certain times of the year to eat slugs and other pests.

The ground is always covered. As well as the clover and weeds, there is the straw from the previous crop, which is used as mulch, and each grain crop is sown before the previous one is harvested. This is done by broadcasting the seed among the standing crop. Fukuoka reintroduced the ancient technique of *Tsuchi Dango* (literally Earth Dumpling) in which the seed for next season's crop is mixed with clay, and formed into small balls. The result is a denser crop of smaller but highly productive and stronger plants.

Fukuoka's method and philosophy are tuned for small scale farming, yet he claims "With this kind of farming, which uses no machines, no prepared fertilizer and no chemicals, it is possible to attain a harvest equal to or greater than that of the average Japanese farm."

In 2005, at the age of 93, Fukuoka still managed to lecture.

5 : One-Straw Revolution

Bill Wolverton is president of Wolverton Environmental Services in Picayune, Mississippi, and author of the book *How To Grow Fresh Air*. A retired NASA scientist, he has studied plants as a way of cleaning the air for many years.

Clean the Air in Your Home with House Plants

B.C. "Bill" Wolverton

Science is now catching up with what gardeners have known for decades – that is, growing plants can relieve stress while helping to clean the environment. Gardening has become the number one leisure activity in the United States and Canada, surpassing even sports. A growing body of research shows that cultivating plants indoors and outdoors may be the best medicine available for improving mental and physical well-being at any age.

Although "green building" is becoming an attractive concept to building managers and building occupants, the use of living plants is not part of the present concept. Architects and engineers are beginning to design buildings with an eye toward low-emitting carpets, paints and furniture. This is good but should only be the first step. A further step should include the design of houseplants into each building, mimicking the earth's natural processes.

Benefits from our botanical friends

Benefits derived from our botanical friends include a wide range of psychological and physiological effects. Studies conducted on plant/people interactions have provided overwhelming evidence that plants do indeed have a measurable beneficial effect on people and the spaces they inhabit.

Plants not only add beauty to a room, but also make it a friendly, inviting place to live or work. Plants symbolize friendship and appear to have a calming, spiritual effect on most people. This perhaps explains why plants play such an important role in human events such as weddings, funerals, holidays, hospital stays and birthdays.

Plants are also used as background props for most important events such as television addresses, commercials, etc. People feel relaxed when they are near or tending to living plants. Corporations install interior landscaping to increase worker productivity and decrease absenteeism. Elite hotels, restaurants and other businesses use plants to help entice customers to their establishments.

During early manned space flights, NASA astronauts and Soviet cosmonauts expressed a desire to have plants on board their space vehicles. Plants can help reduce stressful conditions inside cramped space capsules during long-duration flights.

Nature's bio-cleaning machines

In the past, houseplants were sought only for their beauty and psychological value. Thanks to NASA research findings, houseplants now have a third value. Studies conducted in the early 1980s at the John C. Stennis Space Center in Mississippi provided evidence that houseplants can also improve indoor air quality. The ability of houseplants to improve indoor air quality and one's health is no longer a matter of conjecture – it's scientific fact.

Plants and their root microbes are nature's biological cleaning machines. It is commonly understood that plants purify and revitalize the earth's air and water. In general, we know that the animal/plant/microbial world is harmoniously balanced so that each benefits from the other. We are dependent upon these interactions for our existence.

We are just now beginning to understand some of the mechanisms that create these symbiotic relationships. Approximately 42 species of interior plants have been evaluated for their ability to remove various indoor air contaminants from sealed chambers. Hundreds of experiments have been conducted and technical reports published that seek to answer legitimate concerns about placing plants in buildings for the specific purpose of improving indoor air quality.

After more than ten years of extensive research (both laboratory and "real-world"), we now have a basic understanding of how plants function to remove indoor pollutants. Research conducted by Wolverton Environmental Services, Inc., and supported by the Plants for Clean Air Council in Mitchellville, Maryland, continues to expand on the research begun at NASA. Specifically, we are trying to understand how plants clean and revitalize the air and how to use this knowledge to improve indoor air quality.

Plants use ingenious methods to obtain food and protect themselves from would-be enemies. Each plant has the ability to culture microbes on and around its roots specific for its needs. These microbes biodegrade and mineralize (compost) dead leaves, animal waste, tannic and humic acids and other debris to provide nutrients for the microbes and their host plant. This is basis of organic gardening.

Geographic locations and environmental conditions of the plant's origin determine which microbes it cultures. For example, the microbes associated with plants that evolved underneath the canopy of tropical rainforests (most houseplants) differ from those in arid environments. Tropical plants need aggressive microbes that can rapidly recycle jungle debris. Because rainforests are dark, warm and humid, mold and bacteria thrive.

Tropical plants excrete substances that protect their leaves from airborne molds and mildew. When these plant species are placed in an indoor environment, they continue to suppress airborne mold spores. Because chemical pollutants commonly found indoors such as formaldehyde, benzene and xylene have structures similar to components found in tannic and humic acids, microbes adapt to biodegrade these chemicals also. Thus, the basis for plants' ability to improve indoor air quality is established.

Humidity: the basics

Plants use two well known processes to move chemicals in the air to their roots: Leaves absorb certain chemicals in the air and transport them inside plant tissue down to the roots, and plants pull air down around their roots when moisture is emitted from leaves during transpiration.

Plants with high transpiration rates are able to move greater amounts of air. Therefore, the more efficient air cleaners are plants with high transpiration rates. Plant transpiration rates are controlled by humidity. Plants attempt to balance humidity levels for their optimum well-being by controlled release of moisture from their leaves. When humidity is high, plants emit less moisture into the air than when humidity is low.

Early critics complained that too many plants in buildings would cause the humidity levels to rise and support the growth of mold and mildew. However, findings proved otherwise. Low humidity, most prevalent during winter months, dries the respiratory system and makes one more susceptible to colds, viruses and allergens. Ideally, humidity should range between 40 to 60 percent. Plants produce healthy, microbial-free moisture.

Mechanical humidifiers, when not properly maintained, can become a source of mold and mildew. When plants transpire, they not only add moisture to the air but also emit substances that help suppress airborne mold spores and bacteria. Although these substances are yet to be identified, we do understand their function. Recent findings show that plant-filled rooms contained 50 to 60 percent fewer airborne mold and bacteria than rooms with no plants. Interestingly, air in the plant-filled rooms had fewer microbes, even when temperature and humidity levels were raised – the exact opposite effect predicted by some critics.

Ironically, some doctors advise their allergy patients to avoid house plants. House plants have been falsely accused of harboring mold spores. The real problem is usually overwatering and the growth of mold on wet carpeting. To avoid these problems, use hydroponic (soil-less) methods in water-tight planters to grow house plants. If potting soil is used, cover it with aquarium gravel and feed and water from the bottom to keep the surface dry. There are also many commercial sub-irrigation systems available. When large planters are used, the need for frequent watering can be eliminated.

Healthy air for your home

As a general guide, two or more medium to large plants (14"-16" containers) per 100 square feet of area are recommended. Of course, more plants and larger plants would certainly increase effectiveness.

Plants alone may not be the total solution when serious indoor air quality problems exist. Proper source management (allowing building materials and furnishings to vent volatile fumes before installation), complete air distribution and preventative maintenance are all components of a healthy building.

Fan-assisted planter/air filters

Fan-assisted planter/filters may be needed to rapidly remove pollutants from the air. Once the biological mechanisms of plants were understood, it was only natural to merge man and nature's technologies. By combining the most effective air filtering media, mechanical air flow devices and living plants, WES Inc. has developed a family of enhanced plant/air filters. These aesthetically designed, patented planter units not only increase the air purification capacity of houseplants by as much as 200 times but also help maintain healthy indoor humidity levels.

One of the unique properties of this natural air purification is that under normal operating conditions, the filtering media is bioregenerated (self-cleaned) by the plant's root microbes. Therefore, the filter media does not require periodic replacement, as is the case with other commercial air filters.

We should all breathe easier knowing our beautiful house plants are working so hard to keep us healthy!

This article first appeared at Judy Barrett's *Homegrown: Good Sense Organic Gardening for Texas.*

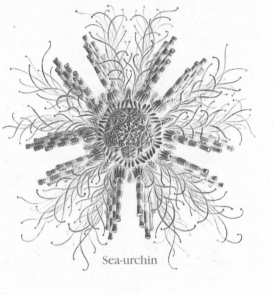

Sea-urchin

Pliny the Elder, a first century Roman scientist and physician, said, "Garlic has such powerful properties that the very smell of it drives away serpents and scorpions." Among the 61 ailments he claimed could be cured with garlic were respiratory and tubercular maladies along with digestive problems, dog, snake, and scorpion bites, asthma, arthritis, ulcers, and convulsions.

From coast to coast, building material stores selling reused building materials are providing markets that channel deconstructed lumber and other materials into homes and factories. It's resource preservation involving the local community.

Too Good To Throw Away

Josh Wachtel

A growing number of reused building materials stores are springing up in the United States – saving consumers much money in their search for hard-to-find items while the new stores quickly become self-sustaining and provide employment in their communities. As nonprofit organizations, many of these stores have stated missions:

Habitat for Humanity's ReStores help raise funds for building projects. Boston's Building Materials Resource Center supports renovations for lower income home-owners. Minneapolis's Reuse Center – perhaps the first enterprise of its kind in the US – focuses on promoting sustainable community development as a whole. In this article, two building materials reuse stores are profiled – one on each coast, with different but parallel missions.

Start-up In Springfield

"Eight years ago, we decided at CET we wanted to open a used building materials store," says John Majercak of the Center for Ecological Technology (CET) and director of the ReStore Home Improvement Center in Springfield, Massachusetts. "I visited other stores across the country, took the best of what I saw, and we set it up in Springfield."

The ReStore – not to be confused with Habitat for Humanity or other ReStores – is a nonprofit enterprise of CET, a 501(c)(3) organization with offices in Northampton and Pittsfield, Massachusetts. CET's mission is to provide residents, businesses and communities with the tools to make it easy and affordable to live in a more environmentally sound manner. With over 30 employees, CET's activities are so broad it is difficult to define. Its programs range from community education about energy efficient technologies and composting, to home energy assessment and paper recycling pick up. CET also hosts an online store selling sustainable products, and conducts school programs, including the "Junior Solar Sprint" in which middle schoolers race solar cars of their own design.

The ReStore is just one of its programs with its own three-pronged mission: 1) Reuse valuable materials; 2) make home improvement affordable for more people; and 3) create local jobs and provide training.

Like other models, CET's ReStore has aimed and succeeded to be fully self-financed after a short period of subsidy. Majercak says that for him there were three years of prep work, fundraising and site selection before the store could actually open in 2002. For the first two years of operation the store was partially subsidized. Grants totaling $240,000 covered start-up costs and absorbed the store's shortfall. Since then, all the costs of operating the ReStore – rent, heating, electricity, advertising, supplies and salaries (60 percent of operating costs) – have been offset completely by sales.

"In the scale of things, this was not a lot of money," says Majercak. "Sales covered 65 percent of operating expenses in the first year, 75 percent in the second year. Since then, as projected, the store has been paying for itself. We were able to do that type of approach because we learned from the pioneers. We waited to open until we had the money, and then we invested in advertising, which has really paid off."

ReStore reports that for fiscal year 2005, its 7,400 customers saved $470,000 compared to purchasing new items, and they helped divert literally hundreds of tons of materials from landfills. Total sales – and operating expenses – were $320,000.

The ReStore has come a long way very quickly. Four years ago, the first employees were just Majercak and Jeff MacFarlane, a volunteer from AmeriCorps VISTA. Now the store employs six to eight full-time staff (depending on the season) and has continued to employ an AmeriCorps volunteer each year. Their first volunteer, MacFarlane, is now a full-time staff member.

Inventory And Markets

Like the growing number of recycled home building stores across the country, ReStore sells everything and the kitchen sink. You can find hardwood cabinets, windows, doors, bathtubs, toilets, light fixtures and more. Inventory is constantly changing because the stock is dependent upon donations. Many people check in every week to see what new items have come in.

Marketing has been a key to ReStore's quick success. In addition to print and other advertising, people can keep abreast of new inventory at the ReStore through its web site – www.restoreonline.org – and there is a page titled "Hot Items." These items have included reclaimed roof slate, salvaged keystone pieces, secure screen doors, a Tiffany style hanging light, oak balusters, a solar hot water system, used pine sheds, an antique Singer sewing machine, radiators and an atrium window. In the future, ReStore hopes to catalog its entire stock. Customers can also sign up on-line or in the store to receive e-mail updates on new products available.

Currently one special offering is "Bowling Alley Lanes" – reclaimed from a local alley that was closing – which the web site states "...make great floors, tables or countertops!" One block of lane has been turned into a table by a local crafts shop, Studio Cochineal, which has begun a partnership with ReStore to make unique pieces of furniture from scrap material. Most of the work will be on a custom order basis and the profits will be divided between the studio and ReStore.

John Grossman, manager of the ReStore, has been working in the store for the last year. He learned of the store as a customer when he was renovating the home he'd bought in Holyoke, Massachusetts. "The bulk of our material comes from our commercial partners," he says. "These are contractors, retailers, wholesalers and manufacturers who donate materials that otherwise cannot be sold or used. After that it's homeowners."

According to ReStore's 2006 progress report, "Donators give materials for many reasons. Some need the space in their warehouses, some want to save on disposal costs and some just can't bear to throw away high quality building materials they know someone else could use."

This is where environmentalism meets good business sense. Explains Grossman, "One customer actually said to me, 'Look, I'm no tree hugger. But this stuff is too good to be thrown away.'"

As a whole, ReStore accepts about a third to half its materials new from distributors, manufacturers and retailers, mostly in big loads, a truck or two at time. "If they don't give it," says John Majercak, "they have to pay guys to break it up and dispose of it."

The other half to two-thirds comes used from contractors and homeowners. "We're picky about what we take back from people," says Majercak. "We only take the cream of the crop. We don't want to be a middle point on the way to the dump, and people understand that."

When ReStore does get something that won't sell or has been damaged, like a door that can be fixed or refinished, they put it in a "free area" where many thousands of items are given away each year.

"A lot of people come regularly to look at this stuff," explains Majercak. "We had some wallpaper rolls and shutters. Later we heard someone had taken them and was selling them on the street in a neighborhood. There's a whole 'scavenger economy' out there and we're happy to be a part of that."

Outreach At Home

Another way ReStore has marketed itself and is promoting its new deconstruction program (see below) is to set up a tent each year at the Western Massachusetts Home Show. At this year's show in March, ReStore's display was the first thing people saw when entering the gates of the Eastern States Expo Center in West Springfield. Samples of stock were on display and ReStore staff gave periodic demonstrations of the denailing gun to promote and inform the public about their deconstruction services.

Last year, in conjunction with its parent organization, CET, ReStore hosted its first workshop for the public. Held in its warehouse where the truck is usually parked, ReStore presented to a full house a training on how to assess one's home for energy loss and basic weatherization. This year the ReStore and CET are planning to host a whole series of "how to" workshops on weatherization, installing a door, installing windows, laying tile, lead safety and possibly home composting.

Additionally, last summer ReStore had two teens working as part of a local youth job training program. The teens were paid by Massachusetts Career Development Institute. To ReStore's great pleasure, far from needing basic training, the high school junior and recent graduate were ready to work. One was a truck helper and the other served customers, worked on the computer and did web updates. ReStore plans to expand their participation in this program this summer.

Deconstruction

In the last two years ReStore has launched a deconstruction program which is yet another way it acquires materials. This is a fledgling program that ReStore hopes to really develop in the coming years. "We purposely didn't get into deconstruction the first few years," says Majercak. "It goes hand in hand with the retail store. We wanted to make sure we had the retail under our belts first and then add deconstruction."

Deconstruction means taking a house apart and recycling as much of the materials as possible rather than simply demolishing and sending all the waste to the dump. It's more labor intensive and can take longer than demolition because deconstruction requires more people rather than heavy machines. But it can divert tons from the solid waste stream.

ReStore deconstructed a 2,600 sq. ft. house in two weeks, for example, whereas a demolition crew could have done it in three days. But doors, windows, cabinets and flooring, metal pipe and all the lumber and plywood were saved and resold at the store. It was estimated that demolition of the house would have sent 15 thirty-yard rolloffs to the landfill. Instead, ReStore only sent six rolloffs, but uncompressed, so the savings in weight were even greater. The main things that couldn't be salvaged or recycled were the drywall and shingles. "But," Majercak says, "there are even markets for drywall and shingles now." All in all, 20 truckloads of reusable materials were taken from the house.

At this point, at least in Massachusetts, "Homeowners who choose deconstruction are motivated by the mission," says Majercak. "Deconstruction is not saving homeowners tons of money." When you factor in the tax deduction homeowners can take for donating materials to the ReStore, the cost can be competitive, but deconstruction is still more costly than demolition. "After a day or two," says Majercak, "the payback of the labor goes down. When you're deconstructing lathe and plaster, for example, you may want a hybrid method."

This hybrid method refers to what may be termed "soft stripping," or cherry picking the house for certain architectural features with resale value, and demolishing the rest. This can be done relatively quickly. Then the demolition can be done by conventional means and the waste landfilled. Some deconstruction firms are forming partnerships of this kind. ReStore recently participated in a big project of this sort in conjunction with Lend Lease Actus at a closed Air Force base in upstate New York where 172 military housing units were being torn down to make way for redevelopment.

Limitations To Lumber Reclamation

Starting in July 2006, new legislation goes into effect in Massachusetts banning the disposal of wood. Majercak isn't yet sure if and how the new law will help tip the equation toward deconstruction rather than demolition. "There may be exceptions to the ban," he says. "Wood can go to an incinerator, and both Pittsfield and Springfield have waste-to-energy incinerators. Also, when a dump is in 'close off mode' and being capped off it may be allowed to continue receiving waste wood."

Since ReStore can only take clean wood that hasn't been painted or treated, this is another limitation to lumber reclamation. "Except for very odd circumstances, we only get lumber when we take a house down," says Majercak. ReStore uses specialized tools like denailing guns to save time when recovering lumber. Right now the lumber is not graded but simply eye-inspected. The purchaser can decide whether it seems usable, and some show it to their building inspector before using the wood. If it looks decent, the lumber might be used for studding out a wall, for example. "But the lumber we salvage hasn't become part of the official lumber economy yet," he says.

At present, deconstruction is a sideline for ReStore, a service that is offered but does not yet provide ReStore enough business to maintain a regular crew. Some of the ReStore store staff double as deconstructionists when projects come along. When ReStore needs to respond quickly, it has had to hire additional help through temp agencies.

Majercak would like to see this change. "Ideally we'd like to be able to hire staff from other mission driven organizations to do the work when we have jobs. I think there's a lot of room for growth in our own deconstruction program. We need to do more marketing to show people that it's an alternative."

Rebuilding Center, DeConstruction Services: Portland, Oregon

In Oregon, Portland's Rebuilding Center is one of the stores Majercak visited when planning his store. In 1998, Our United Villages – a nonprofit organization founded by neighborhood volunteers seeking ways to improve their local communities by fostering dialog among local residents – launched the Rebuilding Center store. Along with two newer programs, DeConstruction Services and ReFind Furniture, The Rebuilding Center currently employs about 50 people and provides exclusive funding for its parent, Our United Villages.

Through the combined efforts of its three programs, the Rebuilding Center salvages 4.5 million pounds of material a year. In 2006, the organization continued to find itself in a period of growth. It has remodeled its store, is expecting to double its salvage rate in the next few years and hopes to add 10 to 15 more jobs.

BioCycle last profiled Rebuilding Center in 2001, two years after its DeConstruction Services had been launched. At that time the potential for deconstruction (as opposed to demolition) was first being demonstrated and DeConstruction Services had quickly increased its staff to 40 or 50 people. The staff has now been reduced to 20 people, but DeConstruction Services has found it can actually do more work with fewer people.

Explains Brian McVay, Chief Estimator and Project Manager of DeConstruction Services, "There are a few helpful innovations that we've come up with, along with a more structured administrative backbone and uniformity of practices."

DeConstruction Services did 175 projects last year, ten of which were full house deconstructions. Fifteen percent of the jobs were on commercial buildings and the rest were residences. This year DeConstruction Services is setting records. In the first quarter alone, 12 houses were deconstructed or were under contract and 64 projects were completed.

"Remodeling is still the bread and butter of the deconstruction industry," says McVay. "We gut kitchens to the studs, roofs to the sub floor, take down falling down garages. We do everything."

On a typical 1920s house, McVay says 65 percent of the materials are recovered and reused, 25 percent are recycled and 10 percent are disposed. The reusables include doors, windows, cabinets, flooring, plywood and lumber. Fiberglass and cellulose insulation that is not wet or moldy is bagged and resold at the Rebuilding Center store, too. Recyclables include broken pieces of clean wood, lath, ferrous and nonferrous metal, nonasbestos roofing material and gypsum wallboard made after 1980 (although markets change and wallboard is not always a viable recyclable). Plaster, painted wood, nonreusable plastics, asbestos, pre-1980 gypsum wallboard, vinyl flooring and lower tier reusables (like damaged and worn hollow-core doors or damaged fiberglass shower tap enclosures) are landfilled.

Recently, DeConstruction Services was offered a unique contract to be sole provider for deconstruction services in Clark County, Washington. This is a two-year contract, renewable for five years, to remove buildings on any public project requiring the service. The main issue is a watershed enhancement program which will require the removal of houses built too close to the waterway. McVay says, "It's the first contract of its kind to exist." He anticipates the deconstruction of six houses in the next couple of years.

Building A Culture Of Safety

One difficulty for the deconstruction industry has been insurers who insist on basing workman's comp rates on statistics for demolition companies. Yet deconstruction companies have asserted that their work is safer and that there are fewer reported accidents. McVay says they've come to accept this situation but that there are things that can be done. "We have to use what we have in the insurance industry which wants to view us as full-blown demolition companies. But we no longer feel threatened and we ask workman's comp providers what we can do to lessen costs. In general our rates have gone down."

McVay describes a "functioning safety culture" that has been developed at DeConstruction Services. A part-time safety manager is employed to handle all communications and paperwork involved in implementing a safety policy. "Our safety policy is not fixed," says McVay. "We are constantly assessing new requirements for safety." One way this is done is by weekly "tailgate chats." These are brief meetings on site where workers can voice safety issues and talk about solutions.

Additionally, DeConstruction Services gives monthly trainings for staff. These trainings include topics such as fall protection, scaffolding, electrical safety and respirator maintenance and fitting.

Competitive Business Practices And The Triple Bottom Line

Trainings extend to other areas as well. For example, DeConstruction Services recently hired a professional speaker to train its entire deconstruction crew in customer service. "It is important to make the right impression on customers," says McVay. "All our actions have a ripple effect."

And there is plenty of competition. McVay knows of three other companies offering deconstruction services in Portland, and some are advertising on *Craig's List*, the free classified ads web site. "There are more providers than ever and increasing numbers of jobs suited to deconstruction," says McVay.

In 2001, BioCycle reported that $100 per house was spent by DeConstruction Services to create a portfolio for customers of their deconstruction projects. McVay says the process has been streamlined to reduce waste. The photos are digital now and customers can request they be emailed or put on a CD, though they can still receive a full portfolio if they want. "A few color pictures and a written inventory are all people need to prove the tax deduction," says McVay.

Currently in Portland, the costs of deconstruction, particularly when prepping for remodeling, are on a par with demolition. For a full house, deconstruction is still a little more expensive. But McVay plays down looking at cost alone and talks about "the triple bottom line." Economic decision-making is one part, but DeConstruction Services urges people to look as well at the social factor – like job creation and Our United Villages' community enhancement programs – and the environmental factor – alternative sources for materials and reduced waste.

In Portland, this theme is resonating. "'Preservation' and 'simplicity' are terms that are more and more used in conversation, planning and policy," says McVay. "Instead of trucking materials across the country, people are looking to find what they need in a 200-mile radius. For example, three bars have been remodeled with salvaged materials, all within walking distance of the Rebuilding Center."

When Things Fall Apart, Make Art

ReFind Furniture, the Rebuilding Center's newest program, assists this mission in another way. Taking pieces of trim, old growth lumber with nail holes and blemishes, and other reclaimed odds and ends with little potential for reuse, it creates a line of one-of-a-kind pieces to be sold in the store.

ReFind has had three managers since its inception, each of whom, says McVay, has brought his own take on reuse and style. Currently the program employs a shop steward and an AmeriCorps volunteer who have started making a line of tables and benches in a very simple, linear "arts and crafts" style with an environmental finish.

Pieces are displayed on Rebuilding Center's web site: www.rebuildingcenter.org/refind. There are all kinds of tables, cabinets, chairs, picture frames and mirrors. Items can be custom ordered as well. One Portland restaurant bought all its tables from ReFind Furniture.

Community Commitment

The Rebuilding Center supports its social mission in many ways. It starts its employees at $10/hr, with benefits after 90 days. These include medical and dental insurance, a small life insurance policy, a cafeteria plan and membership in a recently established 401K. Pay for upper tier management is as high as $25/hr with the average worker earning between $12 and $15/hr.

Rebuilding Center works with other nonprofit organizations as well. Recently it sent four people to train and work with Mercy Corps disassembly staff in New Orleans helping clean up after Hurricane Katrina. Reclaimed materials went to a nonprofit in New Orleans. Rebuilding Center constantly donates materials to other nonprofit organizations who follow a regular procedure for requesting help.

As a nonprofit itself, much of Rebuilding Center's profits go to its parent organization, Our United Villages, which employs three full-time staff to conduct neighborhood discussions in economically depressed areas of North Portland. Changing demographics in these areas create a climate for lack of communication between residents. These workers go door to door asking people what they like about their neighborhoods and what they would like to see changed. These neighborhood surveys give way to discussion groups to facilitate people getting to know one another and developing projects.

Rick Denhart, Director of DeConstruction Services, sums up the recycling activities of the Rebuilding Center and the social activities of Our United Villages like this: "What we're involved in is not just a mechanical process. In a recycling program stuff might be wasted again. We don't say waste management, it's resource preservation. We involve the local community. We're a learning center, to help people understand the world."

The last 10 years have been very fruitful for building materials reuse and recycling. In the coming years it will be interesting to see how markets for reused building materials and deconstruction continue to develop. Already it is economical to reclaim and resell these materials. As oil prices and landfill tipping fees continue to increase, and as public awareness grows around the multiple benefits of reuse, there may be more for-profit companies joining the ranks of the nonprofits which have been paving the way.

Deconstruction Potential In Military Base Redevelopment

One area for development in the deconstruction industry involves military housing. With base closings and redevelopment of military housing, there are tons of material ripe for reclamation.

The Stewart Terrace Military Family Housing Area in Orange County, New York is currently being redeveloped by Atlantic Marine Corps Communities (AMCC), a public/private partnership of the Department of the Navy and Actus Lend Lease created through the Military Privatization Act. The project involves demolishing 296 homes and replacing them with 171 new homes and a community center.

John Majercak of the ReStore in Springfield, Massachusetts got a call from Actus Development Manager Ryan Kleinau after Kleinau viewed a television report on the ReStore in the fall of 2005. "This was a case where there were a lot of materials and a developer who wanted to see the materials reused," says Majercak. "Usually ReStore gets paid for hire, but since there were so many materials and they were easy to remove, we did it for free."

Because of the large number of houses to strip at once and there was time pressure, ReStore engaged the help of Construction Junction, another nonprofit reuse center based in Pittsburgh, Pennsylvania.

Four semitrucks of material were taken from the site, two each for ReStore and Construction Junction. Each truck held seven pine wood storage sheds taken from yards which were filled with kitchen cabinets, windows, handrails and other interior fixtures. Later ReStore made two more trips with their truck and took 13 more cabinet sets, 71 windows and about a dozen handrails. Construction Junction took a total of 20 sheds and 30 cabinet sets. Habitat for Humanity also worked with AMCC to take another truck load worth of material.

"To get so much material is unique," Majercak says. "There's a lot of potential here for the industry. When you look at it, we have barely scratched the surface."

Grading Old Lumber Reuse In Housing

As more buildings are deconstructed nationwide, the question of grading old lumber will become a larger issue. It will affect consumers, deconstruction firms, reused building materials outlets, contractors, architects, engineers, and building regulating agencies.

Bob Falk of the USDA Forest Products Lab in Madison, Wisconsin, says there are two issues. "When it comes to big timbers," he explains, "they are usually resawn into flooring and other nonstructural building materials because of their greater value, or else they are used for timber frame construction. But each timber frame building is individually engineered." In these latter cases, the timber can be graded individually for the structural needs of the building.

"The other case is the ubiquitous 2x4s' material which is used in most single family construction," continues Falk. "That's where you want to have a grade stamp for each individual piece."

In the Pacific Northwest, grading agencies have already trained and certified graders to regrade Douglas fir for structural use. The assumption is generally that old is better when it comes to reusing old growth high density wood. This is true for the ReBuilding Center in Portland where Brian McVay reports its grading stamp never gets used because old growth fir is sold as soon as it arrives.

At this time, though, not all grading agencies will grade reclaimed lumber for structural reuse as they are not yet sure old lumber is adequate for new structural situations. Falk has been working on this issue for some time and has graded and tested thousands of pieces of reclaimed lumber. "Old growth wood in use for 50 or 100 years, with nail holes, notches and other damage from deconstruction, is not the same piece of lumber as when it got its initial stamp," he says.

Currently he is looking at reclaimed lumber, testing it for strength and residual use and analyzing the data gathered in the Forest Products Lab. In the next few months, Falk hopes to report his findings. This may lead to the development of grading standards specifically for reclaimed dimensional lumber. These may include engineering tables (load and span), how to deal with nail holes, splits and damage you don't find in new lumber, and what to do about wood species mixture, since species vary in strength and can often be hard to distinguish, especially when aged.

Falk foresees not only the implementation of standard grading practices, as we now find with new lumber, but a new sub-economy dealing with reused lumber. "I envision, as reuse entrepreneurs market more of this material, a broader acceptance of graded reclaimed lumber for reuse in housing."

For the latest information on conferences and developments in this field, consult www.building-reuse.org.

BioCycle June 2006, Vol. 47, No. 6, p. 21

Lamellibranchian shell

According to author and naturopathic physician Ron Schmid, raw milk has been victimized by the same forces that gave us Wonder Bread, processed American cheese, and pasteurized beer. Rather than dealing with the challenges of handling fresh, unadulterated products, the food processing factories have elected to give us fancier packaging and longer shelf life. The only casualty appears to be our health.

The Rise and Fall of Raw Milk
by Ron Schmid, ND

Human consumption of animal milk is usually linked to the beginnings of grain farming some 10,000 years ago. Most treatises on the history of the human diet assume that animal husbandry began with the dawn of agriculture, making dairy products a relatively recent human food. But archeological evidence indicates that 30,000 years ago people in the High Sinai Peninsula at the north end of the Red Sea used fences to aid in confining and breeding antelope for their milk.[1] They likely were one of many cultures that used milk long before the beginnings of agriculture.

Physically, civilization rests on the soil, because the soil produces the nutrients for the grasses that feed the animals that feed the people. Fertile soil ultimately provided the milk upon which civilization was quite literally built.

In the whole range of organic matter, milk is the only thing purposely designed and prepared by nature as food. Early humans did not hesitate to appropriate this gift of nature for their own use. No state of civilization has ever been attained without the subjugation of animals and the subsequent use of their milk; from the infancy of human society, distinction has been assigned to the bovine species in history. Those species include the bison, buffalo, yak, and domestic animals of the genus Bos, like cows and bulls. Where people have gone, the ox and his kind have followed. In every country, bovines are either indigenous or naturalized. In most, their milk has at one time or another been used as an essential article of human sustenance – in many, as the chief.[2]

The earliest Hebrew scriptures contain abundant evidence of the widespread use of milk from very early times. The Old Testament refers to a "land which floweth with milk and honey" some twenty times. The phrase describes Palestine as a land of extraordinary fertility, providing all the comforts and necessities of life. In all, there are some fifty references in the Bible to milk and milk products.[3] Milk is often used metaphorically to signify privileges and spiritual blessings.

In the New World, the Jamestown colony was established in 1606, and times were very tough for a number of years. Despite several infusions of hundreds of new settlers, by 1610 a pitiful remnant of 60 is all that remained. It was Sir Thomas

Dale's arrival with a hundred cows the following year that marks the beginning of dairying in America, and the beginning of some prosperity for the Jamestown settlers.

An old saying has it that "A young fellow wantin' a start in life just needs three things: a piece of land, a cow and a wife. And he don't strictly need that last." [5] The cow had a pervasive influence on America's history and culture, and no one has written of this more eloquently than Joann S. Grohman in her wonderful book *Keeping A Family Cow*:

> The cow is a primary producer of wealth. She can support a family. She not only turns grass into milk in quantities sufficient to feed a family but also provides extra to sell and she contributes a yearly calf to rear or fatten. The family that takes good care of its cow is well off.
>
> The dairy cow doesn't ask for much but she asks every day. People who are creating wealth with a cow either are hard-working and reliable or they get that way in a hurry. The need to milk the cow twice a day determined the location of churches; people had to be able to walk there and back without disruption to the schedules of cows. It is certainly no coincidence that such a large number of our finest American statesmen were born on farms. Important virtues are nurtured on the farm, including a graphic understanding of the relationship between working and eating. I have come to understand and accept the words of that great 19th Century agricultural essayist, William Cobbett: "When you have a cow, you have it all." [6]

At the end of World War II, 3.7 million of America's 5.4 million farms had milk cows. Most still sold raw milk directly to neighbors and through local distribution channels, a situation that would change drastically under relentless official pressure for compulsory pasteurization of all milk. A series of articles in popular magazines in 1944, 1945 and 1946 served to frighten the public into support of these efforts. A side effect of this movement was the demise of America's small farms.

Ladies' Home Journal began the campaign with the article "Undulant Fever," [7] claiming – without any accurate documentation – that tens of thousands of people in the US were suffering from fever and illness because of exposure to raw milk. The next year, *Coronet* magazine followed up with "Raw Milk Can Kill You," by Robert Harris, MD. [8] The outright lies in this article were then repeated in similar articles that appeared in *The Progressive* [9] and *The Reader's Digest* [10] the following year.

The author of the *Coronet* article represented as fact a town and an epidemic that was entirely fictitious:

"Crossroads, U.S.A., is in one of those states in the Midwest area called the bread basket and milk bowl of America....What happened to Crossroads might happen to your town – to your city – might happen almost anywhere in America." The author then gives a lurid account of a frightful epidemic of undulant fever allegedly caused by raw milk, an epidemic that "spread rapidly…it struck one out of every four persons in Crossroads. Despite the efforts of the two doctors and the State health department, one out of every four patients died."

But there was no Crossroads, and no epidemic! Author Harris admitted this in a subsequent interview with J. Howard Brown of Johns Hopkins University. The outbreak was fictitious and represented no actual occurrence. Harris' own public statements both before and after the *Coronet* article show that not only was the article a complete fiction, but that he knew that such a thing could not possibly happen. In an article he wrote in 1941, Harris stated: "Mortality in acute cases of undulant fever was formerly about two percent, but this has been greatly lowered by modern methods." In a paper he read before the Maine Veterinary Medical Association in Portland in 1946, he stated, "The small proportion of deaths from acute illness, varying from two to three percent, rarely higher, can be made almost, if not quite zero."

The undulant fever epidemic lies and many others like them were repeated in subsequent magazine articles read by tens of millions of people, as well as in countless newspaper articles in the ensuing years. Writing in *The Rural New Yorker* in 1947, Jean Bullitt Darlington made a particularly fine effort to set the record straight with an article titled "Why Milk Pasteurization? Sowing the Seeds of Fear."[11] Darlington exposes the lies and distortions in the magazine article referred to above. Present day attacks on raw milk are often more subtle but no less vicious.

Ron Schmid, ND, is the author of *The Untold Story of Milk*.

Notes

1. Grohman, Joann S. *Keeping a Family Cow*. Dixfield, Maine: Coburn Press, 1981, 272.
2. *Ibid.*, 1.
3. Hartley, Robert M. *An Historical, Scientific and Practical Essay on Milk as an article of Human Sustenance*. New York, J. Leavitt, 1842, 25.
4. Crumbine, Samuel, and Tobey, James. *The Most Nearly Perfect Food*. Baltimore: Williams Wilkins Co., 1930, 58-9.
5. Quoted in Grohman, 13.
6. Grohman, 4-5.
7. Darlington, Jean Bullitt. "Why Milk Pasteurization, Part I: Sowing the Seeds of Fear." *The Rural New Yorker*, March 15, 1947.
8. Harris, Harold J. "Raw Milk can Kill You.." *Coronet*, May 1945.
9. Harvey, Holman. "How Safe is Your Town's Milk" *The Progressive*, July 15, 1946.
10. Harvey, Holman. "How Safe is Your Town's Milk" *The Reader's Digest*, August 1946.
11. Darlington, Jean Bullitt. "Why Milk Pasteurization, Part I: Sowing the Seeds of Fear." *The Rural New Yorker*, March 15, 1947.

"We all advance reasoning through synthesis of the ideas of others. A primary contributor with enormous influence was Lao Tsu, who pierced the veil of the philosophy and religion of his time and produced 72 verses that cut to the quick: the essence of unity and harmony between humans and the flow of the natural world."

— *Albert Bates*
Author, The Post-Petroleum Survival Guide and Cookbook

"Over time, the Buddha will prove the most positive influence on the relationship between humans and the environment by promoting lifestyle choices like vegetarianism."

— *John Elkington*
Author, Cannibals With Forks

"The search for The One Person is a symptom of the kind of obsession with the individual that emerged from capitalist economic demands, which wrench the real economic unit – the community – from its real base in the

natural world – and then thrust an impossible burden onto each person to survive. To me, the people who most impact the human-ecology confluence are all those unnamed folks through history who have either quietly continued their land-based traditions or boldly fought to protect them. In my community I'd name Linda Velarde, Max Córdova, Leonél Garcia, Johnny Chávez, Alfredo Montoya, Floraida and Tranquilino Martinez, Raymond Chávez."

— *Chellis Glendinning*
Author, Chiva: A Village Takes on the Global Heroin Trade
winner of the National Federation of Press Women book award (nonfiction)

" The faithful among us are most able to positively influence the relationship between humans and the environment. Faith in God and faith in man's ability to survive are essential ingredients for an environment that will sustain life."

— *Burr Morse*
Seventh generation farmer and author, Sweet Days and Beyond: The Morse Family — Eight Generations of Maple Sugaring

"According to the Buddha we are all one! "
— *Chris Plant*
New Society Publishers

"Externalities are effects (good or bad) that do not circle back to impact their originator. First raised by the economist Arthur Pigou, the idea of externalities blows standard economic theory out of the water, especially the assumption that the market economy can produce the best possible results for everyone. This only works when markets manage to channel all the effects of economic

actions back to the original actors. When we recognize the prevalence of these effects-unfelt-at-their-source (especially easy to detect in relation to environmental impacts), we realize that our economic system is seriously flawed."

— *Neva Goodwin*
Tufts University

The ancient Hebrews credited garlic for its ability to satiate hunger, give color to the complexion, improve blood circulation, kill parasites, cure jealousy, keep the body warm, and encourage love. The *Talmud*, a book of ancient Hebrew rabbinical teachings, encourages eating garlic on Friday because making love on the Sabbath is considered a good deed. Even fifth century Sanskrit medical documents found in India mention garlic as treatment for heart disease and rheumatism, as well as coughs, colds, fatigue, hemorrhoids, worms, digestive upsets, epilepsy, and leprosy. When the British colonized the country, they noticed that lepers were peeling and consuming garlic non-stop. The British began referring to leprosy as the "peelgarlic disease." Today Hindus and Brahmins eschew garlic and onions, believing they are too stimulating and interfere with the ability to reach a high spiritual plain in meditation and self-reflection. However, Brahmins will allow the medicinal use of garlic.

Ancient China welcomed garlic into its cuisine as far back as 2700 BCE with master chefs incorporating the herb into a banquet of dishes. Later the Chinese employed garlic as an effective food preservative. Garlic was one of 365 plants cultivated in the Far East by about 200 BCE. Chinese culture divides many aspects of life into nature's forces of yin and yang. Garlic falls into the yang category for its pungent, warming, and stimulating effects and is prescribed for patients suffering from depression.

Because of its stimulating qualities, garlic was never part of Buddhist tradition in China or Japan, whose practitioners felt it would upset one's spiritual balance. Garlic was never adopted into traditional Japanese cuisine and was shunned by Zen masters. On the other hand, legend tells of a Japanese Buddhist priest who hid in the mountains and secretly cured himself of tuberculosis by ingesting large amounts of garlic.

Those following the Jain religion do not eat garlic, onions or potatoes, because they practice *ahimsa,* the philosophy of non-violence. Concern that they might be destroying potential life forms or souls, they recognize that a bulb of garlic, with its many individual cloves, could possibly produce many more plants. Potatoes, too, develop many eyes, each one a potential plant.

The New Village Library

Gaia's Garden: A Guide to Home-Scale Permaculture, by Toby Hemenway. Chelsea Green, 2001.

Permaculture, by Bill Mollison. Island Press, 1990.

Cradle to Cradle: Remaking the Way We Make Things, by William McDonough and Michael Braungart. North Point Press, 2002.

Red Sky at Morning: America and the Crisis of the Global Environment, second edition, by James Gustave Speth. Yale University Press, 2005.

6 SMALL IS BEAUTIFUL

Radiolarian

> " *We are now far too clever to survive without wisdom, and further developments of our cleverness can be of no benefit whatever.*"
>
> — E. F. Schumacher

The Farmers' Market in Rutland, Vermont is a "Slowcavore" paradise. The "slow" comes from Slow Food, the international activist organization that glorifies the pleasures of the table, especially when the distance between farm and table is reduced to a minimum. The "local" comes from the small organic farmers and artisans that have germinated in the past decade. Food connects the community, and Rutland Farmer's Market gives many reasons to linger.

There's a backdrop of live music. Today, it's the playful meanderings of a hammered dulcimer, last week an old world Italian accordion player. There's conversation at every stop. The vendor who offers ten varieties of potatoes can tell me the origins of each variety. The lady who gives a sample of her garlic jelly, gives me the recipe as well. The woman who knits hats from alpaca wool tells me why these creatures are well-suited to the terrain of Vermont.

There are several local cheese makers present. They don't worry about commodity prices, because they use their own raw materials, adding value throughout the production process. They are more concerned about quality and identity, knowing that these are the characteristics that bring value to their finished product.

If the Rutland Farmers' Market was the world, a slowcavore could claim victory and declare "Fritz Schumacher was right! Small is, indeed, beautiful." Switching to a wider-angle lens, however, the market is seen to occupy a small corner of an immense parking lot for Wal-Mart. While the market tinkles with happy music, signs on the security lights for the parking lot warn that the premises are fully covered by security cameras. While there is a cluster of cars at the market end of the lot, the traffic is much more brisk near the store's front entrance. Wal-Mart is known for its designated greeter. At the Farmers' Market, every booth has one.

Inside the big box, signage tells me how many articles of clothing to take into the dressing room and reminds me that I am constantly under surveillance. Shoplifting is a crime and those caught will be prosecuted to the full extent of the law. By the rest rooms, not far from the time clock and more signage mandating that employees wash their hands, is posted today's price of Wal-Mart stock. Wal-Mart has made much noise on the public relations front of the company's flirtation with organic food and experimental forays with renewable energy. Ultimately, however, their decisions will be guided by the number posted by the rest room door. The prevailing myth in our society is that size still matters, and bigger is still better. But, at least a different story is now being told on Saturday mornings out in the far corner of the parking lot. Out there, small is becoming even more beautiful.

Ernst Friedrich "Fritz" Schumacher was born in Bonn, Germany on August 16, 1911. His father was a professor of political economy. He studied in Germany, then in England as a Rhodes Scholar at Oxford. Like many Germans living in Britain, he was interned for a time during World War II. Later, he was released to do farm work, an experience that strongly influenced his sensibilities. He completed his studies at Columbia University, earning a doctorate in economics. Back in the UK, while serving as Chief Economic Advisor to the UK National Coal Board for two decades, he became involved in organic farming.

In 1955 Schumacher traveled to Burma as an economic consultant. While there, he developed the set of principles he called "Buddhist economics," based on the belief that individuals need good work for proper human development. He concluded that "production from local resources for local needs is the most rational way of economic life." Continuing his travels through developing countries, he encouraged local governments to create self-reliant economies. Schumacher pioneered what is now called appropriate technology: user-friendly and ecologically suitable technology applicable to the scale of the community. He is best known for his critique of Western economies and his proposals for human-scale, decentralized and appropriate technologies.

Schumacher's interests led him very far from the orthodoxies of modern economics. His book, *Small is Beautiful* (1973), is a collection of essays intended to bring his ideas to a wider audience. *The Times Literary Supplement* lists the book among the 100 most influential books published since World War II. Because Schumacher's work coincides with the growth of ecological concerns and the birth of environmentalism, he is a hero to many in the environmental and community movements. Schumacher died on September 4, 1977.

In *Small Is Beautiful*, Schumacher points out that we treat natural resources (especially fossil fuels) as expendable income, when in fact they should be treated as capital, since they are not renewable and thus subject to eventual depletion. The capacity of nature to resist pollution is similarly limited, and cannot sustainably continue to be abused. Schumacher concludes that we must achieve sustainable development by directly addressing the underlying problems through appropriate, intermediate, local, humane technologies.

“ [A modern economist] is used to measuring the 'standard of living' by the amount of annual consumption, assuming all the time that a man who consumes more is 'better off' than a man who consumes less. A Buddhist economist would consider this approach excessively irrational: since consumption is merely a means to human well-being, the aim should be to obtain the maximum of well-being with the minimum of consumption.... The less toil there is, the more time and strength is left for artistic creativity. Modern economics, on the other hand, considers consumption to be the sole end and purpose of all economic activity ... It is clear, therefore, that Buddhist economics must be very different from the economics of modern materialism, since the Buddhist sees the essence of civilization not in a multiplication of wants but in the purification of human character. Character, at the same time, is formed primarily by a man's work. And work, properly conducted in conditions of human dignity and freedom, blesses those who do it and equally their products.”

“ ...[N]o system or machinery or economic doctrine or theory stands on its own feet: it is invariably built on a metaphysical foundation, that is to say, upon man's basic outlook on life, its meaning and its purpose ... Systems are never more nor less than incarnations of man's most basic attitudes. . . . General evidence of material progress would suggest that the modern private enterprise system is — or has been — the most perfect instrument for the pursuit of personal enrichment. The modern private enterprise system ingeniously employs the human urges of greed and envy as its motive power ... Can such a system conceivably deal with the problems we are now having to face? The answer is self-evident: greed and envy demand continuous and limitless economic growth of a material kind, without proper regard for conservation, and this type of growth cannot possibly fit into a finite environment. We must therefore study the essential nature of the private enterprise system and the possibilities of evolving an alternative system which might fit the new situation.”

— from *Small is Beautiful*

❝ One of the fascinating aspects of the sustainability revolution is that, unlike Mahatma Gandhi who led the Non-Violence movement and Martin Luther King, Jr., who led the Civil Rights movement, there is no single leader. Instead, hundreds of thousands of community leaders and citizens from around the world are taking action through ecological, economic and social projects to improve people's lives and protect the environment. Some of the visionary leaders who are redefining the relationship between humans and the environment are William McDonough, Janine Benyus, Ray Anderson, Paul Hawken, Vandana Shiva, and Sim Van der Ryn."

— Andres Edwards
Author, The Sustainability Revolution
Founder, EduTracks
www.andresedwards.com

❝ Bioregionalism, in combination with deep ecology, is the most important ecological idea of our time. Bioregionalism means living on a particular part of earth, a coherent natural region, with a true affection for its systems and species, making use of its available resources in a careful and respectful fashion, knowing the carrying capacity of the area and living within its limits. Deep ecology reinforces that idea with a sense of the holiness and specialness of all life in full diversity, an understanding that both human and non-human well-being are equally valuable, and a charge that humans must live lightly on the land, using its life systems and fellow creatures only as necessary for our frugal survival. These ideas in tandem provide the only sensible way for humans to live, long-term, on earth."

— Kirkpatrick Sale
Middlebury College

What is
Community Supported Agriculture (CSA)?

by Robyn Van En

CSA is a relationship of mutual support and commitment between local farmers and community members who pay the farmer an annual membership fee to cover the production costs of the farm. In turn, members receive a weekly share of the harvest during the local growing season. The arrangement guarantees the farmer financial support and enables many small- to moderate-scale organic and/or biointensive family farms to remain in business. Ultimately, CSA programs create "agriculture-supported communities" where members receive a wide variety of foods harvested at their peak of freshness, ripeness, flavor, vitamin and mineral content.

The goals of Community Supported Agriculture is to support a sustainable agriculture system which:

- provides farmers with direct outlets for farm products and ensures fair compensation
- encourages proper land stewardship by supporting farmers in transition toward low or no chemical inputs and utilization of energy-saving technologies
- strengthens local economies by keeping food dollars in local communities
- directly links producers with consumers allowing people to have a personal connection with their food and the land on which it was produced
- makes nutritious, affordable, wholesome foods accessible and widely available to community members
- creates an atmosphere for learning about nonconventional agricultural, animal husbandry, and alternative energy systems not only to the farmers and their apprentices, but also to members of the community, to educators from many fields of study, and to students of all ages.

Kinds of CSA Farms

There are many kinds of CSA farms. All include payment in advance at an agreed upon price. In some, members of the community purchase a "share" of the anticipated harvest, while in others they sign up for a predetermined amount of produce over the course of the season. In most cases, this commitment implies a willingness to share with the farmer both the bounty from the land and at least some of the risks involved with production.

In return for fair and guaranteed compensation, consumers receive a variety of freshly picked (usually organic) vegetables grown and distributed in an economically viable and ecologically responsible manner. Some farms also offer fruit, herbs, flowers and other products, such as meats, eggs, cheese, and baked goods. Many farms offer their shareholders the opportunity to work in the fields or distribute produce in exchange for a discounted share price. Others offer sliding scales to accommodate lower income consumers. In this way, farmers and members become partners in the production, distribution and consumption of locally grown food.

One other fact to consider, organic food produced within local communities is not the same as organic food transported over long distances. When members obtain food from local farmers, environmental costs associated with the transport, processing and distribution of organic food and the consumption of fossil fuels are significantly reduced.

What is a Share?

A "share" is usually enough to feed a family of four or a couple on a vegetarian diet. Sometimes "half shares" are available. The price of a share for a season varies widely, depending on each farm's costs of operation, total months of distribution, variety of crops available and productivity of the soil. Most full shares fall with the range of $300 to $700. Actual cost of produce to the member varies, but is generally comparable to prices in the supermarket.

History of the CSA Movement

In 1984 Jan Vander Tuin brought the concept of CSA to North America from Europe. Jan had cofounded a community-supported agricultural project named Topanimbur, a biodynamic farm located near Zurich, Switzerland. Upon researching this type of co-op movement in Europe, Vander Tuin found the first producer-consumer food alliance in Geneva was inspired by European visitors to Chile in the 1970s. Vander Tuin introduced the idea to Robyn Van En at Indian Line Farm in South Egremont, Massachusetts and the CSA concept in North America was born.

Robyn Van En, Jan Vander Tuin, John Root, Jr., Charlotte Zanecchia, Andrew Lorand, and others formed a core group. They began the first season of their CSA with a small apple orchard operation, and gradually began introducing the "share the harvest" concept to the community. By spring of 1986, Hugh Ratcliffe had joined on as the farmer, and they began to offer shares in their produce harvest. Within four years, the Indian Line CSA expanded from 30 to 150 members. Today, thanks to the pioneer efforts of Robyn Van En, the CSA concept has spread across the nation. More than 1,500 CSAs are supported by members of local communities.

In 1985, there started another 'first' CSA farm, Temple-Wilton Community Farm, located in southern New Hampshire. The birth of this CSA farm also followed inspirations and experiences gained in Europe by Trauger Groh, Anthony Graham and Lincoln Geiger. Groh had studied extensively the concepts of biodynamic farming and produce community co-op programs in Northern Germany and brought his ideas here to the United States, likewise contributing to the founding of Community Supported Agriculture.

There is much speculation as to whether the founding farmers knew anything about a concept known as *teikei* that originated in Japan, though their ideas and foundations for action follow an extremely similar path. *Teikei*, the CSA equivalent, which literally translated means "partnership" or "cooperation," was developed by a group of women concerned with the use of pesticides, the increase in processed and imported foods and the corresponding decrease in the farm population. The more philosophical translation for *teikei* is "food with the farmer's face on it." In 1965 Japanese women initiated a direct, cooperative relationship in which local farmers were supported by consumers on an annual basis.

Community Supported Agriculture continues to blossom in North America, and it opens various doors of opportunity everyday for local communities, helping them get back in touch with each other. In a CSA environment, this is possible in many ways: quite simply, the shareholders physically get together at pick-up, socially interact with one another and the farmer(s), and provide economic support for their neighbors, thanks to one thing that every single living person has in common with the next: eating.

Resources

Robyn Van En, *Basic Formula to Create Community Supported Agriculture*, CSANA Indian Line Farm, 1988.

Steven McFadden, *CommUnity of Minds: Working Together*, 2004. According to McFadden, both Vander Tuin and Groh studied the works of Austrian philosopher Rudolf Steiner (1861-1925).

Trauger Groh and Steven McFadden, *Farms of Tomorrow*, Bio-Dynamic Farming & Gardening Association, 1990.

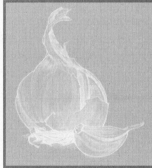

In 2004, at the 27th annual Garlic Festival (held the last weekend in July) in Gilroy, California, the "Garlic Capital of the World," 122,675 garlic lovers gathered to devour over 2 tons of garlic in every form including garlic ice cream.

Greg Pahl is the author of *The Citizen-Powered Energy Handbook: Community Solutions to a Global Crisis*

Community Supported Energy 101
by Greg Pahl

There is no question that we need to start to shift from our current dependence on fossil fuels, nuclear power, and imported electricity as soon as possible. Many places in the United States have the necessary resources and expertise to meet much of our energy needs with local renewable energy, but until fairly recently, states have placed very little emphasis on this potential part of our future energy mix. This is beginning to change, due in part to a growing realization at the grass roots level that, in the absence of strong national leadership on renewable energy issues, it's going to be up to local governments and citizen's groups to take a more active role in the process. This has led to a growing interest in community based, renewable energy projects.

This strategy, when applied to wind power for example, falls in between the large-scale commercial wind farm and the small-scale backyard wind turbine, and has been described as "The Third Way." This middle strategy, also referred to as Community Supported Wind, relies on somewhat smaller scale projects that are developed, sited, and owned by members of the local community rather than out-of-state corporate entities. Community Supported Wind could fill a huge gap in the present wind power sector. And this approach is not just limited to wind power, but can be applied to virtually any type of local renewable energy project such as solar panels, biogas digesters, a variety of biofuels processors, and small-scale hydro.

When applied to a wide variety of renewable energy technologies, this strategy is known as Community Supported Energy (CSE) or sometimes Community Based Energy Development (C-BED). Regardless of the name you use, these projects are somewhat similar to Community Supported Agriculture. The main difference, however, is that instead of investing in potatoes, carrots, or cucumbers, with CSE, local residents invest in energy projects that provide greater energy security and a wide variety of other benefits.

Many Advantages

A cooperative or community owned energy project offers many advantages. It stimulates the local economy by creating new jobs and new business opportunities for the community while simultaneously expanding the tax base and generating new income for local residents. A locally owned energy project also generates support from the community by getting people directly involved in the project from the very beginning.

chapter 6 : Small is Beautiful

Another advantage of community energy projects is that they can be owned co-operatively or collectively through a variety of legal mechanisms. Ownership strategies can include limited liability corporations (LLCs), cooperatives, school districts, municipal utilities, or combinations of these models. Sometimes a partnership with an existing utility can be mutually beneficial. The appropriate model varies from project to project and from state to state, depending on a wide range of variables. What these strategies all have in common, however, is some form of community ownership and group benefit.

The main point is to identify the project as belonging to the community, which may avoid (or at least minimize) the usual conflicts between local residents and developers, whose large-scale, commercial proposals are often viewed as primarily benefiting absentee owners. Local ownership is the key ingredient that transforms what would otherwise be just another corporate energy project into an engine for local economic development and greater energy security.

Community Supported Energy projects offer yet another advantage; they retain a greater amount of income in the local area and increase the economic benefits substantially over projects owned by out-of-area developers. This fact was highlighted by a study conducted by the National Renewable Energy Laboratory for the Governmental Accountability Office. NREL compared the effect of a large corporate wind farm owned out of area with a similar project owned locally. The study found that local ownership yielded an average of $4 million in local income annually, over three times more than the $1.3 million produced with out-of-area control, while job creation was more than twice as large in the local model.

A European Model

With benefits like these, why aren't there more CSE projects? For one thing it's a relatively new concept in this country, although it's a well-established strategy in many European nations. In Denmark and Germany – which are world leaders in wind energy development – many commercial-scale wind turbines are installed as single units or in small clusters distributed across the countryside, or sometimes in or near urban areas. And many of these turbines are either owned by the farmers on whose land the turbine stands, or by groups of local residents. This idea has spread to many other EU nations as well and is beginning to catch on in North America, especially in states like Minnesota and Iowa, where dozens of community owned wind farms are sprouting up like mushrooms after a summer rain.

One of the best examples of community wind in Minnesota is called MinWind. In 2000, a group of farmers in Luverne, Minnesota began to develop a plan for farmer-owned wind turbines that would take advantage of state policies favoring local wind development. Their goal was to find an investment that would generate new income for farmers and provide economic benefits for the local community.

The group finally settled on forming two limited liability companies (LLCs) named MinWind I and MinWind II. This legal structure was the best option because it maximized the companies' ability to use tax credits and other incentives for wind energy while maintaining some principles of cooperatives such as voluntary and open membership, democratic member control, and concern for the greater community.

The MinWind projects were so successful, that the organizers decided to pursue opportunities for additional projects. After a lot of hard work, MinWind Energy dedicated seven new wind turbines in December 2004. These turbines are owned by approximately 200 local investors, following the same principles as the original MinWind I and II projects.

Barriers

The main barrier to wide-scale implementation of Community Supported Energy is a regulatory environment and process that does virtually nothing to encourage these types of projects. For the most part, CSE isn't even on the radar screen of most regulators, and the typical high cost of the approval process (often $100,000 to $500,000 or more) halts most community based initiatives before they even get started. This situation needs to change, and it needs to change soon, because all viable forms of renewable energy, regardless of their size, need to be supported and encouraged if we are going to meet the substantial energy challenges of the next few decades.

One of the best regulatory models in North America at the present time is the new Standard Offer Contracts in Ontario, Canada. Announced earlier this year, the new Standard Offer Contracts (Advanced Renewable Tariffs) are an historic step towards a sustainable energy future. Standard Offer Contracts allow homeowners, landowners, farmers, co-operatives, schools, municipalities and others to install renewable energy projects up to 10 megawatts in size and to sell the power to the grid for a fixed price for 20 years. The Ontario Standard Offer Contracts provide a powerful model that other provinces and states should consider when developing their own renewable energy laws and regulations.

Community Supported Energy is an idea whose time has definitely arrived. I am convinced that if this "Vermont scale" strategy were to be adopted across the state that it could fundamentally alter the entire debate about most renewable energy proposals. It could also go a long way towards meeting a greater portion of the state's energy needs from local resources while simultaneously strengthening the local economy. It's a win-win proposition. Almost every city and town in Vermont has the potential for one or more Community Supported Energy projects. Perhaps you can get one started in your community.

Dave Smith, the "Smith" in Smith & Hawken, presently runs an independent bookstore and lives off-grid.

Friends Meeting
by Dave Smith

While the Vietnam War was still in its infancy, two little old ladies arrived at the Stanford Shopping Center in Palo Alto, California, every Saturday morning at 11:00 and stood silently at the entrance for an hour protesting the war. They were there every Saturday without fail, and they were alone in their protest for months. But as the war became an issue in the press, others began joining them, and in 1968, the year Martin Luther King, Jr. and Robert Kennedy were assassinated and the Tet Offensive in South Vietnam had exposed the futility of the war, hundreds stood with them in protest. Those faithful, steadfast, responsible, unintimidated little old ladies were "bearing witness" to their beliefs, and their efforts were gathering momentum.

As I walked through the crowd to do some shopping, I stopped and asked them who they were. They told me they were Quakers, members of the local Religious Society of Friends. Out of curiosity, I visited their church. They met each Sunday for "Friends Meeting" in their plain, no-frills meeting house, with twenty or thirty chairs on each side facing each other. People quietly filed in, the doors were closed, and there was silence. Some sat with eyes open, others with eyes closed. Some seemed to meditate, others to contemplate, others to pray. This went on for some thirty or forty minutes of increasing uneasiness on my part, when finally an older woman got to her feet and began relating how a book she was reading had challenged her and what it meant in this time of war and social upheaval.

What blew me away, because it was outside the realm of my own experience, was that the book this older, grandmotherly woman talked about was by Hermann Hesse, an author then popular with young people that was also in my stack of bedside reading. These Quakers were people, young and old, who were questioning and examining their values. After she sat down, another two or three people rose and reverently said a few words of faith, inspiration or insight, or quoted scripture. Then there was quiet again before everyone stirred, joining hands all around for a few more minutes of silence. Then, with a hand squeeze passed from one to the other, the meeting was over. No pastor, no sermon, no choir, no organ, no hymnals, no stained glass, no doctrine, no creed, no dogma, and no one in charge. Any "authority" came from within themselves. I was moved and forever changed.

Quakers believe that there is "that of God in everyone," the "inner light." They believe we can have a direct experience of God and therefore we don't need any middlemen to mediate between us and Spirit. They combine mysticism (seeking within) and activism (applying values). Even though their religion is rooted in Christianity, they don't accept the idea of original sin or believe in a God who whimsically rewards and punishes. There was no "fall from grace" because the first woman ate an apple, no need for a redeemer or atonement or plan of salvation. Quakers look for the truth within themselves and within their "Meetings for Worship." By seeing "that of God in everyone," they overcome self-centered individualism. They believe in a life of simplicity, service, and love, and in letting their lives speak for who they are. For them, the Bible is the word of God only as interpreted by each person for themselves. Sacred revelation is not only found in the Bible but continues today. They believe in responding to injustice with peaceful noncooperation rather than either violence or acquiescence. They are pacifists, following the Christian teachings of compassion, not returning evil for evil, and not killing their fellow human beings. In their 1660 statement to King Charles II of England they wrote: "We utterly deny all outward wars and strife and fighting with outward weapons for any end or under any pretence whatsoever, this is our testimony to the whole world." During the Vietnam War, many conscientious objectors and antiwar activists were Quakers.

They believe in walking their talk; they believe that their values apply to what they do every day of their lives. They believe in equality and were involved heavily in the women's suffrage movement – Susan B. Anthony and Lucretia Mott were Friends – as well as the antislavery movement, and the Underground Railroad. And they are strong supporters of the United Farm Workers Union. They may be kind and gentle, but they are definitely not meek and mild. Among Christian communities, Quakers may be the closest of any to practicing the values of fairness and justice that Jesus taught.

And when it comes to meaningful work, their business decision-making process, a version of consensus democracy, is a revelation. The Quaker "Meeting for Business" is based on a reverential "spiritual discernment," a search together for truth, as a group, rather than a pushing of personal desires or agendas. Respect for everyone's point of view, with periods of silence between points offered, and a sober, serious attitude marks the Quaker way of doing church business. It's profoundly moving when first experienced.

The Quaker history of lived values, now extending over hundreds of years, gives us hope that fairness and justice will continue to progress despite the huge steps backward that occasionally occur. Ridicule from those protecting the status quo has failed to extinguish the Quakers' inner light, an insistent beacon of truth and equality for the rest of our culture. There's no better illustration of their commitment than their treatment of women. Many churches still teach that God created women as inferior beings and that women must always obediently submit to their husbands. But the Quakers, way back in the 1700s, had already progressed into the twentieth century, voluntarily relinquishing the privileged positions of men. They recognized that women were not participating fully in their Meetings for Business, as most women would not "nay-say" their husbands. So they decided to form two separate "Meetings for Business." They built their meeting houses with a movable divider down the middle. During Meetings for Worship, the divider was raised, but for business meetings the divider was lowered, creating two rooms so each gender could run separate business meetings. If they needed a common agreement, each group would send an emissary to the other meeting. They continued this practice until there was no longer a concern over whether women would feel free to disagree with their husbands. Their patience and commitment of time to make things fair and just, and to reach agreement, is a commendable and prudent commitment to the most basic democratic values.

As businesspersons in the 1600s, the Quakers' integrity and honest dealing would not allow them to haggle over prices, as was the common practice of their day. Instead, they believed that it was dishonest and deceitful to ask a higher price than what they would accept. Their prices were thus set and non-negotiable. According to *A Quaker Book of Wisdom*, written recently by Robert Lawrence Smith, a practicing Quaker:

> Early in the history of the labor movement, Quaker businessmen recognized that unions were essential as a means of communication between management and workers. Many saw collective bargaining at its best as similar to the search for consensus that goes on at Quaker Meetings for Business. Viewed this way, negotiations become a method for bringing about an enlightened resolution or synthesis of different points of view. One result is that, by and large, workers at Quaker businesses have been able to reach fair contract terms without resorting to strikes. ... The fact is, many Quaker businesses have demonstrated that profit and social responsibility are not only compatible, but interdependent. Big business enterprises today have become increasingly bottom-line oriented. Rather than being accountable to their customers, they are accountable only to their stockholders. They demonstrate their success not by the public regard they've engendered but by pointing to the figures at the bottom of the profit/loss balance sheet. The Quaker business model seeks cooperation, while recognizing the need to compete. Instead of seeing their workers and customers as adversaries, they view them as partners. Quaker businesspeople understand that they are accountable to the individuals they employ, the customers they serve, the community they share, and their own conscience. Not surprisingly, this adds up to both good citizenship and good business.

This unassuming and gentle Quaker meeting house in Palo Alto became my center of comfort and community while I transitioned to a new way of understanding and found a new place in the world. I look back with deep regard and respect to the way of the Friends. They saved me.

John McClaughry is the Director of the Ethan Allen Institute

Memoirs of a Moderator

by John McClaughry

On a brisk March day in 1967, my neighbors rather suddenly chose me to moderate a town meeting.

This struck me as a wholly unlikely event. I had come to the Northeast Kingdom town of Kirby in May of 1963, on foot, with a knapsack, sleeping bag, an axe, and Kephart's *Camping and Woodcraft*. I started to build a log cabin on the 206 acre piece of land on Kirby Mountain that I had bought one year before. The price was $2,400. The payment terms were 6% interest and three years to pay it off.

With the help of two college pals with time on their hands, we got the cabin up and (barely) livable by August. But since I didn't have a source of income, I went off to Washington to work for a short-lived *Republican* magazine, and then as a legislative aide for Vermont Senator Winston Prouty.

Though working six hundred miles away, I was eager to be a freeman of my town. In 1965 I drove all the way up from Washington for a town meeting – only to find out, to my great embarrassment, that town meetings are held in the morning, not at 7:00pm. When town meeting 1966 rolled around, I was there early, listened to the proceedings, but didn't say anything.

A year later, I was slouched in my seat among 35 other townspeople when to my surprise the town Republican chair, Grace Emery of North Kirby, nominated me for moderator. The nomination was seconded by Virginia Wood, the town clerk from South Kirby. One minute later I was handed the gavel. I later learned that the long time moderator, a retired farmer named Theodore Simpson, was ill in the hospital (and soon after, died). There were factions in town, north and south, and my nominators had agreed that as a newcomer and a neutral (the northernmost resident of South Kirby!) my election would not give rise to any factional backbiting.

Having experienced only one town meeting, I was pretty much at sea. I had been in the student senate in high school and college, so I had some idea of the rules of order. In any case, I managed to get through my first trial without making any noticeable mistakes.

I have no recollection of what was debated that day, but one amusing thing happened that I still chuckle about.

My roots were in small town southern Illinois, where I had been raised by grandparents after my mother died suddenly and my father went off to war. Southern Illinois shares an accent with Kentucky and the Missouri Ozarks. By 1967, I had been gone some years, but my accent was still noticeable.

Most Kirby residents really didn't know who I was. I hadn't grown up in or around the town and had no local schoolmates or relatives. To most, I was "the kid from down country who built the log cabin up on the mountain." I was, I suppose, suspect for being a college graduate flatlander with citified values and attitudes, and a curious accent to boot.

I was thus enormously relieved to overhear a white haired gent, in the line at the pot luck luncheon, observe to the person ahead of him: "He ain't from around hyuh, but he's a hick from somewheyuh."

Every year since that meeting, my townspeople have re-elected me to be their moderator. I am enormously proud and honored that they have done so. Kirby is certainly far from the world stage. The town has no retail businesses, no church, no post office, no village center, and no school. Its residents get mail from at least five different post offices. Its population in 1967 was about 250; today it's around 500.

And yet the people of my small town carry on a proud tradition of democratic self-government. Over the years, the subjects of their civic responsibilities have withered. The state took away welfare in 1966. Under state pressure our last (of six) one-room schools closed in 1978; all of our 80 children are tuitioned out to public and independent schools in nearby towns. Act 200 (of 1988) tried (unsuccessfully, as it turned out) to tell us what our townscape needed to look like. We are allowed to do only what state law allows. Today, the town's main functions are record keeping, elections, taxing, planning and zoning, and road maintenance.

Even with this very limited scope for action, there have been some memorable moments. One came in the early 1990s when the selectboard concluded that the town's single truck needed repair or replacement. Should we replace it, or patch it up for another winter? If we decided to replace it, would we buy new or used? GMC or Ford or International?

What was interesting about this discussion was that it drew out the best in two citizens, both of them truck drivers. Neither had ever taken much part in debates over schools, listing, or town spending. But now was their moment. They knew trucks.

The road commissioner leaned toward buying a late model used truck. I can't remember the make – let's say it was a GMC. But Tom (let's call him) protested. "They had one of them Jimmys over in Wheelock, and mister, if that thing hit a frost heave hard it'd bust an axle sure as we're setting here." But Dave (let's call him) took issue. "The engines in them Internationals don't hold up. I had to tear one down after 40 thousand miles, and it was a reg'lar mess inside."

And so it went back and forth for maybe twenty minutes. The townspeople who weren't farmers, logger, or mechanics had a hard time keeping up with this debate. But finally those who knew trucks came to a consensus, and it was duly voted. What I remember was not the outcome – I can't even remember what we decided. What I do remember was that every citizen fully understood that he or she would have his or her moment, when he or she had something knowledgeable to contribute that others needed to hear before making a decision.

Another interesting moment in local democracy occurred in the early 1970s. The legislature had given towns the option of exempting livestock (cows) from property taxation. The town had to make its choice. The dairy farmers thought that their cows ought to be exempt. Thanks to the farms, the town enjoyed open space, landscapes, and the rural character that we all valued. Dairy farming is a tough business. The tax exemption would strengthen farm balance sheets a little, and encourage farmers to keep on farming.

This argument was heard respectfully. No one wanted to say no to the dairy farmers, in Kirby much admired. But exempting the cows meant that everyone else would have to pick up the tax burden. Other folks were pinched financially as well. Some were retired on fixed incomes. Some had to drive considerable distances for jobs paying very modest wages. Some were out of work, or had a lot of mouths to feed.

There were no angry speeches, no finger pointing, no harsh words. Little by little, the farmers saw that they were asking a bit too much. A motion was made to exempt half the cows on each farm. Duly voted.

And so the people of Kirby worked out what to do about the town truck, and how to distribute the property tax burden. Small matters. Insignificant matters. Yes, but in a different way, very important matters.

For every freeman attending those meetings, and many others, understood that "I am a free Vermonter and a citizen of my town. I have the right to stand and speak my piece. I have the opportunity and the duty to work with my fellow citizens toward an outcome that, after debate and reflection, seems right and fair for all of us. In much of America and the world, democracy is little more than casting ballots. Here, real democracy rules."

This core belief among those who venerate town meetings is the wellspring of every free, just and progressive society. Admittedly, town meetings as held in Kirby won't work when towns get too large. But if the spirit of our free institutions is to survive and flourish, Vermonters need to find ways to apply the same principle on a larger scale, so that every freeman and woman can believe that they count, that their voice matters, and that the opportunity for civic contribution and civic virtue lies always before them.

Pennatalucean (Sea pen)

Reprinted by permission. Published originally in *Vermont Commons*

Think clean, think green
Law makes schools use "environmentally friendly" supplies
by Cara Matthews

Products with names such as Earth's Choice, Sustainable Earth and Green Knight will fill janitors' closets this fall as schools around New York State comply with a new law that requires "environmentally friendly" cleaning supplies.

Concerns about the harmful health effects chemicals can have, especially on children, and a realization that cleaners with reduced amounts of potentially dangerous ingredients are increasingly available, prompted the legislation, which takes effect today.

The US Environmental Protection Agency estimates human exposure to air pollutants indoors can be two to five times higher than outdoor levels. Some of the culprits are cleaners, waxes and deodorizers. Reducing or eliminating potentially harmful ingredients helps protect the environment and water supply, according to the legislation's sponsors.

The state School Boards Association supports the measure but has had some questions about the law, such as whether the "greener" products would cost more and clean as well as traditional ones, spokesman David Ernst said.

"There are certainly concerns about student health that may be addressed by some of these products," he said. "(For) a lot of these concerns ... the source of the health problem hasn't been pinpointed, but certainly chemicals can be one."

Prices of the environmentally friendly cleaners are comparable to others on the market, said Christine Burling, At least two districts in Dutchess County will have a jump start on other local schools. The Pine Plains school district has been using green and environmentally friendly cleaning supplies for about four years, while the Rhinebeck school district has been using the products for about two years.

"The products are easier on the people who are applying them," said Thomas Garrick, director of operations and maintenance for Pine Plains schools. "It's just healthier on the people who apply them."

Because the prices are so similar, the district didn't need to make too big an adjustment, Garrick said.

Laurie Rich, president of the Rhinebeck school board, is vice president of programs for Inform, Inc. The nonprofit organization examines the effects of business practices on the environment and on human health.

The Rhinebeck school district made the switch after Inform performed a free audit of its cleaning supplies. She said the greener cleaning products have an immediate benefit not only to the workers who apply them, but to the entire school population.

"It's well documented that when you clean up the quality of the air we breathe indoors, students' attendance rates go up, attention spans in the classroom improve and students perform better," Rich said.

Greg Decker, custodial supervisor at the Rhinebeck school district, said the green products were comparable in performance.

"The transition was difficult because there are a lot of items out there that we had to try out and we were just trying to hope for the best," Decker said. "We wanted to make sure that the products that were on the market could do the same job."

In some cases, it may take a little longer for the green or environmentally friendlier products to work. For instance, environmentally friendly bathroom disinfectant may take longer to work than traditional bathroom cleaners.

Since bathroom cleaners are designed to kill germs, it's impossible to find a cleaner that is completely green.

Grandfather clause

Schools don't have to throw away cleaners that aren't on the state's list of approved products for cleaning products, vacuum cleaners and sanitary paper products, she said. They can use them up before buying green ones. The new law applies to buildings and grounds at all public and private elementary and secondary schools.

A number of groups and parents have criticized the regulations, saying they don't go far enough to protect children. The state stands by the guidelines, Burling said.

"They're a living document. As science and technology evolve, we anticipate that we'll be making changes," she said.

The Office of General Services and the New York State Education Department have to issue a report by June 1 on the law's impact on schools.

The legislation, which passed in 2005, was sponsored by state Sen. Steve Saland (R-Poughkeepsie) and Sen. James Alesi (R-Perinton, Monroe County).

Grassroots Environmental Education, a nonprofit on Long Island, thinks the state should have adopted stricter guidelines, said Patti Wood, executive director. For example, the organization wanted to exclude all products with added fragrances and chemicals that can negatively affect the endocrine system, she said.

"Overall, it didn't go far enough. They missed an opportunity to really protect children, who are uniquely vulnerable to all kinds of environmental exposures," she said.

More susceptible

Children, especially young ones, are more likely to come into contact with cleaning chemicals, and they are more vulnerable than adults because of their size and age, Wood said.

The state's list of products notes which ones have added fragrances, and the guidelines recommend reducing the use of those to the greatest extent possible.

Most cleaners on the state's list are certified by Green Seal or Environmental Choice. According to Wood, the standards are not as strict as the US Environmental Protection Agency's Design for the Environment program, which includes information on eco-friendly cleaning products.

A statement on the Office of General Services' Web site said the agency anticipates working with the Design for the Environment program, among others, in updating regulations, but any changes will be based on "solid scientific studies and research."

Potential harmful effects of cleaners, waxes and deodorizers are skin and eye irritation, asthma attacks and neurological effects, Wood said. Some parents have taken their children out of school because of exposure to chemicals there, she said.

"If there is a single ingredient in any cleaning product that will cause an asthmatic attack, it would be the fragrance, and there are a lot of children with asthma in our schools," she said.

Grassroots Environmental Education will provide information to each school about its own recommendations for green cleaning products, Wood said.

New York State United Teachers, the state's largest union, backed the legislation as a good first step toward making schools healthier and safer for children and staff, spokesman Carl Korn said. But the union has a concern similar to that of Wood's group.

"The legislation requires them to use green, healthy products but not the highest rated ones, and that's something that we're going to be working towards in the future," he said.

The Civil Service Employees Association thinks the law is a good one but will require involvement from community members to make sure it is implemented on a local level, spokesman Stephen Madarasz said.

"I think all habits take a long time to change sometimes, so I think a lot of this will involve some grassroots involvement from people and our members," he said.

Brachiopod
(Lamp shell – cross-section)

Poughkeepsie Journal staff writer Rasheed Oluwa contributed to this report. Latest news www.poughkeepsiejournal.com Founded in 1785, New York State's oldest newspaper

Psychotherapist Linda Buzzell-Saltzman is the founder of the
International Association for Ecotherapy (applied ecopsychology)

How to Turn your Neighborhood into an Eco-Hood!

by Linda Buzzell-Saltzman

What the heck is an Eco-Hood?

Susan DeFreitas defines an EcoHood as "a Permaculture retrofit of a mid-. to low-income neighborhood with a high potential for ecological sustainability." But I think this retrofit can be done in any neighborhood.

One of Permaculture's basic recommendations is to start any project with a Needs and Resources Inventory. So if you're interested in turning your neighborhood into an Eco-Hood, that's a good first step.

Begin with your own home ("Zone Zero" in Pc parlance). Start with the Resources List. What resources do you have to share with others? These could be anything other people might need or could use: surplus food from your garden, balcony pots or fruit trees, equipment or tools you could share, skills, information, compost, transportation, stuff in your garage or closets you no longer use, whatever. Take your time with this list. Every day or so, you may realize you have something else that could be added to the list.

Next, start a Needs List. What needs do you have for things you either don't have or would like to get from greener and/or closer sources? Maybe you could use a daybed, a kitchen table, avocadoes in season (no room for a tree), flowers, childcare, a haircut, a greywater system, alternative energy, a green remodel, etc.

Once you've taken your own inventory, you're ready to approach others who already live in your neighborhood or who might be interested in moving to your neighborhood.

Start by approaching a few neighbors and offering to share your resources. Perhaps you bring over some flowers, fruit, veggies or eggs and end up having coffee at a neighbor's kitchen table. Once you've opened the door this way, you could explain your vision for the neighborhood, with neighbors sharing resources. "Wouldn't it be nice if we shared things, saving us all money?" Start with the easy stuff: home-grown food and crafts are usually welcome.

If your neighbors seem open to it, you can offer to swap. Perhaps they have an orange or avocado tree they never harvest because they're too busy. You could offer to harvest the tree for a portion of the crop. This is what a neighbor of ours did. He heard that the people across from him were going to cut down their tangerine tree as it was "too messy" with fallen fruit. He approached them and offered to solve the problem a different way. He now takes care of the tree, picks the fruit for them, delivers a nice basket to their door and takes half the crop home for his own use! Everyone's happy, everyone's saving money plus a valuable fruit tree is healthier than ever. And no fossil fuel is being used to ship oranges from elsewhere to the local market where our neighbors used to buy them. It's hard to believe, but many people think fruit from their yards is too "dirty" to eat and prefer to buy it at the supermarket!

Community building events can help strengthen the links between neighbors. A garage sale followed by a potluck – these are things that build the social context for Eco-Hood to evolve. Eventually you could have a meeting at your house, with refreshments (very important – food is bonding!) where people could discuss the idea of Eco-Hood and feel part of the creation. It won't work if it's just your idea that you try to impose on your neighbors. They have to buy into the vision and get excited about it too for this to work.

At the meeting, invite neighbors to tell each other about the items on their needs lists, plus any resources they might have to share. Collective thinking can often come up with good ideas to solve the needs. You need babysitting? My son or daughter needs a way to earn money.

This sounds so basic, doesn't it? Everybody used to live like this. And yet in so many neighborhoods, people are totally isolated from each other and only come together in emergencies – and maybe not even then.

This is also a good time to talk about neighborhood needs as well as individual household needs. Are people concerned about street traffic, graffiti or the usual concerns of neighborhood associations? Sharing what other neighborhoods have done to become more sustainable could be appropriate here. Perhaps you could pass around an article on City Repair (www.cityrepair.org)…

From a Permaculture point of view, it's also interesting to explore "outside influencing energies" – things that impact the neighborhood from outside. Fire danger, earthquakes, landslides, crime problems, government issues, water shortages, high heating costs, contaminated creeks, lack of affordable housing, etc. – all grist for the Eco-Hood mill to discuss and for how to mitigate problems at the local-neighborhood level. A pal of mine got together a group of her neighbors and they painted an ugly suburban wall along a busy street and then planted trees and vines to cover it. Simple stuff, but powerful community medicine.

If your neighbors seem open to it, you might also take the next step and discuss the mega-"outside influencing energies" like the end of cheap oil or global climate change and involve everyone in relying less on outside sources of energy, focusing on local solutions to energy, food and product needs.

Another possible action: recruit like-minded friends to move into your apartment building or neighborhood, so you have a set of shared values as a base for further community connection.

The basic idea of Eco-Hood is to move away from the traditional American idea of independence (which is a myth anyway). Each home isn't an island. It's part of an ecosystem. So our goal in creating an Eco-Hood isn't self-sufficiency but rather interdependence. For inspiration, I recommend The Earth Charter, a "declaration of interdependence" and a great document to explore as you turn your neighborhood into an Eco-Hood.

Resources

www.emagazine.com/view/?3066

www.azpermaculture.org

www.sbpermaculturenetwork.org

www.cityrepair.org

www.uvm.edu/~bcmiles/vtfs2005/

www.hopedance.org/new/issues/55/article14.html

www.earthcharter.org

Permaculture Activist, Winter 2005-6 Issue, "Urban Permaculture"

Reprinted with permission from
HopeDance: Radical Solutions Inspiring Hope.
www.hopedance.org

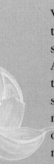

When the Romans conquered Northern Europe, they introduced many vegetables new to Europe, such as the allium family: garlic, leeks, and onions. After the Roman Empire fell, the European Christian monasteries became the libraries that preserved the medical texts of plant remedies. The monks cultivated medicinal plants on the grounds of the cloisters and gained the attention of Charlemagne who decreed that garlic must be grown in the royal gardens. In Shakespeare's *Midsummer Night's Dream*, the character Bottom tells the other actors not to eat garlic or onion, "for we are to utter sweet breath." When the British Admiralty learned that the French navy was giving its men garlic and brandy to keep them warm and prevent scurvy, the British also took up the practice.

The seventeenth century British view of garlic was solidly negative, with expressions like, "not fit for Ladies' Palates, nor those who court them," or that eating garlic "was part of the Punishment for such as had committed the horrid'st Crimes." When famous poet Percy Shelley visited Italy with his friend Lord Byron, he was shocked and appalled to see his friend eating the garlic that was served at a social gathering.

British army doctors created a juice of raw garlic diluted with water and applied it directly to wounds to control infections during World War I. The garlic juice was so successful in treating infection that Russian army physicians employed the same technique in World War II along with garlic and onions given internally to increase resistance to infections.

Debbie Bennett is a Transitions Weight and Lifestyle management coach as well as a nutritional counselor and vegan/raw food chef. Shelley Massa-Gooch teaches yoga.

Think Globally, Eat Locally

by Debbie Bennett & Shelley Massa-Gooch

Throughout the discussions on global warming and Peak Oil concerns, there is one aspect often overlooked. The continued use of massive quantities of petroleum in the production of synthetic fertilizers, in the farm machinery, and in the transportation of food across the globe is clearly unsustainable. Not only is oil a finite natural resource, but CO_2 emissions from a petroleum-based food economy also contribute to air pollution, related health problems, and global warming. We often discuss the use of alternative-energy vehicles, human-powered vehicles, etc., while overlooking the examination of our food's cultivation and origin.

In human history, we have become quite adept at developing new methods for increasing the amount of energy and food we are able to obtain from the environment. The harnessing of fire, domestication of plants and animals, adoption of tools, and use of irrigation have allowed our species to increase our energy-gathering abilities while expending less and less energy in the acquisition. This change was a long, slow evolution that took tens of thousands of years and took place within natural limits. When natural crises occurred, we developed new ways of growing and cultivating our food. The use of fossil fuels to make fertilizer and later to power farm machinery allowed more food to be produced for the rapidly growing population. The internal combustion engine overrode the use of horses and made more land available to feed humans instead of animals. Pesticides and herbicides were developed to "advance" growing techniques. Transportation advances made it possible to trade food items across the globe; first by rail and steamship and then by truck and airplane. These advances not only increased the availability of food across the globe but also led to an explosion in the human population.

When taken individually, these advances would be well and good. Unfortunately, they have proven not to be sustainable. The question for us today is: What can the average person do to help change our current food consumption and cultivation practices while also improving our health and the health of the planet?

- First, take an inventory of your current consumption practices. Knowing where we are is the first step in making changes.
- Exchange non-organic items for organic equivalents. Removing chemicals from the food is not only beneficial to our planet but also to our individual health.

- Remove genetically modified items from the house. Nature has provided a bounty of foods for our consumption, and the less we interfere, the healthier we will be.
- Purchase food from local growers. Ask questions when purchasing food to find out where it's grown and how it's transported. Shift your focus to local sustainability.
- Move towards seasonal eating to enhance our local farming community and also individual health.
- Participate in local community supported agriculture, farmers' markets, and food cooperatives. Take advantage of the bounty we have in this area and support the financial balance in our community.
- Eat less processed food. Not only will this increase your overall health, but less natural resources will be used.
- Buy less plastic-wrapped produce.
- Support the small family farmers. Encourage the rebirth of food variety and farming knowledge that we are losing at a rapid rate.
- Stop before eating the apple from Australia and consider the global impact. As with anything else, think before you act. Simply because we have the financial ability to purchase foods out of season, etc., does not excuse us from playing an active role in the health and longevity of our planet. In addition, the longer the time from the harvesting to your table, the more nutrient-deficient the food becomes.
- Patronize food establishments that use local products. Become knowledgeable about local businesses and their practices. Encourage them to use local products.
- Plant a garden in any space you have; backyards, rooftops, etc. Plant items that you can eat. They are beautiful and can easily be added to any landscape.
- Support educational efforts in the use of organic and local farming and school gardens.
- Help to reform government subsidizing of industrial agriculture.

These are just a few of the practices that each of us can incorporate into our daily lives in order to reduce fossil fuel use and the overtaxing of the globe. The alternatives to doing nothing or attempting to solve our food production problems simply by applying more technology will certainly result in dire consequences, some of which we are witnessing already. Overcoming our fossil-fuel-dependent food production system is an immense global challenge, but we are all in control of our individual consumption on a daily basis. An army of one speaks softly and an army of hundreds will be loud.

Reprinted with permission from
HopeDance: Radical Solutions Inspiring Hope.
www.hopedance.org

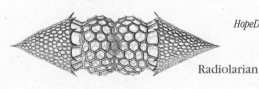

Radiolarian

This article won first place in an essay contest answering the question: "Why Bike to Work?"

Why Bike to Work
by Alexander Asper-Nelson

Why ride a bicycle to work, or anywhere, instead of driving? Math.

- A new car costs about $20,000. A new bicycle costs about $450.
- When a car breaks down it can require lengthy, costly repairs, often exceeding the value of the car. When a bicycle breaks down, the cost is rarely beyond that of a new tire or chain, and folks at the local bike shop will often fix it for the cost of the materials.
- A car requires insurance, registration, and a valid California license. A bicycle requires the sense of balance that god gives eight-year-olds.
- Car lanes are 12 feet wide. Bike lanes are about 2 feet wide. Consider the savings in asphalt alone.
- Gas prices exceed $3 a gallon, while water bottles average approximately $1.07 with tax. And many people in cars drink bottled water anyway.
- Bicycling releases adrenalin, endorphins, and hormones, resulting in a sense of energy and well-being. Driving releases carbon monoxide and pollutants, resulting in greenhouse gases and skin cancer.
- Road-rage abounds. Bike-lane rage is as yet unheard of.
- Cars require airbags, safety restraints, seatbelts, anti-lock brakes, and dozens of other safety mechanisms. Bicyclists are required to wear a helmet if they are under the age of 12.
- Driving too much results in eye-strain, backaches, migraines, weight gain, and highway hypnosis. Bicycling too much results in sexy calves and thigh muscles.
- To date, no one has ever been involved in a deadly alcohol-related hit-and-run on a bicycle.
- Drivers who fall asleep at the wheel result in 20,000 accidents a year. Bicyclists who fall asleep simply fall down.
- Most people drive to work and bicycle on weekends to relax. In fact, some people drive elsewhere on vacation in order to bicycle there. This seems like an unnecessary extra step.
- Between traffic, circuitous routes, one-way streets, etc., it takes about 15 minutes to get from one end of San Luis Obispo to the other by car. On a bicycle it takes about 20. Which is about the minimum amount of aerobic exercise you're supposed to do anyway.

§ In fact, the Surgeon General has determined that 20 minutes of exercise 3-4 times a week increases life expectancy up to 30 years. So then, with this 60 hours of exercise a year spread over those 30 extra years, you lose only 75 days to that exercise, leaving you 10,883 you wouldn't have otherwise.

§ Finally, bicycling takes less real "energy" than any other form of transportation. From walking to air travel, in terms of caloric cost (a calorie literally being a unit of energy-producing potential equal to the amount of heat released upon oxidation, whether that fuel be in the body or from gasoline, electricity, or any other fuel source), bicycling is the absolute most efficient means of transport that has ever been invented. Anywhere. Ever.

So hurrah for bicycles. And share the road. We bicyclists take up one sixth as much of it as automobiles do.

Reprinted with permission from
HopeDance: Radical Solutions Inspiring Hope.
www.hopedance.org

During the ninth century Baghdad flourished as the center of the Moslem world. Philosopher and scientist al-Kindi created the medical text *Medical Formulary* in which he describes the treatment for ear infection that begins with eleven cloves of garlic that are prepared in an elaborate process with lovage, pine oil, and Persian verdigris.

Dr. W. T. Fernie, an old-time Irish physician, mentions in his book *Meals Medicinal* that some physicians used garlic to treat whooping cough and tuberculosis as well as gall bladder problems. Dr. Fernie also recommended using garlic as a suppository to cure the body of thread worms and prescribed garlic by mouth for eliminating round worms. During the Middle Ages, the Irish cure for constipation was garlic smothered in hen broth.

While there was much disagreement among nineteenth-century botanists and historians about the exact country of garlic's origin, some speculated it may have its roots in Asia, others said Europe. Today's botanists believe garlic first appeared in West Central Asia and Southwest Siberia and migrated both east toward China and west into Europe. USDA researcher Dr. Philip Simon discovered garlic's closest wild cousin, Allium longicuspis, growing in the region of Afghanistan's northern border neighboring Turkistan and Uzbekistan. Even today, wild garlic can be found growing in the southern portion of the Ukraine, towards the east into China, and southward into Turkey, Iran, and Afghanistan.

Mid-Course Correction: Toward a Sustainable Enterprise: The Interface Model, by Ray Anderson. Chelsea Green, 1999.

Earth Democracy: Justice, Sustainability, and Peace, by Vandana Shiva. South End Press, 2005.

Cadillac Desert: The American West and Its Disappearing Water, by Marc Reisner. Penguin Books, 1985.

Desert Solitaire: A Season in the Wilderness, by Edward Abbey. Ballantine Books, 1985.

The Toilet Papers: Recycling Waste and Conserving Water, by Sim Van der Ryn. Chelsea Green, 1999.

Biomimicry: Innovation Inspired by Nature, by Janine Benyus. William Morrow & Co., 1997.

7 WHOLE EARTH CATALOG

❝ *Civilization's shortening attention span is mismatched with the pace of environmental problems. . . Environmental health requires peace, prosperity, and continuity.*"

— Stewart Brand

The original *Whole Earth Catalog* was not "given" to me; it was "laid on" me by someone who had moved on to a newer edition. It was dog-eared then. It's more dog-eared now. It has survived more than forty years of moves and life changes.

The publication of the *Whole Earth Catalog* was fueled by new technology. The IBM Selectric typewriter now had changeable type fonts, bringing the world of typesetting, hitherto the exclusive province of printers and publishers, into the home.

That was enough to convince a bunch of Berkeley counterculture mavens that the time was right to reinvent publishing. Stewart Brand enlisted family members, design instructor J. Baldwin, Kevin Kelly, and others to identify products, organizations, and services that passed the criteria of being useful as a tool, relevant to independent education, high quality or low cost, and easily available by mail.

The idea was to provide "access to tools," and the *Catalog*'s combination of youthful arrogance, orientation towards practicality, and haphazard (but groovy) organization were perfect for the nation's first attention-deficit generation raised in a post-war era that had migrated to suburbia to watch television. It was a generation starved for real experience.

The publishing industry regarded the *Catalog* with a curled lip. It was everything that a real publisher detested. It was undisciplined, eclectic, with a chorus of widely varying voices. It was also a smash success, and it didn't take long for the publishing business to change their definitions of what constituted a "book." By 1972 Random House had come calling and had taken over the national distribution and the *Catalog* had been named winner of the National Book Award.

The ripples from the original *Whole Earth Catalog* continue to be felt. The *Catalog* was published sporadically until 1998. Its alumni have been a vocal and visible lot. Kevin Kelly still publishes a weekly eZine called *Cool Tools* (find it at kk.org). Illegitimate step-child *The Solar Living Sourcebook* is in its thirteenth edition and has been continuously in print for the last twenty years.

The founders of the *Whole Earth Catalog* cast a long collective shadow, but it was their ability to look forward that earned their niche in publishing history. Steve Jobs, no stranger to start-ups that begin with a few geeks in a garage, says this of the *Whole Earth Catalog*: "It was sort of like Google in paperback form, 35 years before Google came along: it was idealistic, and overflowing with neat tools and great notions."

Stewart Brand was born on December 14, 1938 in Rockford, Illinois. His father worried that school was not stimulating Stewart to independent, creative thinking, and so when he was old enough, he was bundled off to Phillips Exeter Academy. From there, he went on to study biology at Stanford, graduating in 1960. In the US Army, he was a parachutist and taught infantry skills; he was later to express that his experience in the military fostered his competence in organizing. In 1962 he studied design at San Francisco Art Institute, photography at San Francisco State College, and took part in a scientific study of the then-legal drug LSD in Menlo Park.

In 1966, Brand conceived and sold buttons which read, "Why Haven't We Seen A Photograph of the Whole Earth Yet?" He thought the image of our planet might be a powerful symbol. In a 2003 interview, Brand explained that the image "gave the sense that Earth is an island, surrounded by a lot of inhospitable space. And it's so graphic, this little blue, white, green and brown jewel-like icon amongst a quite featureless black vacuum."

In 1968, using then primitive typesetting and page-layout tools, he and cohorts created the *Whole Earth Catalog*, an oversized compendium of useful "tools": books, maps, garden tools, specialized clothing, carpenters' and masons' tools, forestry gear, tents, welding equipment, professional journals, early synthesizers, and personal computers. The 1972 edition sold 1.5 million copies and won a National Book Award in the US. Many people first learned about the potential of alternative energy production (e.g., solar, wind, small-hydro, geothermal) through the *Catalog*.

A world-class dilettante and advocate of the unusual perspective, Brand's other works include *The Media Lab*, *How Buildings Learn*, and *The Clock of the Long Now*. "What do I do?" Brand asks at his own website. "I find things and I found things. Things I find include tools, ideas, books, and people, which I blend and purvey. Things I've founded and co-founded include the Trips Festival (1966), *Whole Earth Catalog* (1968), Hackers Conference (1984), The WELL (1984), Global Business Network (1988), and The Long Now Foundation (1996)."

Stewart Brand:

66 Environmental health requires peace, prosperity, and continuity."

66 Information Wants To Be Free. Information also wants to be expensive. Information wants to be free because it has become so cheap to distribute, copy, and recombine — too cheap to meter. It wants to be expensive because it can be immeasurably valuable to the recipient. That tension will not go away. It leads to endless wrenching debate about price, copyright, 'intellectual property,' the moral rightness of casual distribution, because each round of new devices makes the tension worse, not better."

Spoken at the first Hackers' Conference, and printed in the May 1985
Whole Earth Review. *It later turned up in his book,* The Media Lab:
Inventing the Future at MIT, *published in 1987*

66 All historians understand that they must never, ever talk about the future. Their discipline requires that they deal in facts, and the future doesn't have any yet. A solid theory of history might be able to embrace the future, but all such theories have been discredited. Thus historians do not offer, and are seldom invited, to take part in shaping public policy. They leave that to economists.

"But discussions among policy makers always invoke history anyway, usually in simplistic form. "Munich" and "Vietnam," devoid of detail or nuance, stand for certain kinds of failure. "Marshall Plan" and "Man on the Moon" stand for certain kinds of success. Such totemic invocation of history is the opposite of learning from history, and Santayana's warning continues in force, that those who fail to learn from history are condemned to repeat it."

From Brand's newest enthusiasm, Applied History,
http://sb.longnow.org/Applied%20history.html

" The *Whole Earth Catalog* was an important catalyst, but there were others, too. In spite of David Suzuki being called the Pope of Ecology in Canada, I don't think we have one. Paul Hawken has pointed out that the health of the movement lies partly in the fact that there is no one leader or center. The center is everywhere and so much of the action is appropriately regional.

— *Nancy Jack Todd*
Author, A Safe and Sustainable World

The counter-cultural explosion not only led to lasting changes — startling changes — in the way we think about race, women, sexual orientation, food, shelter, energy, environment, and just about everything else, but it also galvanized the US far-right to engage in a long-term (and superbly orchestrated) effort to take over the government. It worked. Time to take it back.

When *The Whole Earth Catalog* was published in 1968, it announced that we can be a part of our environment, find our proper place within it, and shape it — as humans seem bound to do — cooperatively and positively rather than competitively and negatively. And it provided the physical and intellectual tools to begin that work.

— *John Abrams*
President, South Mountain Company
Author, The Company We Keep:
Reinventing Small Business for Community, People, and Place

" Amory and Hunter Lovins and colleagues at the Rocky Mountain Institute have helped delineate a soft energy path based on radical efficiency and renewable energy. Their work underscores the economic benefits of environmentally sustainable strategies.

— *Dan Chiras*
Author, The Natural House

On Biophilia and Houses

Alex Wilson interviewed by Stephen Morris

Biophilia is, literally, a love for nature. "It is a concept that should guide building design," says Alex Wilson of Brattleboro, Vermont, author of the book *Your Green Home* (New Society Publishers, 2006). Wilson knows what he is talking about. As founder and currently executive editor of *Environmental Building News*, he has "green cred" within a state that is an epicenter of enlightened building practices.

The state is dotted with examples of biophilia, from the space-age company headquarters of NRG in Hinesburg (that produces 90% of its own electricity), to the madcap houses of Prickly Mountain outside Warren built by young designer/builders in the 1970s, to the permaculture features of the 10 Stone development in Charlotte, to the Yestermorrow Design/Build School in Waitsfield where the alumni of Prickly Mountain now dominate the faculty, to the offices of the trend-setting *Journal of Light Construction* just outside Richmond. Even if they can't spell or define it, Vermonters take biophilia seriously.

But being ahead of the rest of the world isn't good enough for Wilson. "Given the magnitude of the benefits that can be realized through biophilic design – especially the healing benefits – it is remarkable that there hasn't been more interest in carrying out research."

Now, for really the first time, Wilson has distilled his thoughts on biophilia and encyclopedic knowledge of green building into a book aimed squarely at homeowners looking to build an environmentally responsible home.

Wilson, and his company, have been incredibly prolific in generating and cataloging information on green building. The organization has been producing its definitive paper newsletter since 1992. Its roster of products now includes *Green Building Products*, a book featuring nearly 1,600 products from its GreenSpec® database, BuildingGreen Suite, a powerful online tool that integrates articles, reviews, and news with product listings and project case. It also sponsors an annual conference held in Boston in March where the greenest of the green builders, architects, and product designers gather to explore the future of building.

We caught up with him in *EBN*'s decidedly high-tech offices located in the low-tech former warehouse complex that formerly housed the Estey Organ Company on Birge Street in Brattleboro.

QUESTION: *Who is driving the demand for "green" homes: enlightened consumers or enlightened contractors? Or is it technological advances?*

ANSWER: It's being pulled by homeowners wanting healthier, more affordable, and more environmentally responsible houses; and it's being pushed by design and construction professionals who are committed to these issues and wanting to make a difference. In some cases, incentives are helping to advance green building.

How did you personally become involved in this field?

At a young age, 12 or 13, while my friends were thinking fireman or astronaut, I was thinking environmental protection. I became active in the late 1960s to ban DDT and to protect wilderness. My college degree is in environmental biology, but in 1976 I got involved in renewable energy. I saw it as a chance to be for something, rather than opposing things like power plants or chemicals or pollution. After college (and following six months in Washington learning that I didn't want to live in a city) I got a job with the New Mexico Solar Energy Association, where I began writing about renewable energy. In 1980, I was offered a job as executive director of the New England Solar Energy Association, then in Brattleboro. After five years, I ventured out on my own in 1985, starting what is now a 17-person company, BuildingGreen, Inc.

Can you comment on the fact that most renewable energy installers and green builders in the area seem to be working on huge second homes? Is that an accurate generalization?

There certainly is a lot of work being done on these "starter castles." For better or worse, the wealthy often have the available money to invest in the more expensive and highly visible systems like PV arrays. I always push for downsizing a home as the best starting point in home design.

Any truth to the statement that houses are more toxic today than the average house of 100 years ago due to the use of high-tech building materials produced by the petroleum industry and construction techniques that make houses too tight without enough natural air infiltration?

Yes, there is certainly some truth to that. One hundred years ago, we didn't use binders to create plywood and particleboard, we didn't have wall-to-wall carpeting made from various plastics, we didn't have brominated flame retardants and phthalate plasticizers. On top of that, our houses were really leaky, so any indoor contaminants inside a house would quickly leak out. On the other hand, we burned wood in open fireplaces and coal in boilers, and pollutants from those made people sick, and we didn't use fans to bring fresh air into homes and exhaust stale air — lots of fresh air came in on very cold or windy days when there was a pressure difference between the indoors and outdoors, but during swing seasons, spilled smoke in a house might remain there for a long time.

Meanwhile, on the average building site, the construction process seems to be a study in creating waste, much of which could be recycled, but is instead hauled to the local landfill. Is the ecological message getting through to the average builder?

Probably not to the average builder — yet. In commercial construction, the mainstream industry has come along a little faster. The mainstream homebuilding industry has some catch-up to do.

What are the most encouraging trends in green building today?

Growing awareness about three things: 1) the volatility of energy prices and the generally upward pressure; 2) our health and the fact that since we spend 90% of our time indoors we better make sure that our homes and workplaces are healthy; and 3) the changing environment and the realization that global climate change is real and that we need to collectively do something about it.

The most discouraging...?

The magnitude of change that is needed to head off the truly frightening prospects of full-blown global warming — with tens of meters of sea level rise, Atlanta's climate coming to Vermont, loss of sugar maples in the autumn — things like that.

For whom is Your Green Home specifically written?

It's mostly written for people thinking about building a new home and wondering what the questions are that need to be asked and the decisions that need to be made.

Foraminiferan

Alex Wilson's *Environmental Building News* has become the national library of enlightened building practice.

Garlic was brought to the Americas by the Spanish during the late 1400s and through mid 1500s. The explorer Cortes planted garlic in Mexico and noted even the Indians of Peru took a fancy to the herb. Native Americans used wild garlic, along with its wild shallot, onion, and leek relatives for food and medicine. Eaten raw, the green shoots were their cure for scurvy.

During the early 1800s, the Shakers, a communal religious sect that lived in upstate New York, grew, packaged, and sold herbs, including garlic, for medicinal use as a stimulant, expectorant, and tonic for cough, asthma, and respiratory infections.

Your Green Home
by Alex Wilson

There are many reasons to build a green home. Perhaps you want to provide a safe, healthy place for your children to grow up. Or maybe you're concerned about rising energy costs. Your priority might be comfort, or durability — knowing that the house will last a long time with minimal maintenance. For a growing number of us, building a green home is about doing our part to protect the environment, helping to make the world a better place for our children and grandchildren. A green home is all of this, and often much more.

What Is Green Building?

The term green building is used to describe design and construction of buildings with some or all of the following characteristics:

- Buildings that have minimal adverse impacts on local, regional, and even global ecosystems;
- Buildings that reduce reliance on automobiles;
- Buildings that are energy-efficient in their operation;
- Buildings and grounds that conserve water;
- Buildings that are built in an environmentally responsible manner from low-environmental-impact materials;
- Buildings that are durable and can be maintained with minimal environmental impact;
- Buildings that help their occupants practice environmentalism, e.g., by recycling waste; and
- Buildings that are comfortable, safe, and healthy for their occupants.

Quite often, when people think of green building, what comes to mind is the use of recycled-content building materials — insulation made from recycled newspaper, floor tiles made out of ground-up light bulbs, and so forth. Materials are indeed an important component of green construction, but this way of building goes much further.

Green building addresses the relationship between a building and the land on which it sits; how the structure might help to foster a sense of community or reduce the need for automobile use by its occupants; how to minimize energy use in the building (energy consumption being one of the largest environmental impacts of any building); and how to create the healthiest possible living space.

A Short History of Green Building

Green building can trace its origin, in part, to builders of solar homes during the 1970s and '80s. Many of the architects, designers, and builders who were involved with solar energy back then had gotten involved because of concerns about energy shortages and the environment. Since solar energy is a clean, renewable energy source, designing and building homes to make use of solar was a way to reduce impacts on the environment, creating homes that required less fossil fuel or electricity.

These designers and builders began to realize, however, that their focus was too narrow, that reducing conventional energy use was just one part of a much bigger picture of resource efficiency and healthy building. Sure, those solar pioneers could build a house that used solar energy to keep its occupants toasty on cold winter nights, thus saving money and helping the environment at the same time. But what about where these houses were being built? What about their durability? What about the materials used in construction? Was the wood coming from clear-cut old-growth forests in the Pacific Northwest? What about the alarming increases in asthma among children? What about ozone depletion? And what about comfort? Some of those houses with extensive southfacing glass overheated or experienced glare problems during the day.

Environmentally aware designers and builders began to broaden their focus. They recognized that North America's buildings accounted for a huge percentage of its energy use, greenhouse gas emissions, ozone depletion, resource use, and health problems. And instead of simply being part of the problem, these pioneers wanted to be part of the solution. A few professional organizations, including the American Institute of Architects and the Urban Land Institute, formed new committees or divisions to address environmentally responsible building. New organizations were created, including the US Green Building Council. New publications were launched addressing green building, such as *Environmental Building News*. Even the mainstream industry magazines, such as *Builder* and *Architectural Record*, began running feature articles on green building. A shift began that will forever change the way we design and build.

Homebuyers and commercial building owners are also encouraging the green building movement. People want to live or work in buildings that are healthier and better for the environment.

Opinion polls regularly show that the public is willing to spend more for something that's better for the environment; it only makes sense that this concern extends to our homes and workplaces. In commercial buildings, research shows that people working in green buildings (with features like natural daylighting, healthy air, and operable windows) are more productive; they get more done in less time, whether manufacturing widgets or processing insurance forms. Because the labor costs of running a business dwarf the costs of operating a building, improving the productivity of workers can yield tremendous financial returns. Similar studies are showing that students learn faster in classrooms that have natural daylighting. A highly detailed 1999 study of hundreds of classrooms in the San Juan Capistrano School System in southern California, for example, correlated the rate of learning with the presence or absence of natural daylighting. The researchers found that learning progressed 20% faster in math skills and 26% faster in verbal skills in classrooms with the most natural daylighting compared to classrooms with the least daylighting.

While much of the green building movement is very new, there are also aspects that have been around for a long time. Many of the ideas being advanced by environmentally concerned designers and builders are drawn from the past. Landscape architects in the American Midwest are studying how Native Americans managed the tall-grass prairies using fire and are using those practices at some large corporate office parks. Ideas from pioneering individuals – such as Frederick Law Olmstead, 19th-century designer of New York City's Central Park, Frank Lloyd Wright in the early 1900s, and landscape architect Ian McHarg beginning in the 1950s – are referenced widely in the green building field today. Some of the underlying principles of passive solar design date back to prehistoric cliff dwellings. Green building is still in its infancy. Not only does the building industry not yet have all the answers about how to build green, it often doesn't even know the right questions to ask. There have been tremendous strides made since the early 1990s in understanding the environmental impacts associated with building (for example, scientific studies of the life-cycle impacts of building materials), but we still have a very long way to go. Some of the ideas presented in this book will probably become obsolete as the green building movement matures over the coming years and decades. But we now know enough to provide clear guidance to someone who wants a home that will have a lower impact on the environment, and that is the purpose of this book.

Liverwort

Though garlic was consumed with passion throughout the world, Americans considered its odor offensive and socially unacceptable. During the early part of the 20th century some cooks would season their foods with only minute amounts of garlic salt or garlic powder. Even the well-respected Fannie Farmer, who created *The Boston Cooking School Cookbook*, omitted garlic in her Italian and Provençal dishes, substituting onion instead.

The Earth Roof Factor
by Rob Roy

I t is not absolutely necessary to put an earth roof or lightweight living roof on an earth-sheltered house, but not to do so, it seems to me, is a great opportunity lost.

I share seven different advantages to earth roofs with my students, and pull out a timeworn placard to illustrate the points, which are:

1. INSULATION. I can hear it now: "Hold on there, mate, you just told us earth is poor insulation!" Well, yes, it is. Author and earth-shelter owner-builder Dan Chiras reckons earth is worth about a quarter of an R (R-.25) per inch of thickness, and that rings true with me, particularly for earth a few inches down. But the first three or four inches of earth, where the plant roots aerate the soil, is considerably less dense and, therefore, has some insulation value. The grass or wildflowers – don't mow 'em – also flop down in the autumn and add more insulation. And, finally, the earth roof holds snow better than any other roof surface, and light fluffy snow is worth a good R-1 per inch of thickness. We notice that our home is even cozier and requires less fuel to heat with a cap of two feet of snow overhead.

2. DRAINAGE. With non-earth roof systems, you need some sort of drainage system to remove a lot of water quickly from the roof during a downpour: gutters, downspouts, storm drains, etc. The earth roof drainage – particularly where the roof drains at a single pitch directly onto berms, such as the Log End Cave design – is slow and natural. Even a freestanding earth roof, like the one at Earthwood, must fully saturate before runoff must be attended to.

3. AESTHETICS. The earth roof is hands-down the most beautiful roof you can put overhead, particularly one of natural wildflowers.

4. COOLING. The sun beating down on most roofing causes high surface temperatures. You can literally fry an egg on some of them. The living roof, however, stays nice and cool because of the shading effect of plants, the mass of the earth, and the evaporative cooling effect of stored rainwater. Stick your finger into the living roof and you can feel the cool.

5. LONGEVITY. Built properly, the roof will require very little maintenance. We don't even mow ours anymore. All other roofs are subject to deterioration from the ultraviolet (UV) rays of the sun, from wind and water erosion, and from

something called freeze-thaw cycling. In our climate near Montreal, most roofs are subjected to between 30 and 35 freeze-thaw cycles each winter, and each occurrence breaks the roofing down on the molecular level. Sun, wind, and frost never get to the roofing surface, so, protected by the earth from these adverse conditions, the waterproofing membrane is virtually non-biodegradable. It should last 100 years or forever, whichever comes first.

6. Ecology. While not the right place to grow shrubs, trees or root vegetables, the earth roof can support all sorts of plants and microbial life. Instead of killing off – say – 1,500 square feet of the planet's surface to yet more hot, lifeless black tarscape, we can return the home's footprint to cool green oxygenating living production.

7. Protection. Just a few inches of earth afford all sorts of protections not found with other roofing surfaces: fire, radiation, and sound, just to name three. In combination with a Log End Cave-type berm, the earth roof can also contribute to tornado, hurricane, and earthquake protection, as well.

The seven advantages to an earth roof all occur with just a few inches of earth on the roof. Doubling the thickness, from – say – 6 inches to 12 inches does not double the value of the advantage. With fire and sound protection, for example, extra earth beyond six inches adds little advantage; you've still got windows, doors and some portion of above grade walls influencing these considerations. But doubling the earth does double the potential saturated load of the earth component of the roof. And this extra load greatly increases the structural cost of the home. I accent timber framing (also called "plank and beam" roofing) as the most suitable roof structural system for the inexperienced owner-builder. Other options, such as pre-stressed concrete planks (which are very expensive and must be installed with a crane), or poured-in-place reinforced concrete roofing (which should be professionally installed), not only add greatly to the structural cost, but also don't look nearly so nice overhead as a ceiling.

Roy's General Theory on Earth or Living Roofs

This is as good a time as any to tell you about the realities of the earth roof with regard to its weight, or load. Calculating the desired load is the first step towards designing.

But, first, a clarification of terms might be in order. I use the term "earth roof" to describe a roof system that relies primarily on a certain thickness of earth or topsoil to nurture the desired vegetation or ground cover. A "living roof" might have earth on it, or it might have some other growing medium for the plants, such as straw. Or it might combine earth with another medium, as we have done on the roof of our straw bale guesthouse. Lots of work has been done in the past ten years in both Europe and North America on these alternatives that eliminate or considerably diminish the need for placing heavy earth overhead. And the reason is usually an effort to keep the structural cost down.

Because of the heavy weight of saturated earth, my theory for 25 years has always been – and still remains – that we want to use enough earth to maintain the green cover, and not a whole lot more. The reason, as we will soon see, is that wet earth is very heavy, and a great depth of it – while technically possible – adds unacceptably to the structural cost for owner-builders who want to own the home themselves, and not have a bank own it for them.

At Log End Cave and at Earthwood, we had good success with maintaining a green cover (mowed grass at the Cave, wild at Earthwood) with an earth roof with a final compacted depth of about six inches of soil. A couple of times at Earthwood, during its so-far 23-year life, the roof almost died off during drought. We never watered it. But always, after some compensating rain, the roof would come back and flourish once again.

Back in the 1970s, several builders were placing from 18 inches to 3 feet of earth on the roof, and, yes, they engineered the structure properly to support that kind of load. But these homes were very expensive, with a good part of the expense caught up in the roof support system. Why they did it remains a little unclear to me. After you've got an honest 6 inches of earth on the roof, the seven advantages listed above are present. If additional insulation is desired, earth is a poor choice. An extra inch of extruded polystyrene, which weighs practically nothing, will yield as much additional R-value as an extra foot of earth. And neither do the other advantages listed increase proportionally to the use of greater amounts of earth.

In the early 1900s America experienced a changing population with the influx of Europeans. Garlic slowly acquired an acceptable reputation when the Jews and Italians introduced their garlicky cuisines to the East Coast states. Along with their traditional foods were their strange folk remedies, many that relied on garlic to cure everything from colds to stomach aches. However, it wasn't until the 1960s that cooking with fresh garlic became the norm, prompted by the popularity of ethnic cuisines that have now become mainstream.

During World War II, the US government appealed to farmers to produce dehydrated garlic and onions that could be shipped overseas with food supplies for the troops. A small group of California farmers responded and planted a few acres of garlic. That was the beginning of what was to eventually become a huge, successful commercial venture. Most of the present US supply of garlic is grown in California, though some is grown in Mexico. A large percentage of the garlic grown today is incorporated into sauces, pickles, spices, condiments, and sausages. Estimates on fresh garlic consumption note that each adult ingests approximately two pounds of garlic a year.

The Precautionary Principle

by Stephen Morris

Earlier in this book, New Society Publisher Chris Plant cites the "Precautionary Principle" as an important evolution in our collective awareness, and the authors of *Naturally Clean* make frequent references to the concept. In 1998 a conference of scientists and environmentalists first put the idea into words in the historic Wingspread Statement: "When an activity raises threats of harm to human health or the environment, precautionary measures should be taken even if some cause and effect relationships are not fully established scientifically."

Critics have called the principle too vague to provide meaningful guidance, but in an article published by the Environmental Research Foundation (August 2005) author Peter Montague provides a sharper focus: "1) When we have a reasonable suspicion of harm, and 2) scientific uncertainty about cause and effect, then 3) we have a duty to take action to prevent harm.

The precautionary approach suggests five actions we can take:

1. Set a goal (or goals);
2. Examine all reasonable ways of achieving the goal, intending to choose the least-harmful way;
3. Monitor results, heed early warnings, and make mid-course corrections as needed;
4. Shift the burden of proof — when consequences are uncertain, give the benefit of the doubt to nature, public health and community well-being. Expect responsible parties (not governments or the public) to bear the burden of producing needed information. Expect reasonable assurances of safety for products before they can be marketed — just as the Food and Drug Administration expects reasonable assurances of safety before new pharmaceutical products can be marketed.
5. Throughout the decision-making process, honor the knowledge of those who will be affected by the decisions, and give them a real 'say' in the outcome."

We apply the Precautionary Principle every time we buckle a seatbelt. Why doesn't it make sense to do the same with the chemicals that surround us?

A Book for the Generations

book review by Stephen Morris

aturally Clean is a "company book," meaning that it quietly, but unabashedly, promotes awareness of issues that are addressed by the products it sells. The company, in this case, is Vermont-based Seventh Generation, the nation's leading provider of natural and non-toxic cleaning products and household goods. Proponents of journalistic independence might argue that such a book is inevitably biased by business self-interests, to which this reviewer responds:

"Yeah, but so what?" Companies, especially in Vermont, have learned that it can be a good brand strategy to have a strong and very public sense of values.

There are other strengths to "company" books. Businesses have in-depth product knowledge; businesses have broad experience with consumers; and businesses have resources that run much deeper than the average freelance writer toiling away on a laptop. The team that Seventh Generation President Jeffrey Hollender has assembled for *Naturally Clean* includes a wordsmith (Geoff Davis), a researcher who specializes in product analysis (Reed Doyle), and — nice touch — a representative of the next generation (Jeffrey's daughter Meika, a student at New York University).

Companies are also well-connected on both the technical and promotional fronts. *Naturally Clean* benefits from glowing testimonials from eco-celebrities Nell Newman and Robert Kennedy, Jr. At the other end of the spectrum its content was influenced by, and in some cases scrutinized by, prominent doctors, scientists, and environmentalists.

The result is a credible, attractive volume broken into forty-seven brief chapters with several useful appendices including a resource guide and glossary. There's enough science for the skeptic, but not so much that the reader needs to revisit high school chemistry class.

The "why" of this book is deeply troubling and the authors spend nearly the first one hundred pages explaining why a company like Seventh Generation is necessary. Under the guise of progress we have surrounded ourselves with products that poison us. "Clearly, chemistry itself is not a bad thing," say the authors. "It's the kinds of chemicals we make and use that matter. Like most anything else, there is a good side and a bad side to all the molecular manipulation chemists practice. There are safe chemicals, and there are unsafe chemicals. Our problem today is that we don't really know which are which."

I thought this book might fall into the trap of "don't buy their bad chemicals, buy our good ones," but, refreshingly, many of the recommended cleaning solutions are in the "less is more" category. You will find yourself wanting to go out and buy economy-sized packages of baking soda and vinegar, two inexpensive, non-toxic products that can be used for an infinite number of cleaning challenges. To wit:

Baked-on goo at the bottom of your oven? Been ignoring it since Thanksgiving? Just sprinkle on baking soda and moisten with water. Leave overnight, then wipe off with a wet paper towel the next day. No spray cleaner, no rubber gloves, no fumes, no energy-gobbling oven to run, and no threats of divorce!

This book is not for everyone, however. It is not, for instance, for people (like me) who like to keep their heads in the sand about certain unpleasant subjects. When grilling, for example, my approach to sanitation is to scrape the grill with the spatula. No stranger to the cliche "a little dirt never killed anyone" I've been called a guy who keeps the "fun" in "fungus."

Thus, it was difficult for me to read about the myriad of nastiness that could be lurking in my cutting board. It was stressful to learn that up to half of the weight of my pillow could be dust and other mites (half?). I could live easily without knowing the difference between a perfluorochemical (the basic compound used in non-stick pans)and a phthalate (an industrial compound used in a variety of products to make them more pliant).

This is not a book for people who want to believe that our governmental institutions are keeping them safe from toxic products. On the contrary, of the 80,000 chemical compounds now in use, only a tiny percentage (one half of one per cent) have ever been tested for carcinogenicity. The rest? We simply do not know.

The operative standard in this country is to base most regulation on a system that says an activity is innocent until proven guilty. While this is effective in keeping Big Brother at bay, it means there are a huge number products in everyday use whose impact on your health is unknown. Seen from this perspective *Naturally Clean* becomes an important tool to empower individuals to make their own regulatory decisions.

The cheapskate in me loved *Naturally Clean* for its alternatives to expensive household cleaners. My rebel, pagan, and nostalgic sides were similarly delighted. "Once upon a time, things were different in America's cleaning cupboards. In the days before the chemical revolution of the 20th century, our ancestors relied on naturally occurring materials and substances to help them with the housework. These included things like pure vegetable soaps, grease-cutting vinegars, abrasives like calcium carbonate and baking soda, citrus oils to remove odors and grime, and essential oils of plants like birch and lavender to sanitize surfaces in the home.

DuPont promises "Better Living Through Chemistry." Seventh Generation promises to consider the impact of their deliberations on the seventh generation (adapted from a Native American proverb).

I will take my chances with them.

From *Naturally Clean*

A critical epicenter of activity in our kitchens is the dishwasher. Fifty-one percent of all American homes have one of these time- and labor-saving devices, yet it surprises many to learn that they're the most toxic appliance in the modern home.

Over the course of approximately 30 experiments, researchers at the EPA and the University of Texas recently documented the dishwasher's role as a leading cause of indoor air pollution. Pollutants released by dishwashers include the chlorine added to both public water supplies and dishwasher detergents, volatile organic compounds like chloroform, radioactive radon naturally present in some water sources, and other volatile contaminants that have worked their way into public water supplies. When these materials are exposed to the piping hot water that circulates through your dishwasher as it cleans, they are easily "stripped out" and evaporated into the air.

Depending on the material in question and your water temperature, dishwashers can reach 100 percent efficiency when it comes to transferring water pollutants and detergent chemicals to indoor air. Because these machines vent about six liters of air per minute into your home as they work, they're continuously releasing any water-borne toxins throughout each operating cycle. Even more problematically, the air pollution created by routine venting is often exceeded by the single large burst of contaminated steam that's released whenever a dishwasher is opened before its contents have cooled.

Although it certainly sounds a little odd to say, protecting yourself from your dishwasher means taking steps like these:

- Use a chlorine-free dishwasher detergent. This will greatly reduce the burden of chlorine and other chemicals in its water, which in turn reduces your exposure to them.
- Ventilate your kitchen during and after dishwasher operation. This can mean opening windows, running your stove's ventilation fan (assuming it vents outside and not back into your kitchen), and using window fans.
- If you're connected to a public water system that's using chlorine to treat drinking water, filter your home's water supply. An activated carbon filter placed where water enters your home will remove chlorine and most volatile chemicals. It will also filter water used in your washing machine and shower – two other hot-water sources of chlorine fumes.
- Have your water tested for radon. If results are positive seek solutions from radon abatement professionals.
- Keep your dishwasher closed and sealed for at least an hour following a completed cleaning cycle. This will prevent the hot burst of pollutant-laden steam that escapes when dishwashers are opened immediately following their use.
- If you have a "no dry heat" option on your dishwasher, use it. This prevents the activation of its heating coils. These coils heat up the inside of your dishwasher and quickly evaporate the final rinse water, which allows that water to transfer its toxic load to indoor air. Deactivating the heated dry cycle also saves energy.

- 🖤 Only run your dishwasher when it's completely full. Running a dishwasher when it's less than full means you're using it more often than necessary and increasing its contributions to unhealthy indoor air. And it means you're using more water and energy than needed.

- 🖤 Make sure your detergent is phosphate-free, too. Contrary to popular belief, phosphate use is still legally permitted in dishwasher detergents, and phosphates may constitute as much as 20 percent of a product's formula. (Dishwasher detergents contain levels of phosphorus as high as 8 percent, which translates to a phosphate level of 20 percent.) Once phosphates are discharged into the environment they promote massive algae growth in local waters. These sudden blooms of algae trigger a process called eutrophication in which local waters become starved of oxygen and devoid of life. This issue is of special concern to anyone living near a lake or pond.

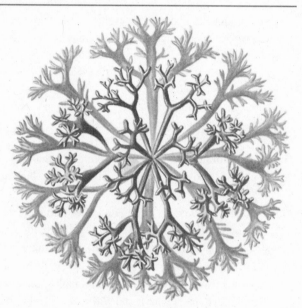

Red algae (Rhodophyceae)

Andrew Korfhage is the online editor for
Co-opAmerica.org

Try A Solar Water Heater
by Andrew Korfhage

With a solar water heater, you'll get the hot water your household needs while saving money and energy and reducing your dependence on coal-fired power.

After a year with their solar hot water heater, homeowners Bob Allen and Lyle Rudensey say they'll never go back to relying on a conventional water heater. Even in gloomy, rainy Seattle, they are saving money and energy by heating all of their water with the power of the sun.

"With a lack of leadership at the federal level, I feel it's very important that we all do what we can to reduce our dependence on fossil fuels and reduce greenhouse gases," says Lyle. "Solar hot water systems are a great place to start. They're not as expensive as solar photovoltaics, and they'll save you substantial amounts of energy and money."

Looking at his household energy bills, Lyle notes that it's hard to quantify the exact dollar amount the new water heater has saved, because he and Bob also installed energy-efficient appliances and a solar photovoltaic system last year, as part of an overall strategy to reduce their dependence on fossil fuels. Still, according to the American Council for an Energy-Efficient Economy (ACEEE), water heating uses more household energy than any activity other than heating and cooling, so replacing your household's water-heating energy with free power from the sun will have a significant effect on your bottom line. With all their savings combined, Lyle points out that his and Bob's electric bills have dropped to a low of $5.

"Plus, the water heater increased the value of the house," Bob adds. "And it's a hedge against future energy cost increases."

Bob and Lyle installed an "active" solar water heater with "evacuated tube" collectors, which they say works great in the Pacific Northwest, because the heater keeps working even on overcast days or when temperatures are freezing outside.

"I can't think of anything negative to say about it," says Lyle. "It never ceases to amaze me to see our solar hot water system still pumping 80- to 100-degree water late into the evening on a day when it isn't even sunny."

Active and Passive Heaters

When you select a solar water heater for your home, you can choose between an active system (like Bob and Lyle's), or a passive system. *Active* systems use a pump to move water through their heating system, and this requires a source of energy (often a solar photovoltaic panel). *Passive* systems use no pumps or electrical components.

Because of their design, passive systems are the simpler of the two. They work essentially like a garden hose left out in the sun, except the container for the water is much, much larger. The sun directly heats the water in a large, rooftop tank, which then flows down into your plumbing system. If the water has not yet reached the temperature you've selected on your thermostat, your conventional water heater will need to kick in to finish the job. Passive systems are best suited for warm climates where your rooftop storage tank is in no danger of freezing.

Because of their simplicity, passive systems are usually cheaper and can last longer than active systems. The drawbacks are that they can be less reliable, and require a heavy water tank, or collector, to be mounted on your roof. (Depending on your roof's design, this may require structural support.)

An active system stores water in a tank inside your house, and uses its pump to move either water or a "heat exchange" fluid through a "collector" on your roof. Collectors are the components of your solar water heating system it needs to heat your water. Used in freezing climates, the heat-exchange fluid is a non-freezing liquid that carries the sun's heat from the roof to your tank, where it transfers the heat to your water. The fluid re-circulates to the roof to be heated again, while the water flows on to your tap. (This fluid is usually propylene glycol, which the FDA has approved as an additive in food and medicine. However, it is a suspected neuro- and respiratory toxin, according to the National Institute of Occupational Health and Safety.)

Although active systems are more expensive but more reliable than passive ones, you may still wish to keep your conventional water heater for a back-up. In fact, in many areas, local building codes require conventional back-ups, so be sure to check with your contractor or local government. Active systems using the "heat exchange" method are best for areas where freezing temperatures are likely.

Keep in mind that solar water heaters also work great for your outdoor hot water needs, like pools and hottubs.

Two Types of Collectors

If you choose an active system, you'll need to consider two types of collectors:

1. FLAT-PLATE COLLECTORS: These are metal boxes with glass or plastic covers (called glazings) on top and a dark-colored "absorber plate" covering a system of pipes on the bottom. Sunlight passes through the glazing and is collected by the absorber plate, which converts the sunlight into heat that is passed on to the liquid (either water or a heat-transfer fluid) in the system of pipes. The advantage of this type of collector is the price – it's cheaper than evacuated-tube collectors.

2. EVACUATED-TUBE COLLECTORS: Best visualized as a series of tiny, open-ended thermoses, these collectors consist of individual glass vacuum tubes surrounding a secondary inner tube, through which the liquid or heat-transfer fluid flows.

The most efficient (and most costly) collector, the evacuated-tube model works somewhat better than the flat-plate model in cold climates.

Depending on the type of system you choose, a solar water heater can cost from $2,000 to $6,000, and begins paying for itself right away with your reduced energy bills. The amount you save will depend on many factors, including how much hot water you use, your system's performance, sunlight in your area, and the local cost of conventional fuels, but the US Department of Energy estimates than on average, your bill should decrease by between 50 and 80 percent.

The Tax Incentives

A federal incentive went into effect on January 1, 2006, making a solar water heater a more affordable addition to your home than ever.

For any solar water heater placed in service between now and the end of 2007, you can receive a federal tax credit for 30 percent of the system's cost, with the maximum credit capped at $2,000. Be sure to save documentation of all costs associated with the system's installation (including the labor of any installers, plumbers, or electricians you use), and note that to claim the credit your system must be certified by the Solar Rating Certification Corporation.

Also, to find additional state-level tax incentives, including rebates, property tax credits, sales tax exemptions, and more, visit the Database of State Incentives for Renewable Energy.

Remember that no matter where you live or what your climate, a solar water heater can be a great way to reduce our country's dependence on fossil fuels, and position you to not only start saving money today, but to save a lot more money in the future as the cost of fuels like natural gas and heating oil continue to rise.

"Some people might think that solar water heaters aren't worth installing in a climate like the Pacific Northwest, but that's not true," says Lyle. "Germany gets about 70 percent as much sunlight as Seattle does, and they are the biggest users of solar power in the world. This is something everyone can do that really makes a huge difference."

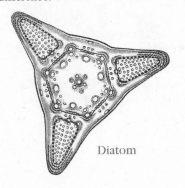

Diatom

Visit Co-op America's family of Web sites for information on socially and environmentally responsible purchasing and investing.
www.coopamerica.org
www.responsibleshopper.org
www.greenpages.org

Tamsyn Jones is a recent graduate of the University of Missouri
at Columbia, currently pursuing further study in Tasmania.

The Scoop On Dirt
Why We Should all Worship the Ground We Walk On
Tamsyn Jones

I t's one of nature's most perfect contradictions: a substance that is ubiquitous but unseen; humble but essential; surprisingly strong but profoundly fragile. It nurtures life and death; undergirds cities, forests and oceans; and feeds all terrestrial life on Earth. It is a substance few people understand and most take for granted. Yet, it is arguably one of Earth's most critical natural resources – and humans, quite liter-ally, owe to it their very existence.

From the food we eat to the clothes we wear to the air we breathe, humanity de-pends upon the dirt beneath our feet. Gardeners understand this intuitively; to them, the saying "cherish the soil" is gospel. But for the better part of society, dirt barely gets a sideways glance. To most, it's just part of the background, something so ob-vious it's ignored.

Even among the environmentally minded, soil sags well below the radar of im-portant causes. But the relationship between soil quality and other aspects of envi-ronmental health is intricately entwined. What's more, it's a relationship that encompasses a vast swath of territory, from agricultural practices to global climate change, and from the well-being of oceans to that of people.

Despite humankind's long relationship with soil, the stuff remains a mystery. Even our language manages to maligns it. Somehow, "dirt" has acquired a bad rep-utation. And it's been codified in some of our most common idioms, with people de-scribed as "dirty rotten scoundrels," "poor as dirt" or "dirtbags." The modern word "dirt" itself descends from the less than complimentary Old English word "drit," meaning "excrement." Instead of marveling at the mystery of soil, we have mocked it, by dredging and paving; desiccating and polluting; and working it to exhaustion.

Now our poor husbandry of this essential resource is catching up with us, in the form of disconcertingly rapid erosion and loss of farmland, widespread agricultural pollution, damage to fisheries, and alarming levels of pesticides and other chemi-cals building up in our bodies. The subject of soil is rarely billed as glamorous or sexy, but it should be. From its remarkable properties to its critical ecological im-portance, the dirt under our feet is a goldmine of scientific wonderment, and it's about time people got excited about soil.

Soil is Special Stuff

Soil types vary considerably on our planet, from the hottest deserts to the coldest poles. Soil directly and indirectly affects agricultural productivity, water quality and climate. Thanks to the Earth's soils, most of the rainfall hitting our planet is trapped and absorbed, watering plants and replenishing aquifers, rivers, lakes and streams. If soil didn't catch and apportion this water, it would run off the land into the oceans, and the continents would be barren wastelands.

If it weren't for the stabilizing effect of soil, ancestral plants could never have survived the fierce, raw weather of primordial Earth. Over millions of years, these plants and their offspring created the life-sustaining atmosphere required for land animals to evolve. Essentially an organ of Mother Earth, soil is a vital living system – the very skin of our planet – that nourishes the plants we eat, the animals we use for food and fiber, and the thriving underground kingdom of bacteria, fungi, protozoa, earthworms and other microbes that are critical to the planet's food webs.

To put it another way, without soil humans would be creatures of the sea. Only about 20 percent of the Earth's surface is covered by land. However, much of this land is too inhospitable to support our species. Only about eight percent of the planet's soil surface is actually arable. This means, explains Wes Jackson of the Land Institute, that all six billion people living today have but a tiny fraction of soil to thank for their survival and diverse ways of life.

Anatomy of Healthy Soil

So what is healthy soil? Deceptively simple to the naked eye, healthy soils are dynamic ecosystems made up of a mixture of minerals, air, water, organic materials and a healthy population of microorganisms. The range and concentration of minerals present depends on the parent bedrock. Healthy soil is also extremely porous: Air accounts for about half its volume, providing channels for water to flow, pathways for roots and space for organisms to move around. Compaction, primarily the result of heavy farm machinery and livestock, squeezes air out of soil, depleting available oxygen.

When soil is healthy, however, it is a hotbed of thriving biological activity. We can't see most of that ongoing work, save perhaps on particularly rainy days when earthworms flock to the surface or a large insect scuttles across the ground. But a single gram of fertile soil can contain several million microbes. One heaping tablespoon of healthy soil may contain up to nine billion microorganisms, which is more than the human population on Earth, points out Harvey Blatt, author of the 2004 book *America's Environmental Report Card*. An acre of healthy topsoil can contain 900 pounds of earthworms, 2,400 pounds of fungi, 1,500 pounds of bacteria, 133 pounds of protozoa, 890 pounds of arthropods and algae, and in some cases, even small mammals. When this diverse soil community is disrupted or damaged, the consequences may be dire.

Plants are the first to suffer from damage to the soil community. Interestingly, soil microbes play a critical role in plant health. Long ago in Earth's evolutionary history, early soil microbes forged one of the first symbiotic relationships with early land plants when some algae and bacteria developed the ability to "fix" nitrogen, a nutrient essential for plant growth. Nitrogen is plentiful in the atmosphere, but plants can't use it in that pure form. They can only use nitrogen that's been incorporated into compounds like ammonia or nitrate. Once nitrogen-fixing organisms evolved billions of years ago, pioneer plants were able to creep onto the land. As these early plants gained a foothold on the rocky ledges poking out of the primordial seas, they helped build the terrestrial soils.

Today, the symbiosis between soil organisms and plants is deeply intertwined. Many soil microbes feed on by-products from growing roots and, in turn, help plants by extracting minerals and vitamins from the soil. Like microscopic farmers plowing and tilling their subterranean plots, these organisms enhance soil structure and help control plant-preying pests, cultivating an underground ecosystem.

Construction and urbanization pose significant challenges to soil health. A single rainstorm can wash away centuries worth of dirt.

These "chthonic" (pronounced "thonic" and meaning "of the Earth") creatures also provide another overlooked but critical function: They are perhaps the world's most prolific recyclers. Without the help of soil microbes to break down decaying plant and animal matter, fertile soils would not exist. Dead animals would never decompose, and the litter of leaves dropped from trees every autumn would soon bury buildings and roads.

The Carbon Link

Soils also play an important role in the process of recycling carbon, the most vital element for living beings. Healthy soils can be an important carbon sink, binding up carbon that might otherwise enter the atmosphere, potentially contributing to global warming.

According to the Environmental Literacy Council (ELC), soils contain twice the amount of carbon found in the atmosphere, and three times more carbon than is stored in all the Earth's vegetation. Thanks to soil microbes, as plants and animals decompose, some of their carbon becomes part of the organic matter in soils instead of escaping into the atmosphere as carbon dioxide. Paul Hepperly of the Rodale Institute's experimental research farm in eastern Pennsylvania defines organic matter as "mostly the resistant remains of plants." When this material combines with the mucus, slime and digestive products of soil organisms, it forms the material known as humus – an extremely rich component of soil the color of dark chocolate. Hepperly explains that humus is saturated with carbon.

"Carbon is really the glue that holds everything together in fertile soil," Hepperly says. "When you introduce tillage and compaction, there's excess air, and humus breaks from long chains of carbon into carbon dioxide, which then goes into the air." Since humus is highly concentrated organic matter, soils with a lot of humus tend to be more fertile. By the same token, damaged soils have less organic matter, hold less carbon, harbor a much more fragmented community of soil microbes, support fewer plants and animals, and are much more vulnerable to erosion and other problems. "Organic matter is really what holds water in the soil when you have droughts or floods," Hepperly says. "If you take away the glue, everything falls apart."

Soils in Trouble

Unfortunately, in many parts of the world, that "glue" is deteriorating rapidly. The explosion in human population, fuelled by agricultural and technological advancements, has led to soil erosion, compaction, salinity and loss of fertility. As the figurative "lifeblood" of many organisms, including humans, problems at the level of soils may reverberate through entire ecosystems – or civilizations.

In the 1930s, Hugh Hammond Bennett – a USDA scientist widely regarded as the "father of soil conservation" – commented, "Soil erosion is as old as agriculture. It began when the first heavy rain struck the first furrow turned by a crude implement of tillage in the hands of prehistoric man."

Any discussion about the health of soil ends up addressing agriculture. Since Neolithic times, when our ancestors adopted settled agriculture, our relationship with soil has been intimate and intense. Throughout history, the story has repeated itself: Great civilizations have grown where soils were fertile enough to support high-density human communities, and fallen when soils could no longer sustain our rough treatment. According to the International Task Force on Land Degradation, the great early civilizations of Mesopotamia arose because of the richness of their soils, and collapsed because of declines in soil quality. Poor land management and excessive irrigation caused soils to become increasingly degraded, leading to power struggles, migrations, and ultimately, the collapse of the Fertile Crescent civilizations.

Ancient Greece suffered a similar fate. The philosopher Plato, writing around 360 BCE, attributed the demise of Greek power to land degradation: "[In earlier days] Attica yielded far more abundant produce. In comparison of what then was, there are remaining only the bones of the wasted body; all the richer and softer parts of the soil having fallen away, and the mere skeleton of the land being left."

Many experts also blame the collapse of the great Mayan civilization and the peaceful Harappan society of the Indus valley on soil exhaustion and erosion, resulting from agricultural practices and clear-cutting of forests. According to Jared Diamond, a UCLA professor and author of the books *Guns, Germs and Steel* and *Collapse*, 90 percent of the people inhabiting Easter Island in the Pacific died because of deforestation, erosion and soil depletion. In Iceland, farming and human activities caused about 50 percent of the soil to end up in the sea, explains Diamond. "Icelandic society survived only through a drastically lower standard of living," he says. Not surprisingly, the practice of destroying soils by torching or salting farms and fields has been employed by armies in wars, from Alexander the Great to Napoleon.

Today, we are facing many of the same issues as these former civilizations: forest loss, over-consumption, dwindling freshwater supplies, overpopulation and overworked soils nearing the brink of collapse. While other social and economic factors also threaten soils, intensive, unsustainable agricultural practices continue to bear the brunt of the blame, despite lessons from history. Non-agricultural activities such as logging, construction, off-road vehicles, floods, droughts and fires also increase erosion, but the Natural Resource Conservation Service (NRCS) reports that agriculture is responsible for at least 60 percent of the erosion afflicting the US.

In America, our history has arguably been shaped from the outset by unsound farming practices. From the moment the first Europeans stepped off the boat, we set plow to earth and began to dredge the soil, overworking it through constant tilling and planting. "The farming practices of our forebears caused a one percent per year breakdown of essential organic matter, so that in 50 to 100 years families could no longer farm their home plots," explains Hepperly. He adds that the need to seek new fertile soils and farmsteads was a major factor in the westward movement of settlers.

Fortunately for those early colonists, there was always an abundance of fresh, new land. Today, humans have colonized just about every viable land surface on the planet. No fabled fresh frontiers remain. As the world's human population continues to grow, placing ever more strain on already stressed soils, will human societies find themselves near the brink of collapse?

Threats to Soils

Not all soil problems are equal everywhere. In many regions, including the US, Australia, China and Mexico, wind and water erosion are major threats. In the arid southwest of the US, massive irrigation is causing soils to become salty, in some cases to the point that plants can no longer grow. Soil compaction abounds wherever massive farms or livestock operations (especially confined livestock operations) exist; and in many countries with naturally acidic soils, such as Australia and Ghana, overuse of fertilizers is causing soils to become even more acidic. In the case of Ghana, Hepperly says that the soil has become so unnaturally acidic that it can no longer grow its native sorghum crop. Declining soil fertility – the result of over-intensive farming – is a serious problem worldwide, but it is particularly acute in Sub-Saharan Africa, where severe depletion of soil nutrients is a major cause of poverty and hunger.

EROSION: Among the soil problems, it is generally agreed that soil erosion is one of the most serious, in part because it often precedes or accompanies other forms of soil degradation or environmental problems. While erosion occurs naturally because of wind, water and ice acting on any exposed rock or soil surface, the process has been tremendously exacerbated by human activities, especially agriculture, logging and construction. It is now estimated that humans are responsible for 60 to 80 percent of all erosion. According to the American Society of Agricultural and Biological Engineers (ASABE), lost food production is the direst consequence of erosion.

The 1930s Dust Bowl is perhaps the most extreme example of this consequence in modern US history. For nearly a decade between 1931 and 1939, prolonged drought acted on severely misused land to cause massive erosion over millions of acres in southern Great Plains states. Destruction of a significant portion of agricultural acreage caused a mass exodus of millions of people and bogged down an already depressed national economy. According to the United Nations Convention to Combat Desertification, during the Dust Bowl years, "At least five inches of top-soil were lost from nearly 10 million acres."

While erosion isn't as dramatic in the US today as it was in the 1930s, the problem continues to haunt farmers and urban developers. In a 2002 position paper adopted by ASABE, the group estimated that soil erosion is damaging the productivity of 29 percent (112 million acres) of US cropland and is adversely affecting the ecological health of 39 percent (145 million acres) of rangeland. Worldwide, erosion is one of the biggest causes of soil degradation. "An outrageous amount of soil is being lost," says Craig Minowa, an environmental scientist with the Organic Consumers Association (OCA).

In many places, soils are eroding faster than they can be rebuilt. Though a renewable resource in theory, soil forms very slowly, measured in centuries. For all practical purposes, the soil we lose to erosion will never be replaced in our lifetimes.

"The fastest soil regeneration is about 200 years, but it can take a million years, depending on the geologic processes," says Dan Yoder, a professor in the Department of Biological Systems Engineering and Soil Science at the University of Tennessee. "Coarse sand, for instance, doesn't form soil very easily."

Hepperly says that each American erodes an average of 3.5 tons of soil yearly. "In fact, it is our biggest national export," he quips. A single rainstorm can wash away centuries-old accumulations of soil from damaged, neglected or badly managed ground.

Human-caused erosion (also known as "accelerated erosion") is most damaging to topsoil, the soil's uppermost layer. In addition to being the most productive soil layer (it contains the highest concentration of organic material), topsoil is also the layer in which plants grow best. But topsoil is also the thinnest layer, usually not more than a foot deep. Preston Sullivan of the National Sustainable Agriculture Information Service says that soil lost to erosion contains about three times more nutrients and 1.5 to five times more organic matter than the soil that remains behind. Further, loss of topsoil increases a soil's overall vulnerability to erosion, thus creating a vicious, exponentially worsening cycle of damage.

The developing world is especially at risk from the negative effects of soil erosion and declining soil fertility. In Africa, many nations are facing a veritable soil health crisis, due in large part to increasing population pressures, poverty, and the limitations inherent to many tropical soils. Tropical soils are naturally lower in fertility, and also foster increased weeds and pests, says Hari Eswaran, national leader of the NRCS-affiliated Office of World Soil Resources and an expert on soil erosion problems.

"In Nigeria two to three years ago, I visited a farmer growing tapioca, a tuber which is a staple crop there. His average yield was about three tons per acre," Eswaran says. "In contrast, the average yield is 30 tons per acre in India...You combine these problems, and that's why they practiced shifting cultivation. After two years, production decreased and people moved on. That only works with lower population.

Population pressures are now forcing farmers to remain on the same nutrient-depleted land to grow their crops year after year – a practice known as "mining," because nutrients are literally extracted from soil with nothing given in return. Among other problems, farmers often have practically no access to soil-enriching fertilizers.

"Here in the US land starts to degrade and farmers see it in terms of decreased productivity. They counteract it with massive amounts of fertilizers and chemicals," Eswaran says. But in Africa, farmers often have to walk for miles to buy fertilizer, he explains. Many are also ignorant of proper fertilizer use and simple farming techniques that could significantly minimize soil damage. The result is that at least a third of sub-Saharan Africa's population is chronically undernourished, according to a study released this year by the International Center for Soil Fertility and Agricultural Development (IFDC), a US-based nonprofit. The study tracked soil health across Africa from 1980 to 2004, and describes the situation now facing Africa as a "soil health crisis." Some 75 percent of Africa's farmland is severely degraded and rapidly losing basic soil nutrients needed to grow crops, the report states. Many sub-Saharan countries can't feed themselves," says Eswaran.

A 1995 study published in *Science* concluded that the loss of soil and water from US cropland decreases agricultural productivity by about $27 billion per year. A 2000 story in the Australian rural weekly paper *Landline* estimates that soil degradation costs Australian farmers $2.5 billion a year in lost production. It added that nobody has even calculated the off-farm costs of soil degradation, such as salt-polluted rivers or the loss of biodiversity and wildlife habitat.

AQUATIC POLLUTION: When soils erode, much of the displaced sediment – as well as the pesticides and excess nutrients mixed with it – ends up washing into streams, rivers and eventually oceans. The World Resources Institute says that the surfeit of excess nutrients on the land – primarily from a massive surge in fertilizer use since the 1940s, deforestation and the burning of fossil fuels – has resulted in "a glut of nitrogen," the effects of which "reach every environmental domain, threatening air and water quality, and disrupting the health of terrestrial and aquatic ecosystems." The Institute adds, "Aquatic ecosystems have probably suffered the most so far. They are the ultimate receptacles of much of the nutrient overload."

The Environmental Protection Agency (EPA) reveals that at least 40 percent of the affected stream miles and 45 percent of lake and reservoir areas were damaged because of eroded sediments. More broadly, Blatt writes that farms produce 70 percent of all stream pollution in the US.

Agricultural pollution originating in the Midwest is the primary cause of a chronic pollution problem in the Gulf of Mexico known as hypoxia. When excess nutrients pollute water, toxic algal blooms grow, which suck up most of the available oxygen. This leads to the death of aquatic organisms. The mouth of the Mississippi River now has a yearly dead zone larger than the size of New Jersey, says

Hepperly, and brown shrimp harvests have routinely been 25 percent of their historical catch size. The problem is similar in the Chesapeake Bay.

URBAN EROSION: Erosion isn't just an agricultural phenomenon. Urban erosion is an equally significant problem – one that has often been overlooked, but is becoming more serious as population pressures fuel development and urban expansion. Housing and construction projects gouge the soil and strip its vegetation, leaving it exposed to the elements for long periods of time. Erosion rates remain higher after construction is completed, as vegetation is reduced and rooftops shed water that would have been trapped by plants. When it rains, the soil washes away like sand from a shovel, eventually finding its way into city sewers and gutters, and eventually, streams and waterways.

"One of the hot areas of soil science is erosion at construction sites," says the University of Tennessee's Yoder. "In agriculture, I think we have a pretty good handle on how to control soil erosion. Construction sites are something else. You have steep slopes, and they're completely bare."

One of the major problems with urban erosion, Yoder explains, is that there is currently no unified national standard for erosion monitoring and control at construction sites. While soil conservation measures on farms were adopted in the 1970s and '80s requiring farmers who receive federal support to prove they had adopted conservation practices, no such regulatory structure exists at construction sites. "You have the EPA watching, but each state has its own agency for permitting of construction sites," Yoder says. "There's not much concentration on soil conservation."

The available statistics on construction site erosion are disconcerting. According to Cathy Rofshus, an administrator for the Shell Rock River Water District in Minnesota, "The Environmental Pollution Control Agency estimates that 20 to 150 tons of soil per acre runs off construction sites with rainwater. That would be 1,600 to 12,000 tons of soil for an 80-acre site." Wal-Mart alone may thus be responsible for between 1.5 million and 11.25 million tons of soil erosion in the US through construction of its stores. According to AlterNet, Wal-Mart's 3,600 US stores and 100 distribution centers, including their parking lots, currently occupy roughly 75,000 acres.

To minimize erosion at construction sites, Yoder says there are a number of fairly simple measures developers can employ. Silt fences can be placed at the bottom of slopes to stop sediment from getting into waterways. A wall of soil may build up behind them, which is then returned to the hillsides. Sediment basins are more permanent versions of these structures that trap run-off and allow the suspended soils to settle out before water carries sediments into streams. Erosion-control mats are usually made out of straw and placed on the tops of slopes so that wind and rain will be less likely to carry soil away. Hydro-mulching is a similar measure whereby a water-seed-straw mix that will absorb rain is blown over the bare land.

The Funding Erodes, Too

Even as soil problems have increased in severity, federal funding of soil research and conservation has steadily declined over the years. Whereas the government practically lavished money on soil projects in the 1930s and '40s, scientists proposing soil-focused research projects today are having trouble getting funded. They have to compete with research proposals on "hot" science topics that are more attractive to major grantees, or they have to adapt their research to fit the funder's interests, Yoder says.

Staff in Eswaran's World Soil Resources office once traveled extensively in developing countries educating farmers about soil management and providing support. For the past 10 years, however, Eswaran says the office "has had no funds to travel." Most of the direct scientist-to-farmer work once possible with federal funds – primarily from USAID – has had to be aborted. USAID gave Eswaran's office about $65 million in the early 1980s for agricultural research. By the early 1990s, his funding had dropped to about $10 million, a decrease of almost 85 percent.

And yet in some African countries, simple education of farmers in better land management techniques and better access to fertilizers could arrest the worst of problems. In Yoder's view, part of the problem is that "nobody thinks long-term anymore."

Is Bigger Better?

One reason why agriculture can be so detrimental to soils is because of the sheer scale of most farming operations today. According to USDA, since 1900 the number of farms has fallen by 63 percent, while the average farm size has risen by 67 percent. In 1900, the average farm size was less than 100 acres; in 2002 it was more than 400 acres. Farm operations have also become increasingly specialized, from an average of about five commodities per farm in 1900 to an average of one per farm in 2000. Most important, the USDA says that all of this has taken place with no variation in the amount of land being farmed. Small family farms have steadily disappeared in the midst of increasing urbanization and decreasing profitability, and the mega-farms that now dominate US agriculture have transformed into "agribusinesses" that receive most federal farm subsidies. What this means is that the intensity of agriculture has dramatically increased.

While individual farms have shrunk, yields have increased, thanks to growing reliance on pesticides, herbicides and fertilizers. But while this practice has allowed farmers to control pests and nutrients in the short term, the net result is artificial enrichment of overworked soils that often lose stability.

According to David Tilman, who wrote the 1998 *Nature* article "The Greening of the Green Revolution," only about half of all fertilizers are absorbed by plants. The remaining chemicals pollute the atmosphere, soils and waterways. OCA's Minowa attributes much of this chemical overuse to a comparative detachment of industrial farm workers from the land. "Farmers working their family land knew they'd be working that plot, and their children would be working that plot, for a long time, so they would take care of it and respect it more," he says. "Agribusinesses, on the other hand, are primarily concerned with profitability, which means using the land more intensively."

Yoder cautions against placing all the blame on agribusiness, however. Sustainable management of farms can be expensive, he says, and small farms sometimes can't afford the risk.

Farmers generally apply some fertilizer to their crops, although some are "natural," including cover crops used in winter to help feed nutrients back into the soil. However, most fertilizers employed by conventional farmers are synthetic versions of the NPK (nitrogen, phosphorus, potassium) formula. These nutrients are depleted from intensively worked soils over time. But synthetic fertilizers can also wreak havoc on the underlying ecology, as well as on humans and ecosystems far away from the farms on which they are used. EarthWorks News reported, "The high salt content of many synthetic fertilizers... may overwhelm the natural balance of organic decomposition taking place in the soils."

Pesticide Profiteering

Like fertilizers, pesticides are often over-applied. According to Blatt, pesticides have become 10 to 100 times more toxic than 30 years ago, which has resulted in about 3.5 to 5 million acute poisonings each year. Farmers who work with certain kinds of pesticides have been found to get Parkinson's disease and several types of cancer more often than the general public. Pesticides have also been linked to learning disabilities, hyperactivity, emotional disorders, weakened immune systems, birth defects and low sperm counts. Further, Blatt says that while less than one percent of pesticides applied to fields actually reach the target pests, at least 53 carcinogenic pesticides are presently applied in massive amounts to major crops. Many of the chemicals developed for agricultural use have not been tested for their effects on humans or are poorly regulated.

For instance, the manufacturers of Atrazine, one of the most commonly used pesticides, recommend that farmers apply two pounds per acre, Hepperly says. However, only half of it breaks down in a year, so at the end of the planting season, one pound still remains through the following year.

Why do farmers continue to apply so much? By recommending that farmers apply more of the pesticide than is needed, the chemical manufacturers reap a bigger profit. What is particularly troubling about Atrazine, though, is that recent studies have linked very low doses to developmental problems in frogs, which are experiencing global declines. Several European countries have now banned the chemical.

Gradually, the world's soils have been accumulating pesticides and fertilizers, and as these soils erode, their chemical burdens pollute the surrounding environment or enter the food supply. According to a Food and Drug Administration (FDA) study, more than 80 percent of conventional, non-organic produce tested in grocery stores had measurable levels of pesticides. Minowa says that most pesticides accumulate for years in people's bodies, collecting in fat cells and other tissues. Children are particularly vulnerable to pesticides, with studies showing numerous detrimental effects to their health.

Hepperly believes our continued use of pesticides and fertilizers has made the soil problems we faced 20 or 30 years ago much more severe. "This can be measured in water quality," he says. "Dead zones in ocean environments have expanded in size and number around the globe."

Factory Farming and Feed Lots

Another side effect of modern agribusiness is that instead of raising livestock and crops together, animals are now raised on enormous Confined Animal Feeding Operations (CAFOs), while crops are mass-produced on separate farms. Concentrating so many heavy-hoofed animals in a relatively small space wreaks havoc on soil health, ruining its porous structure. Excess animal waste over-fertilizes soils, and pollutes the environment.

Once upon a time, small farms used the manure generated by their animals to naturally fertilize their crops. Today, however, it is too costly to transport the mass quantities of manure generated on CAFOs to the big crop-producing farms. As a result, these farms make heavy use of synthetic fertilizers in order to support high-intensity monocrops, while the CAFOs generate huge amounts of animal waste, which eventually pollutes the surrounding land.

Some would argue that commercialized agriculture has been necessary to feed the world's growing population, and that as a result, it has been beneficial to society. While this is true in some respects – particularly in our ability to supply starving people in developing nations with food, and in our ability to allow cities to grow even as farmland has been shrinking – agribusiness has, on the whole, fostered some disturbing social and environmental trends. In the long run, dramatic increases in crop yields may have disastrous implications.

Minowa likens the current state of modern agriculture to speeding up on the highway. "People have their foot on the pedal and don't see how much gas they're using," he says. "But intensive agriculture is disrupting the microorganism and nutrient ratios in soil, and causing a build-up of pesticides." At some point, the system may run out of gas and crash.

Some Solutions

Fortunately, there are measures we can take today to help save our soil. Educating farmers in the US and abroad about the damaging effects of intensive agriculture and over-application of synthetic fertilizers and pesticides is a good place to start.

SUSTAINABLE FARM MANAGEMENT: Progressive farmers can reduce damage to soils by reducing tillage, managing irrigation to minimize water loss (and hence salt build-up from evaporation) and planting cover crops. Planting wind barriers on hillsides (also known as "shelterbelts") and maintaining healthy grass cover on pastures can help prevent erosion. If streams run through a farm property, planting grassed waterways along the stream banks can help trap eroded sediment and bind it up, keeping it from entering and polluting larger water bodies.

Tillage, a standard procedure during planting season, is extremely damaging to soils over time. While it has historically helped increase plant yields, it also fosters erosion and breakdown of organic matter by killing worms, chopping up residual root and plant parts, and disrupting the microbe community. Ultimately, farmers are forced to make up for declining soil fertility by relying on synthetic fertilizers.

No-till has been touted as one alternative, but it has drawbacks of its own. Hepperly says that no-till often leads to greater rather than less pesticide use (about four times as much, he says), and ends up costing farmers more money. Because of this, the pesticide industry is one of the bigger proponents of no-till. "Is tillage the lesser evil, or reduced pesticides the lesser evil?" Hepperly asks. He argues that a combination of no-till for some crops and tillage for others will help reduce both damage to soil structure and use of synthetic chemicals.

Pesticide use can be greatly reduced by adopting an integrated pest management system, which relies on such practices as crop rotation (which deters plant-specific pests from taking up long-term residence in soil) and natural biological controls. Planting marigolds around tomato plants in gardens to discourage pests is one such example. Many other plants or insects have similar beneficial pest-deterring properties when intermixed with agricultural crops. Jerry Bisson, an environmental compliance officer with USAID, says his agency promotes developing world farmers using simple technologies to improve land management. "Farmers can be taught to use string, rock and wood as barriers, for example. They can see how they benefit."

THE ORGANIC REVOLUTION: Renewed interest in organic and locally grown food has been a boon to smaller, family-run farms with good soil husbandry.

Even without becoming organic farmers ourselves, we can do a lot to help soils. Buying organic food is one of the first actions consumers can take to support sound conservation practices. Organic agriculture is based on the principle that healthy soil is the foundation of the food chain. In order to be certified "organic" by the US Department of Agriculture (USDA), stringent requirements must be met. As a result of these standards, organic farms employ only natural fertilizers. Healthy populations of soil microbes thrive on organic farms, and effects of erosion and soil compaction are greatly minimized.

Supporting organic farming also tends to support strong local communities. Mega-farms have no obligation to circulate their profits back into local communities, and often don't. Buying locally has the double effect of encouraging investment in healthy towns and a healthy environment. Even if organic goods aren't from a local farm, buying them still sends a powerful message that sustainable soil is a national priority. That message seems to be getting through: in March 2006, statistics showing a leap in organic food sales caused Wal-Mart to announce plans to stock more than 400 organic items in its stores.

While industrial agriculture currently dominates the market, it may not remain king of the hill indefinitely. As the costs of oil and natural gas go up, the price of fertilizers, a majority of which are fossil fuel based, is also increasing. According to Yoder, the price of nitrogen fertilizer has almost doubled in the last two years. Because mega-farms rely so heavily on fertilizers, and then must pay for transport to supermarkets scattered around the country or globe, these farms are seeing costs skyrocket.

Organic farming is the fastest growing sector of the farm industry, and is becoming increasingly profitable. Can organic farming achieve the same high yields as conventional agriculture? For 25 years, the Rodale Institute has been conducting a continuous experiment on its Pennsylvania farm, comparing organic and conventional methods. Throughout the study, the organic plots have repeatedly performed better than the conventional plots, especially during severe weather events.

The Big Picture

There are deeper societal issues that need to be addressed when looking at soil conservation on a global scale. First, urbanization needs to be better managed. The wholesale conversion of rural lands to concrete jungles consumes and degrades vast amounts of soil. In many places, particularly much of the developing world, the roots of mass migration to cities – poverty, war, desperation – need to be addressed. Franklin suggests, "The more small farmers have control over their land, the less likely they'll be to mine the soil." In addition, cities can mitigate damage to soils by supporting low-impact development and construction of eco-roofs and integrated parking lots.

Fundamentally, Hepperly believes people need to reestablish their connection to the land. "We need people to grow something – tomatoes, raspberries, flowers – so they understand why the land, returning soil to its rightful place in the very center of our lives."

Reprinted with permission from E Magazine. Their
weekly Q&A column, Earth Talk, can be found at
www.emagazine.com

Basidiomycete

Excerpted from *The Solar Food Dryer,* this article reminds us that solar energy can be as delicious as it is practical.

Why Dry?
This Summer Try Solar Drying
Eben Fodor

Each day the sun rises, warms the Earth back up, and powers the entire biosphere. There is plenty of extra sunshine available to dry your food. On a clear day, up to 1,000 Watts of solar energy are available for our use per square meter of area of the Earth's surface. This means that a solar food dryer with a horizontal window (or glazing) area of one square meter will have up to 1,000 Watts (3,413 Btu/hr) of solar power available to dry food. However, this is at noon on a clear summer day. Typical operating conditions for a solar dryer will vary depending on weather, geographic location, season, and of course, time of day. Solar food drying is a great way to learn more about the sun and solar energy. By using a solar dryer you will gain an appreciation for the remarkable potential of this plentiful energy source. You will learn how to efficiently harness solar energy and put it to work preserving your food. And you will discover that it's easier than you might think.

More and more people are discovering the joys and benefits of growing their own food and buying fresh, local produce. Garden foods are seasonal, resulting in the boom-and-bust cycle. First, you can't wait to savor your first vine-ripe tomato. In no time you've got more tomatoes than you can give away. Then frost hits and the party's over. Some gardeners turn to canning and freezing to preserve their nutritious bounty. Drying is a third option that has some distinct advantages. Drying is simple and easy: If you can slice a tomato, you can dry food. Dried foods retain more nutrients than canned foods and don't require the energy of a freezer. Dried food is concentrated, reducing bulk and weight to ½ to 1/15th that of hydrated food. Drying requires fewer containers and less storage space. A power failure (or mechanical failure) can result in the loss of all your frozen foods, but your dried foods will be A-ok. Dried foods are convenient and easy to handle. Use as much as you want, and put the rest back for later. Take them with you on hikes, camping, or vacations – they're light and hold up well under a wide range of conditions. Dried foods can last about as long as frozen foods, which are subject to freezer burn. Drying can actually improve the flavor of many foods. Bananas are fantastic fruits, but dried bananas are heavenly. A Roma tomato is almost too bland to eat fresh, but dried it's a treat your tastebuds will savor. Watery Asian pears are sometimes a little disappointing. Dried, they are among the finest treats on the planet. Indoor electric food dryers have become very popular in recent years. These dryers generally work well. But they do have some drawbacks. They require electricity around the clock – 100 to 600 Watts is typical. An electric dryer costs about one to two dollars per load for the electricity to operate it. These electricity costs eat into the savings of doing it yourself. Electric dryers also take up vital counter space and release all the moisture, heat and odors indoors. The heat and moisture from electric dryers comes at the most unwelcome time of year – the summer harvest, when it's still hot outside. Sometimes the odors are pleasant, but when they continue for days and weeks, they become a nuisance and can attract pests, like ants and fruit flies, into your home. And there is the constant humming of the electric fan. If you have a sunny area on your patio, deck, or back yard, a solar food dryer can produce outstanding results without any of these hassles. Solar food dryers have zero operating costs. Dry all you want – it's free! Solar food dryers are easy to use and fairly easy to build – if you know just a few simple solar design concepts. Once you learn how to put the sun's energy to work, you can experiment with many possible designs. Or simply follow the detailed instructions provided here to build a high-performance solar dryer of your own. Using the sun to dry food may be the oldest form of food preservation, dating back thousands of years. For many prehistoric people, dried fruits, berries, grains, fish, and meat were essential to surviving the cold winters. Hanging or laying food out in the open air and sunshine was the simplest method available for drying and preserving the food collected over the summer. Native Americans dried meat, fish, berries, and roots in the sun. But simple outdoor sun drying leaves a lot of room for improvement. Your precious food will take a while to dry and will be subject to possible rotting and assault from rain, wind, dust, rodents, bugs, and, well, you get the idea. These problems are readily solved with a well designed solar dryer that uses a few modern materials such as glass, plywood, screens, and adjustable vents. While "solar dryer" could refer to a tray set out on your deck, in this book, the term is used to refer to a durable, enclosed, weatherproof design that takes advantage of basic solar energy design principles to efficiently and securely dry food. "Sun drying" refers to simply placing food out in the open sunshine to dry. The solar food dryer stays outside and efficiently harnesses the sun's power to dry food much faster than ordinary sun drying. The sun has a surprising amount of energy and a solar food dryer is a great way to get acquainted with the impressive nature of solar power. A well designed solar dryer dries food quickly – typically in one to two days – by capturing the sun's energy to produce heat and move air across the food. Warmer air is lighter and rises (like a hot air balloon) in a process called natural convection. Natural convection can be used like a "solar fan" to speed drying.

Designs for solar food dryers and solar cookers proliferated in the 1970s as interest in alternative energy and solar-heated homes peaked. Far too many of these designs used cardboard, tin foil and plastic wrap. The solar dryer designs described in this book are sturdy, dependable, highly effective, easy to use, weather resistant and will provide many years of enjoyment and savings.

Is Solar Food Drying Right for Me?

At this point, you may be asking "Is solar food drying really a good idea, and is it right for me?" With a little guidance, you will never regret going solar. If you are not technically inclined and don't want to learn the details about solar energy, you will still be successful, because using solar energy is intuitive. You just have to do what's obvious. In fact it's hard to screw it up. Occasionally I find disparaging comments about solar food drying, such as "solar dryers are not suitable for humid climates," or "solar dryers won't work in areas without lots of sunshine." A good solar dryer will work well in most of the world and anywhere in the Lower 48 states where you can get two days of sunshine in a row with some regularity. In fact, just about anywhere you can grow a successful outdoor vegetable garden, you can use a solar dryer. Outdoor temperature and humidity levels have only minor impact on solar food drying. You can successfully dry foods in the muggiest climates and at outdoor temperatures down to about 45° F. Clouds, however, will diminish drying quite a bit. An overcast day will leave your solar dryer sputtering. For this reason, a backup electric heat option is a good idea to protect against unpredictable weather changes.

Why Haven't I Heard More About Solar Food Dryers?

If solar food dryers are so great, why aren't lots of people using them? Solar food drying started to take off in the late 1970s when energy prices spiked and interest in solar technology peaked. There was quite a bit of experimentation, and many solar food dryer designs emerged. But with little research funding and no promotion, they never achieved much popular status. The 1980s and 1990s were periods of economic expansion and interest in energy conservation and renewable energies was all but forgotten. But energy prices are heading skyward again, resulting in a broad reawakening of the importance of sustainable alternative energies. Along with the growing awareness of our overreliance on fossil fuels, we are seeing an increased interest in healthy eating, high-quality organic produce, local food production, and sustainable living. Solar food drying is an obvious part of the solutions to these challenges. Another factor that may have held solar food drying back in the past was a perceived lack of convenience and performance. Designs for solar dryers have ranged from shoe boxes covered with plastic wrap (a good science experiment) to big bulky contraptions that have to be assembled every time they're used. There is a happy medium. There is plenty of power in the sun to dry food quickly, so good performance simply requires proper design. Solar dryers can be highly effective and on par with the best electric dryers. Because solar dryers need to collect sunshine for power, they must have a certain bulkiness associated with the glazing area. The larger the capacity of the dryer, the more sunshine is needed to power it.

This book features an original dryer design – the SunWorks SFD – which was originally constructed from scrap and recycled materials. This provided me with the added pleasure of minimizing consumption of natural resources. The design is built with new materials to standardize the construction process. Once you have materials on hand, you can build this dryer in a weekend. Several other designs are illustrated to give you an idea of the range of design possibilities. The SunWorks dryer described in this book was designed to be compact, lightweight, and portable, but still have enough capacity for the serious home gardener. Since there are many ways to harness the sun, a number of other good solar dryer designs are also described in this book. Everyone with a vegetable garden or a passion for locally grown produce should consider getting a solar food dryer. If you haven't been hearing about them yet, you soon will!

The Bigger Picture

I often get blank looks when I mention solar food drying to people. But then I ask them to think about how important food is, how dependent we are on importing foods from far away, how the quality of those foods is often not the best, and how our long-distance food supply depends on fossil fuels for shipping and storage. The alternative is to expand the local food supply. But when the local growing season is over, what can we do to extend our local self-reliance in a sustainable manner? It all starts to become clear: Solar food drying is the renewable energy solution to the local food supply challenge. Sure, as long as fossil fuels remain cheap, lots of people will continue to buy winter grapes and plums from Chile, peppers from Mexico, tomatoes from artificially heated hothouses, and apples and pears from refrigerated storage warehouses. But this energy-intensive food supply system seems vulnerable and beyond our control. And the nutritional quality and safety of the food is often questionable. Solar food drying is simply the healthy, sustainable alternative. And it's ready to work for you today!

Additional information (including dryer plans):
solarcooking.org
knowledgehound.com/topics/solarcoo.htm
www.epsea.org/dry.html

Hydrodictyacean

chapter 7 : Whole Earth Catalog

Green Weddings (and More)

by Tracy Fernandez Rysavy

Make your wedding, anniversary party, or commitment ceremony green – for a personal celebration you and your guests won't ever forget.

New York is a city known for lavish parties and people who embrace the latest material trends. But when Baly Lau and Craig Cooley decided to get married there last year, they made their wedding a simple affair, incorporating as many socially and environmentally responsible touches as they could.

"We wanted a celebration that was meaningful to us, instead of just traditional," says Baly, a Co-op America member. "Going green and keeping as many purchases local as possible meant a lot to us."

So Baly and Craig held a small wedding in a friend's garden – where they'd planted flowers and greenery the year before in preparation for their nuptials. They chose wedding attire they could wear again for other occasions, and decorated with soy candles, potted bamboo, and lights they'd bought secondhand. They decided to forego an engagement ring because of social and environmental problems with the diamond industry, and they bought all of the reception food and drinks from locally owned stores.

Baly and Craig ended up with a celebration that saved them money and was socially and environmentally responsible. They also look back on a wedding that was elegant, special, and deeply personal.

"It wasn't a sacrifice to green our wedding. I feel we gained more," says Baly. "Our wedding reflected our values, our personalities, and our relationship to our community. Most of our friends said it was the best wedding they had ever been to."

If you or someone you know is about to plan a wedding, anniversary celebration, or commitment ceremony, consider adding in some green touches. Not only will you save money and resources, but you'll be able to personalize your celebration by bringing in your values.

Go Simple

The first step to planning a green celebration can often be choosing what not to buy, says Michelle Kozin, author of *Organic Weddings: Balancing Ecology, Style, and Tradition* (New Society Publishers, 2003) and founder of OrganicWedding.com.

"The wedding industry is notorious for promoting excess," says Kozin. "Your dream wedding can become a reality without overspending and overconsumption."

Tradition dictates you need party favors, rice to throw at the happy couple, and virgin-pulp paper invitations that come with three envelopes and a sheet of tissue paper, for example. But ask yourself, could you do without these or other things, or replace them with pared-down and green alternatives?

Simplifying your celebration isn't just a money-saving step – it can help you make sure that everything involved in your wedding is personal and meaningful.

The Ring's the Thing

Whether your celebration is a wedding, a commitment, or an anniversary, you may want to exchange rings, whose circular shape symbolizes eternal love. But there are social and environmental problems connected to diamonds, gold, and platinum – the most common materials used for such rings. For example, gemstone and metal miners often work in cramped and unsafe conditions, and mining itself can damage local ecosystems and watersheds. Also, children often labor in diamond mines around the world, and some countries use diamond sales to fuel armed conflicts.

If you'd like to exchange rings, consider purchasing from a sustainable company like Leber Jeweler or GreenKarat, which sell wedding, anniversary, and commitment bands made from recycled gold and platinum – no new mining required. Leber also offers rings with responsibly mined gems and conflict-free diamonds from Canada, and will do custom designs. And Sumiche sells handcrafted gold and platinum rings from responsibly mined sources. You can even send Sumiche your own ring design, and co-owners Susan and Miché Onaclea will make it an eco-friendly reality.

Eco-paper Invitations

Invitations are the perfect place to go green when it comes to your celebration, because recycled and tree-free paper options abound – and they look as pretty as their virgin-pulp paper counterparts.

You can pick up eco-paper sheets from your local office supply store and design your own, or there are several sustainable companies that offer recycled or tree-free paper invitation packages.

For example, Green Field Paper Company offers handmade paper cards, envelopes, and sheets for invitations made from a blend of recycled paper and hemp. It also offers a "gourmet line" of recycled papers infused with hemp threads, roasted coffee chaff, garlic skins, or junk mail for a unique look. Green Field's signature product is its handmade Grow-A-Note paper, which has wildflower seeds embedded inside so guests can plant the paper and watch the flowers grow. Grow-A-Note paper comes in sheets or blank invitations and is made from a blend of recycled paper, seeds, and hemp. You can either have Green Field print the invitations for you, or arrange for your own printer. (Be sure to choose one that uses nontoxic soy-based inks.)

Twisted Limb Paperworks offers wedding, commitment, and anniversary celebration invitations, envelopes, and reply cards made of 100 percent post-consumer waste fibers. Twisted Limb artists handcraft the paper from recycled office paper, junk mail, grocery bags, flowers, and grass cuttings, giving each piece a unique, artistic look. No new dyes are used – the colors come from the recycled materials, and the company prints with soy-based inks. Couples can work directly with an artist to ensure that their invitations are unique and individualized.

OrganicWedding.com also offers a variety of recycled and tree-free invitations,such as paper made with hemp, kenaf, recycled cotton, wildflower seeds, and coffee.

For a truly green option, consider forgetting paper invitations altogether and using e-mail instead. Evite.com, for example, offers a free electronic invitation service, complete with RSVP tracking.

What to Wear

You can always look in your closet for an outfit you already own to wear to your wedding, commitment ceremony, or anniversary celebration. But, if you're craving a special, new-to-you garment, try these eco-friendly options:

- Men are simple to outfit – it's long been a tradition for men to rent tuxedos for weddings. But did you know that women can also rent formalwear, including wedding gowns, thereby saving money and resources? Check the "Formalwear Rental" category of your local Yellow Pages to see what options are available.
- Local upscale consignment or vintage boutiques often offer used wedding gowns or formals at a fraction of the price of a new gown – and they may even have suits for men. Or, check out classified ads from people around the country selling secondhand wedding gowns and tuxes at NearlyNewBridal.com. Women can also call the Making Memories Breast Cancer Foundation to see when it will be holding a bridal gown sale near you. Making Memories sells used bridal and bridesmaid gowns to raise funds for their nonprofit organization, which grants wishes to terminally ill breast cancer patients. You can donate your gown back to Making Memories when you're finished with it, if you choose.
- Have a tailor make your gown or suit from natural eco-fabrics, which, unlike synthetics, are made without non-renewable petroleum. Eco-fabrics include peace silk (made without killing silkworms), hemp, organic cotton, or hemp-silk blends. OrganicWedding.com offers hemp-silk blend fabrics for gowns in various shades of ivory or a white bleached without toxic chlorine. Aurora Silk sells peace silk. And Near Sea Naturals offers notions, as well as fabrics, made from organic cotton and organic wool, hemp, and silk.
- If you buy a new gown or suit, stay with natural fabrics, rather than synthetic, and purchase from a local formalwear shop to keep the money in your local economy. Or, buy from a green company like The Emperor's Clothes, which offers hemp-silk-blend, three-piece suits for men that are perfect for grooms and groomsmen.

- If you'd like a new bridal veil, Kozin suggests one made from silk organza rather than petroleum-based nylon tulle.

A Place for Everything

When choosing the location for your celebration, consider these steps to make it green:

- The same location twice. If you can, hold your ceremony and reception in the same location – or at least within walking distance – to minimize guest travel. Many houses of worship have banquet halls, or you can ask your officiant to come to the reception location for the ceremony.
- Go local. Choose a locally owned hall to keep money in your local economy.
- Go green. Consider using the ballroom at a green hotel, so your money supports an establishment that goes the extra mile for the environment. To find a green hotel near you, contact the "Green" Hotels Association.
- Help a nonprofit. If you'd like your reception room fee to bolster a local non-profit organization, Kozin suggests choosing a reception room at your house of worship, a museum, or a local historic building owned by a nonprofit.
- Green decor. When it comes to green decor, consider buying organic flowers from a local shop or OrganicBouquet.com, or using 100 percent soy or vegetable wax candles, rented plants, potted plants, or rented or secondhand lights.
- Or, you could choose to have your ceremony outside in a garden, to take advantage of the free natural decor. Your reception party can be outdoors too, under a rented tent. Just make sure your outdoor location won't be ruined by having a bunch of guests treading on the premises. Also, be sure to have a back-up plan for inclement weather.
- Buy green tags. Consider purchasing green tags to offset the energy used during your ceremony and reception, as well as for guest travel.

Favor, Food, and Fun

You'll probably want to serve food and drinks at your reception party, and you may even want to provide favors. Here are some ways to green those:

- Look for a local caterer that will serve organic foods. If you're serving meat, make it organic, available at local natural food outlets or by mail-order from the Wholesome Harvest Organic Meat Farmer Coalition. Or, you can choose meatless dishes, which save money and are less taxing on the Earth.
- Offer organic and Fair Trade beverages, such as Fair Trade coffee and tea, readily available at local health food stores. You may also be able to find organic beer, wine, and soda locally.
- Avoid using disposable dishware. Most caterers provide washable dishes and will take them away for you for cleaning when guests are finished with them.

If you must use disposables, use recycled paper options, like those from Seventh Generation, or choose compostable, plant-based dishes and cutlery, such as those from Greener Earth Marketing. You'll want to use an industrial composter for disposal, which you can find through your local waste authority.

To give your guests a memory of your special day that isn't hard on the Earth, Kozin recommends several unique party favors on OrganicWeddings.com, from a Tree in a Box seed kits with personalized labels, to organic lavender keepsake sachets from Lavender Green, to homemade organic cookies with your names in frosting.

Gift Registry

Finally, your guests may want to bring you gifts to celebrate your special day. Consider registering at a green company like Gaiam or EcoExpress Gifts. You can also ask guests to donate to a charity or nonprofit in your name through JustGive.org. The site offers a gift registry option, so your guests can easily find out which of the million charities available you would like to support.

Another charitable option is to create a "Personal Giving Page" on the Internet through First Giving. By using First Giving's simple interface, you can make a Web page with your pictures and a personal message to send to guests, asking them to make a donation to your favorite cause instead of bringing a present. Co-op America has set up an account with First Giving, so if you'd like to create a Personal Giving Page to support our work to grow a green economy, please visit www.firstgiving.com/coopamerica.

There are many ways to color your party green, but what all such celebrations have in common is that they're unique, eco-friendly, and unforgettable.

If you're stumped finding a local green alternative, check the appropriate category in Co-op America's *National Green Pages*™.
For a free copy, join www.coopamerica.org

Foraminiferan

About two-thirds of the garlic grown in the US is dehydrated and formulated into a variety of products such as garlic flakes, garlic powder, garlic salt, or garlic and herb blends.

In Asia, garlic is important to today's medical community that is formulating it into antibiotic remedies either alone or in combination with pharmaceuticals. In some cases the garlic-based antibiotics are replacing drugs. Latin America, too, is employing garlic for its medicinal effects. Native healers and midwives encourage its use to treat vaginitis and worm infection.

This article was written for the University of Tennessee – Knoxville Waste
Management Institute

Safe Substitutes:
Non-toxic Household Products
by Gary Davis and Em Turner

Toxic chemicals in the home can be eliminated simply by making thoughtful choices in the supermarket after educating oneself about where the hazards are in common consumer products. How can you determine what toxics you have in your home? Take this "toxics tour."

In the Kitchen

All-purpose cleaner, ammonia-based cleaners, bleach, brass or other metal polishes, dishwater detergent, disinfectant, drain cleaner, floor wax or polish, glass cleaner, dishwashing detergent, oven cleaner, and scouring powder contain dangerous chemicals. Some examples are:

- Sodium hypochlorite (in chlorine bleach): if mixed with ammonia, releases toxic chloramine gas. Short-term exposure may cause mild asthmatic symptoms or more serious respiratory problems;

- Petroleum distillates (in metal polishes): short-term exposure can cause temporary eye clouding; longer exposure can damage the nervous system, skin, kidneys, and eyes;

- Ammonia (in glass cleaner): eye irritant, can cause headaches and lung irritation;

- Phenol and cresol (in disinfectants): corrosive; can cause diarrhea, fainting, dizziness, and kidney and liver damage;

- Nitrobenzene (in furniture and floor polishes): can cause skin discoloration, shallow breathing, vomiting, and death; associated with cancer and birth defects;

- Formaldehyde (a preservative in many products): suspected human carcinogen; strong irritant to eyes, throat, skin, and lungs.

In the Utility Closet

A number of products are likely to contain toxic ingredients: carpet cleaner, room deodorizer, laundry softener, laundry detergent, anti-cling sheets, mold and mildew cleaner, mothballs, and spot remover all usually contain irritant or toxic substances. Examples:

- Perchloroethylene or 1-1-1 trichloroethane solvents (in spot removers and carpet cleaners): can cause liver and kidney damage if ingested; perchloroethylene is an animal carcinogen and suspected human carcinogen;
- Naphthalene or paradichlorobenzene (in mothballs): naphthalene is a suspected human carcinogen that may damage eyes, blood, liver, kidneys, skin, and the central nervous system; paradichlorobenzene can harm the central nervous system, liver, and kidneys;
- Hydrochloric acid or sodium acid sulfate in toilet bowl cleaner; either can burn the skin or cause vomiting, diarrhea, and stomach burns if swallowed; also can cause blindness if inadvertently splashed in the eyes;
- Residues from fabric softeners, as well as the fragrances commonly used in them, can be irritating to susceptible people;
- Possible ingredients of spray starch (aside from the starch) include formaldehyde, phenol, and pentachlorophenol; in addition, any aerosolized particle, including cornstarch, may irritate the lungs.

In the Living Room and Bedroom

Even the furnishings of the typical American home can be harmful. Fabrics that are labeled "wrinkle-resistant" are usually treated with a formaldehyde resin. These include no-iron sheets and bedding, curtains, sleep wear – any woven fabric, but especially polyester/cotton blends, marketed as "permanent press" or "easy care." More modern furniture made of pressed wood products emits formaldehyde and other chemicals. Carpeting is usually made of synthetic fibers that have been treated with pesticides and fungicide. Many office carpets emit a chemical called 4-phenylcyclohexene, an inadvertent additive to the latex backing used in more commercial and home carpets, which is thought to be one of the chemicals responsible for "sick" office buildings.

In the Bath

Numerous cosmetics and personal hygiene products contain hazardous substances. Examples:
- Cresol, formaldehyde, glycols, nitrates/nitrosamines and sulfur compounds in shampoos;
- Butane propellants in hair spray (replacing carcinogenic methylene chloride), as well as formaldehyde resins;
- Aerosol propellants, ammonia, formaldehyde, triclosan, aluminum chlorhydrate in antiperspirants and deodorants;
- Glycols, phenol, fragrance, and colors in lotions, creams, and moisturizers.

In the Studio or Hobby Room
Although legislation controlling many of the dangerous ingredients in hobby materials has recently been passed, exposure to certain art materials remains a health risk. Dangerous chemicals and metals include:

- Lead in ceramic glazes, stained-glass materials, and many pigments;
- Cadmium in silver solders, pigments, ceramic glazes, and fluxes;
- Chromium in paint pigments and ceramic colors;
- Manganese dioxide in ceramic colors and some brown oil and acrylic paint pigments;
- Cobalt in some blue oil and acrylic paint pigments;
- Formaldehyde as a preservation in many acrylic paints and photographic products;
- Aromatic hydrocarbons in paint and varnish removers, aerosol sprays, permanent markers, etc.;
- Chlorinated hydrocarbons (solvents) in ink, varnish and paint removers, rubber cement, aerosol sprays;
- Petroleum distillates (solvents) in paint and rubber cement thinners, spray adhesives, silk-screen inks;
- Glycol ethers and acetates in photography products, lacquer thinners, paints, and aerosol sprays.

In the Garage

A number of dangerous substances are frequently present, including paint, paint thinner, benzene, kerosene, mineral spirits, turpentine, lubricating/motor oils, and gasoline. Hazards among them include these chemicals:

- Chlorinated aliphatic and aromatic hydrocarbons in paint thinner can cause liver and kidney damage;
- Petroleum hydrocarbons, an ingredient of gasoline, motor oils, and benzene, are associated with skin and lung cancer;
- Mineral spirits in oil-based paint are a skin, eye, nose, throat, and lung irritant. High air concentrations can cause nervous system damage, unconsciousness, and death;
- Ketones in paint thinner may cause respiratory ailments; vary according to specific form of the chemical;
- Ketones and toluene in wood putty; toluene is highly toxic, may cause skin, kidney, liver, central nervous system damage; may damage reproductive system.

In the Garden Shed

Pesticides, one of the most important single hazards in the home. Around 1,400 pesticides, herbicides, and fungicides are ingredients in consumer products. Combined with other toxic substances such as solvents, pesticides are present in more than 34,000 different product formulations.

On the Patio

Charcoal lighter fluid contains petroleum distillates. Besides being flammable and imparting a chemical taste to food, some petroleum distillates contain benzene, a known human carcinogen.

Safe Substitutes for Household Toxics

Until World War II and the zenith of the Chemical Age that followed war-related research, householders used a limited number of simple substances to keep most objects in the house clean, odor-free, and pest-free. Soap, vinegar, baking soda, washing soda, ammonia, borax, alcohol, cornstarch, and certain food ingredients were used to lift out spots and stains, deodorize, polish wood or metal, disinfect, scrub, repel pests, clean pets, wash and starch clothes, and to perform countless other household tasks. Simple cosmetic preparations kept hair lustrous and skin supplied with the aid of ingredients such as eggs, oil, clay, vinegar, and herbs.

The garden was fertilized and pests were kept down with naturally occurring substances. Weeds were weeded by hand. Even though some natural pesticides, like nicotine and rotenone, were indeed toxic to humans, they were not persistent in the environment. They degrade soon after application. Pyrethrum, a pesticide derived from a variety of chrysanthemum which is nontoxic to mammals, controlled a wide spectrum of pests. Although it is still widely used, it is usually mixed with other chemicals to increase its potency.

Buildings of the past were made with wood, brick, stone, glass, plaster, and cement. Furniture was made of solid wood, oiled to keep it polished. Rugs or carpets were made of wool or cotton. Insulation was built in by making walls thick, and roofing was constructed from wood shingles or tiles of clay or stone. Walls were plastered. Windows were made to be opened, so at least in good weather there was plenty of natural ventilation.

But toxic materials also were present in homes of the past. Not knowing enough about their hazards, housewives used such chemicals as arsenic, lead, and mercury to perform certain household chores. Interior and exterior paints were often made with lead; many American children are still living with the legacy of lead poisoning caused by eating chips of leaded paint. Asbestos, called a miracle mineral when its fire-resistant properties were discovered, is now known to be a cancer causer that contaminates hundreds of thousands of residences, schools, and other buildings in this country.

We do not need to return to the ways of the past to avoid exposure to house toxics, but we can take some lessons from the past for a better future. How can we do this?

Buy Safe Substitutes. For example, search for a soap-based garden insecticide (at least one national brand is available) instead of chemically-based ones.

When in Doubt, Leave it Out. In cases where there is no effective safe substitute for a toxic product, reevaluate how important the goal really is. Must you absolutely get rid of all insects in your garden, or can you live with some chewed-up leaves? If the goal is absolutely imperative, such as ensuring that termites do not invade your house, it is important to educate yourself thoroughly. You may have more healthful alternatives than your local pest company tells you.

Safe Substitutes in the Kitchen and Bath

One shelf of simple and relatively safe ingredients can be used to perform most home cleaning chores. All that's needed is a knowledge of how they work and how different ingredients should be combined to get the cleaning power needed for a specific job.

Baking Soda is sodium bicarbonate. It has a number of useful properties. It can neutralize acid, scrub shiny materials without scratching, deodorize, and extinguish grease fires. It can be used as a deodorizer in the refrigerator, on smelly carpets, on upholstery and on vinyl. It can help deodorize drains. It can clean and polish aluminum, chrome, jewelry, plastic, porcelain, silver, stainless steel, and tin. It also softens fabrics and removes certain stains. Baking soda can soften hard water and makes a relaxing bath time soak; it can be used as an underarm deodorant and as a toothpaste, too.

Borax is a naturally occurring mineral, soluble in water. It can deodorize, inhibit the growth of mildew and mold, boost the cleaning power of soap or detergent, remove stains, and can be used with attractants such as sugar to kill cockroaches.

Cornstarch, derived from corn, can be used to clean windows, polish furniture, shampoo carpets and rugs, and starch clothes.

Isopropyl Alcohol is an excellent disinfectant.

Lemon Juice, which contains citric acid, is a deodorant and can be used to clean glass and remove stains from aluminum, clothes, and porcelain. It is a mild lightener or bleach if used with sunlight.

Mineral Oil, derived from seeds, is an ingredient in several furniture polish and floor wax recipes.

Soap (NOT detergent) is made in several ways. Castle soap can be used as a shampoo or as a body soap. Olive-oil based soap is gentlest to the skin. An all-purpose liquid soap can be made by simply dissolving the old ends of bar soap (or grated slivers of bar soap) in warm water.

Steel Wool is an abrasive strong enough to remove rust and stubborn food residues and to scour barbeque grills.

TSP is trisodium phosphate, a mixture of soda ash and phosphoric acid. TSP is toxic if swallowed, but it can be used on many jobs, such as cleaning drains or removing old paint, that would normally require much more caustic and poisonous chemicals, and it does not create any fumes.

Vinegar is made from soured apple juice, grain, or wine. It contains about 5 percent acetic acid, which makes it a mild acid. Vinegar can dissolve mineral deposits, grease, remove traces of soap, remove mildew or wax buildup, polish some metals, and deodorize. Vinegar can clean brick or stone, and is an ingredient in some natural carpet cleaning recipes. Use vinegar to clean out the metallic taste in coffeepots and to shine windows without streaking. Vinegar is normally used in a solution with water, but it can be used straight.

Washing Soda or SAL Soda is a sodium carbonate decahydrate, a mineral. It can cut stubborn grease on grills, broiler pans, and ovens. It can be used with soda instead of laundry detergent, and it softens hard water. These items are available from drug and chemical-supply stores.

For common household tasks, try these nontoxic strategies using the above ingredients:

- Freshen air by opening windows and doors for a short period; distribute partially filled dishes of vinegar around the kitchen to combat unpleasant cooking odors; boil cinnamon and cloves in a pan of water to scent the air; sprinkle 1/2 cup borax in the bottom of garbage pails or diaper pails to inhibit mold and bacteria growth that can cause odors; rub vinegar on hands before and after slicing onions to remove the smell; use bowls of potpourri to give inside air a pleasant scent.

- All-purpose cleaner can be made from a vinegar-and-salt mixture or from 4 tablespoons baking soda dissolved in 1 quart warm water.

- Disinfectant means anything that will reduce the number of harmful bacteria on a surface. Practically no surface treatment will completely eliminate bacteria. Try regular cleaning with soap and hot water. Or mix 1/2 cup borax into 1 gallon of hot water to disinfect and deodorize. Isopropyl alcohol is an excellent disinfectant, but use gloves and keep it away from children.

- Drain cleaner. Try a plunger first, though not after using any commercial drain opener. To open clogs, pour 1/2 cup baking soda down drain, add 1/2 cup white vinegar, and cover the drain. The resulting chemical reaction can break fatty acids down into the soap and glycerine, allowing the clog to wash down the drain. Again, do not use this method after trying a commercial drain opener – the vinegar can react with the drain opener to create dangerous fumes.

- Floor cleaner and polish can be as simple as a few drops of vinegar in the cleaning water to remove soap traces. For vinyl or linoleum, add a capful of baby oil to the water to preserve and polish. For wood floors, apply a thin coat of 1:1 oil and vinegar and rub in well. For painted wooden floors, mix 1 teaspoon washing soda into 1 gallon hot water. For brick and stone tiles, use 1 cup white vinegar in 1 gallon water and rinse with clear water.

- Metal cleaners and polishes are different for each metal – just as in commercial cleaners. Clean aluminum with a solution of cream of tartar and water. Brass may be polished with a soft cloth dipped in lemon-and-baking-soda solution, or vinegar-and-salt solution. Polish chrome with baby oil, vinegar, or aluminum foil shiny slide out. Clean tarnished copper by boiling the article in a pot of water with 1 tablespoon salt and 1 cup white vinegar, or try differing mixtures of salt, vinegar, baking soda, lemon juice, and cream of tartar. Clean gold with toothpaste, pewter with a paste of salt, vinegar, and flour. Silver can be polished by boiling it in a pan lined with aluminum foil and filled with water to which a teaspoon each of baking soda and salt have been added. Stainless steel can be cleaned with undiluted white vinegar.

- Oven cleaner. Sprinkle baking soda on moist surface and scrub with steel wool. Or use Arm & Hammer Oven Cleaner, declared nontoxic by Consumers Union.
- Scouring powder can be made from baking soda or dry table salt. Or try Bon-Ami Cleaning Powder or Bon-Ami Polishing Cleaner.
- Toilet bowl cleaner can be made from straight bleach (do NOT mix with any other substance except water), baking soda and vinegar, or borax and lemon juice.
- Tub and tile cleaner can be as easy as rubbing in baking soda with a damp sponge and rinsing, or wiping with vinegar first and following with baking soda as a scouring powder.
- Window and glass cleaner is easy with these tips: to avoid streaks, don't wash windows when the sun is shining. Use a vinegar-and-water solution, cornstarch-vinegar-and-water solution, or lemon-juice-and-water. Wipe with newspaper unless you are sensitive to the inks in newsprint.

Safe Substitutes for Laundry Products

Detergent is specially adapted to clean synthetic fabrics, and it has the added advantage of not leaving soil residues even in hard water. However, detergents are generally derived from petrochemicals, and people sensitive to these compounds may find it hard to tolerate detergents or the fragrances they are scented with. In addition, most detergents contain phosphates, which build up in streams and lakes and upset the natural balance in waterways, causing blooms of algae which deplete the dissolved oxygen fish need to live. Some detergent may even contain naphthalene or phenol, both hazardous substances.

An effective alternative to using detergents is to return to soap. Soap is an effective cleaner for natural fabrics, leaving such items as diapers softer than detergent can. For cotton and linen, use soap to soften water. A cup of vinegar added to the wash can help keep colors bright (but DO NOT use vinegar if you are using bleach – the resulting fumes are hazardous). One-half to three-quarters of a cup of baking soda will leave clothes soft and fresh smelling. Silks and wools may be hand washed with mild soap or a protein shampoo, down or feathers with mild soap or baking soda.

For synthetic fabrics or blends (including most no-iron fabrics), there are biodegradable detergents on the market that do not contain phosphates, fragrances, or harsh chemicals. They are often imported from Europe and are available at health food stores or by mail order.

Safe Substitutes for Personal Hygiene and Cosmetic Products

We use cosmetics and hygiene products for a fairly narrow range of reasons: to keep skin moist and supple; to clean hair without stripping it of natural oils; to eliminate unpleasant body or mouth odors; to prevent skin oiliness and clogged skin pores; and simply for the pleasure of relaxing and pampering ourselves with body-care or facial-care treatments. The following ingredients can help achieve these purposes without the use of toxic additives, synthetic fragrances, or artificial colorings:

- ✍ Moisturizers and conditioners: egg yolk, milk, yogurt, safflower oil (for light moisturizing), olive oil (for dry skin or hair), water, oatmeal, jojoba oil.
- ✍ Astringents/after shaves: witch hazel, diluted isopropyl alcohol.
- ✍ Deodorants: baking soda, white clay, deodorant crystals.
- ✍ Toothpastes: baking soda, salt.
- ✍ Soaps/cleansing agents: castle soap, olive-oil based soap.
- ✍ Perfumes: essential oils provide nontoxic fragrances that can be used to scent shampoo, bath soaks, or even, in the case of peppermint, to flavor toothpaste.

Although it's easy to make healthful alternatives to many cosmetic and hygiene products, any natural-foods store has a fairly wide selection of shampoos, moisturizers, toothpastes, after shaves, soaps, and bath products that do not contain the harmful ingredients in many commercial preparations.

Safe Substitutes for Art and Hobby Materials

There are some nontoxic choices that can be made when buying art or craft supplies, but because some techniques require certain materials, minimizing exposure may be the best you can do.

In painting and print making, ready-mixed water-based paints or inks can be used. If you must be exposed to paint dust, use a toxic dust respirator approved by the National Institute for Occupational Safety and Health (NIOSH). Ventilate the space thoroughly whenever using any kind of solvents, whether in painting or in lithography, intaglio, or photoetching. Solvents also should be avoided while pregnant.

Enamels are usually lead-based, and can contain other toxic metals such as cadmium and nickel. Use lead-free enamels whenever possible, and make sure kilns are vented outside.

In pottery as well, outside vented kilns are important, as is a careful choice of materials – most potters know to avoid lead glazes and lead frits, but many don't know that flint, feldspars, fluorspar, and some compounds containing barium, lithium, manganese, or nickel can also be toxic. Children should avoid the pottery studio, as they are more highly susceptible to the toxics used in pottery than are adults.

Photography presents a number of toxic hazards which are difficult to avoid. Minimize exposure to photo chemicals by using gloves, mixing chemicals in a mixing box with holes in the sides for gloved hands, and providing adequate ventilation. The Health and Welfare Office of Canada suggests at least 10 room air changes per hour. Children under 12 should avoid the darkroom.

Safe Substitutes for Pesticides in Home and Garden

Against pests in the home, the best offense is a good defense. The first step is to make the house – especially the kitchen – unattractive to insects by cleaning up food spills immediately, keeping hard-to-reach areas reasonably clean, and removing clutter that can hide pests. Store foods attractive to pests, such as flour, in the refrigerator. Water attracts pests, so leaky faucets and pipes should be promptly repaired. Doors and windows should be well screened. Cloths should be regularly cleaned and aired, and properly stored in paper or cardboard boxes sealed against moths.

A number of nontoxic substances can be used to repel insects. Generally, they are highly fragrant or volatile herbs or spices. Powdered red chili pepper, peppermint, bay leaves, cloves, citrus oil, lavender, rosemary, tobacco, peppercorns, and cedar oil can repel various types of insects.

Insects can be trapped and killed without resorting to dangerous chemicals: generally a poison nontoxic to humans is mixed with a food that insects find attractive, and spread in the infested area. Examples are oatmeal (attractive) and plaster-of-Paris (poisonous), and cocoa powder and flour (attractive) and borax (poisonous). Old-fashioned flypaper – not a hanging strip of insecticide – is an effective trap. For specific house pests, try these solutions:

- For ants: sprinkle powdered red chili pepper, paprika, dried peppermint, or borax where the ants are entering.
- For beetles: Kill manually when you see them.
- For cockroaches: Mix by stirring and sifting 1 ounce TSP, 6 ounces borax, 4 ounces sugar, and 8 ounces flour. Spread on floor of infested area. Repeat after 4 days and again after 2 weeks.
- For fleas: Feed pet brewer's yeast in powder mixed with food or by tablets.
- For moths: Air clothes well in the sun; store in airtight containers, and scatter sachets of lavender, cedar chips, or dried tobacco in with clothing.
- For rats and mice: Again, prevention may be the best cure. Holes in exterior or interior walls should be closed off and storage spaces kept orderly. Garbage should be kept tightly covered. To catch rodents, the most efficient system is the oldest: a cat. Next best are mouse and rat traps.
- For termites: Any wooden parts of the house should be at least 18 inches off the ground, as subterranean termites cannot tolerate being exposed to air and light. They have to build easily visible mud tunnels to get at available wood. However, most existing houses have only about an 8-inch clearance between wooden parts and the ground, which makes the wood vulnerable. Metal shields may help discourage termites, but they cannot prevent infestations.
- To treat existing termite infestations, there are a few nontoxic alternatives: the "Extermax" system, available in California; and the use of a particular species of nematodes to eat them, a system available from N-Viro Products, Ltd.
- For gardens: In hardware stores, look for new brands of safer insecticides that use soap-and-water solutions to get rid of aphids, or pyrethrum for a number of applications. As more and more people understand the hazards of organic chemicals in the home, market pressure will encourage the introduction of safer products.

Several naturally derived pesticides exist which, in some cases, are less toxic to humans than the organophosphates, carbamates, or organochlorines now widely used. Nicotine is the most toxic, poisonous both to humans and to other mammals, as well as to birds and fish. It is not available commercially for home gardeners because of its hazards. Rotenone, moderately toxic to humans, kills a wide range of insects; however, it should never be used near a waterway, as it is very toxic to fish. Ryania kills only a few species, including the European corn borer, codling moth, and cranberry fruit worm. Pyrethrum is relatively nontoxic to humans and only slightly toxic to aquatic life, so it may be the best choice for home gardens. Sabadilla controls lice, leafhoppers, squash bugs, striped cucumber beetles, and chinch bugs. It has low toxicity to wildlife, but it may be toxic to bees.

✿ For lawns: Herbicides are most often used to kill "unsightly" weeds in gardens and yards, and by lawn care companies to maintain the perfect appearance of turf around homes and on lawns and golf courses. Basically, the safe alternative to herbicides is simple: pull weeds by hand. There are no really safe herbicides.

Safe Substitutes for the Patio

A simple and much more effective alternative exists for the charcoal lighter fluid used to start the backyard barbeque. A metal, chimney-pipe cylinder, which holds the charcoal above a burning piece of newspaper and relies on the air flow under the charcoal to quickly bring it to glowing hot, is available at most discount stores. It readies the charcoal for cooking much more quickly without the chemical taste and fire hazard of lighter fluid.

The Safe Home of the 21st Century

Because Americans spend approximately 90 percent of their time indoors, it is crucial to make the home environment as safe as possible. Indoor pollutants have proliferated in recent years, often either because modern construction techniques and furnishings manufacturers utilize hazardous materials or because consumers do not know enough about the products they buy to make informed choices.

But safe, nontoxic alternatives exist for nearly every real need around the home, and the search for them may help consumers distinguish between what they really do need, and what may be "luxuries" that could compromise their families' health.

Sea-squirt

Whole Earth Catalog
The New Village Library

How Buildings Learn: What Happens After They're Built. Stewart Brand. Viking, 1994.

The Clock of the Long Now. Stewart Brand. Basic Books, 1999.

The Natural House: A Complete Guide to Healthy, Energy-Efficient, Environmental Homes. Dan Chiras. Chelsea Green Publishing, 2001.

Earth Sheltered Houses: How to Build an Affortable Underground Home. Rob Roy. New Society Publishers, 2006.

The New Independent Home: People and Houses that Harvest the Sun. Michael Potts. Chelsea Green Publishing, 1999.

Naturally Clean: The Seventh Generation Guide to Safe & Healthy, Non-Toxic Cleaning. Jeffrey Hollender, Geoff Davis, and Meika Hollender. New Society Publishers, 2005.

The Solar Food Dryer: How to Make and Use Your Own Low-cost, High-Performance, Sun-Powered Food Dehydrator. Eben Fodor. New Society Publishers, 2005.

Your Green Home: A Guide to Planning a Healthy, Environmentally Friendly New Home. Alex Wilson. New Society Publishers, 2006.

The Sacred Balance: Rediscovering Our Place in Nature. David Suzuki. Greystone Books, 1999.

Natural Capitalism: Creating the Next Industrial Revolution. Paul Hawken, Amory Lovins and L. Hunter Lovins. Back Bay Books, 2000.

Organic Weddings: Balancing Ecology, Style and Tradition. Michelle Kozin, New Society Publishers, 2003.

Soft Energy Paths: Towards a Durable Peace. Amory Lovins. Harper Collins, 1979.

Solar Water Heating: A Comprehensive Guide to Solar Water and Space Heating Systems. Bob Ramlow with Benjamin Nusz. New Society Publishers, 2006.

8 THE GOOD LIFE

Hydrodictyacean (colonial algae)

66 *During the whole period of written history, it is not the workers but the robbers who have been in control of the world."*

— Scott Nearing

Were the Nearings the visionary pioneers who escaped the chains of modern civilization to lead lives of harmony and balance first in the woods of Vermont and later on the coast of Maine? Or were they the equivalent of trust fund hippies, the original greenwashers who maintained a veneer of simplicity while feeding off the good intentions of those people who they duped?

Both sides of the story have been told and the truth surely lies in-between. Ultimately, however, the reality is only what the culture makes of it. From this vantage the Nearings are the contemporary story from which all others flow.

The story begins with a fiery intellectual at odds with the academic establishment. Was it his passion for intellectual honesty that got Scott into trouble or a cantankerous personality?

Then there is a love affair with a younger woman whose physical beauty is matched by her sweetness on the violin. Is it the love affair of the century, or an exploitive relationship in which the talents of the woman are subjugated by the ego of the man?

There is a lifestyle of self-reliance in harmony with nature with enduring images of Scott and Helen making maple syrup to pay their taxes, of Scott and Helen carrying stones from the beach to build their home. Images of wooden spoons and crisp apples and rich compost. But was it a lifestyle enabled by unmentioned bank accounts and fueled by the free labor of bright-eyed enthusiasts?

And finally and ultimately it is the story of a heroic passing. Scott, at age 100, carries in the wood for the last time, lies down, and refuses food and water until he finds a quiet, dignified death. Is this what happened, or what Helen wants us to believe is what happened in her elegant memoir *Loving and Leaving the Good Life?*

These are not questions for the historian, but the viewer of *Entertainment Tonight*, forever in search of titillation. The foundation of the Nearing legacy is solid. There is a good life that is a better life when it is in balance. The Nearing division of their days to allow 4 hours of bread labor, 4 hours of community service, and four hours of free time is a touchstone to measure the balance in life. The good life also balances the needs of humans and the natural world and allows for both.

Scott Nearing (1883-1983) was born to a wealthy family in Morris Run, a Pennsylvania mining town. By 1905, he was speaking out on liberal issues, including the treatment and working conditions of miners. He graduated from the University of Pennsylvania's Wharton College of Economics in 1906, where he taught until he was fired in 1915 for his outspoken opposition to child labor.

Helen Knothe Nearing (1904-1995) was born in Ridgewood, New Jersey, the middle child of intellectual middle-class Theosophist parents, and traveled widely as a child and teenager, took music lessons, and was well-educated. As a young woman she joined J. Krishnamurti during his "enlightenment" experience under the pepper tree.

The two met briefly in 1921, then again in 1928, and were together from then on. They left New York City in 1932 for a simple life in rural southern Vermont, where they homesteaded and ran a maple-sugaring business, but felt frustrated by local household independence — which they felt contrasted unfavorably with the reality in many rural parts of Europe. Their valley neighbors in Vermont, the Nearings wrote, "...looked upon cooperative enterprise as the first step toward super-imposed discipline and coercion. They were suspicious of organized methods and planning. They would have none of it." In 1952 they relocated to Harborside, Maine where they started over again, building their own house, outbuildings, and a business raising blueberries. Together, they wrote what they lived — *Living the Good Life* (1954) and *Continuing the Good Life* (1979) — and are often credited with being a major spur to the US back to the land movement that began in the late 1960s.

Helen and Scott usually divided a day's waking hours into three blocks of four hours: "bread labor" (work directed toward meeting requirements of food, shelter, clothing, needed tools, and such); civic work (doing something of value for their community); and professional pursuits or recreation (for Scott this was frequently economics research, for Helen it was often music, but they both liked to ski). They made good and regular use of the volunteer labor of young idealistic visitors who were always warmly welcomed and fed a hearty meal of fresh greens, Helen's famous soup, and Scott's gruel — a combination of raw oats, raisins, peanut butter and honey.

The Nearings read widely and were willing experimenters who found wisdom in some of the attitudes of the past, but did not feel tied to the life patterns or technologies of the past. During a period when manufactured fertilizers and pesticides were becoming standard practice, they pursued the organic approach to food gardening. In Maine, without sugar maples to provide a cash crop, they cultivated blueberries. The Nearings utilized new techniques of building houses and outbuildings from stone and concrete (the Flagg method). The Nearings built 12 stone structures, from small to large, on their Vermont land, and nine on their Maine land. Helen was more the stone mason than Scott, though Scott (21 years older than Helen) also worked hard physically, into advanced age. Due to the publication of their books, and to their open-house practices toward guests, the Nearings' approach was emulated by thousands of people who wanted a life that afforded play and contemplation in addition to work.

Scott's death by self-starvation at Harborside on August 24, 1983 moved Helen to write her own heartfelt works about age and death, *Loving and Leaving the Good Life* (1992) and *Light on Aging and Dying* (1995).

Despite having been critical toward the electric transmission grid and its pitfalls (a nuclear power plant was once proposed for Cape Rosier), the Nearings built a new house with normal modern conveniences, including grid electricity, next to the original Cape Rosier house. That house is now home of The Good Life Center, where the Nearing's work is continuing (www.goodlife.org).

> 66 No meal is so good as when you have your feet under your own table."
>
> 66 Following the rhythms of nature provides more than a formal education; it stimulates unfoldment and growth, and attaches the fortunate individual irrevocably to Mother Earth.
>
> Every day, every week and every year every adult should renew his contacts with nature. He may walk in the woods, sit on the grass, breath deeply of pure air, bask in the sunshine, dig in the earth, enjoy the storms or watch the stars. But not for long should he allow his Earth contacts to be broken.
>
> The gardener should defend with passionate determination his right to grow flowers, vegetables and fruit. No aspect of life is more important to his well-being."
>
> — Helen Nearing, *Simple Food for the Good Life*

Living the Good Life by Helen and Scott Nearing is the book that most influenced our choices in how we relate to the world we live in. The Nearings walked their talk and created a living example that "A man's reach should always exceed his grasp." No one worked harder than the Nearings. If they created a larger than life example that is impossible to duplicate, they still established a standard for which we can strive.

In an age when mythic figures are rare and heroes are usually celebrities or sports stars, I'll take a stooped and craggy Scott Nearing, who never stopped teaching real, earth-changing, human values.

Helen Nearing provides a truth so honest some find it threatening. The Nearings stand for good food, an honest day's work, the straight talk on child labor, civil rights, the economics of oil, wars, the use base economy, and freedom. The Nearings vision of a future in a United, confederated World eerily parallels that of Star Trek creator, Gene Rodenberry's. It's a future of hope. That's why I try to "Live the Good Life" everyday.

Scott and Helen Nearing were the John and Yoko of the Back to the Land movement. They teach, preach, and embrace voluntary simplicity, respect for the earth, and the brotherhood of life. They advocate ownership of your own life, and of working damn hard to keep this experiment called humankind evolving.

— Dave Bonta
USA Solar Stores

Conventional "wisdom" dictates that Festivals can't be Green. Hogwash! Here's how they do it in Seattle, possibly one of the US's three greenest cities.

Sun, Fun, and Diversion
bySam Wilder

Festival season is a great time to think about sunny days, music, and food – as well as how to capture food residuals! Two major festivals in Seattle recently conducted pilot food waste collection programs at the Seattle Center. These programs provide a framework for other festivals and collection strategies.

Seattle Public Utilities (SPU) partnered with Seattle Center and two city festivals in 2005 to trial vendor food recycling – the first during three days in July with an estimated 400,000 attendees and 45 vendors; the second during four days in August with an estimated 150,000 attendees and 60 vendors. SPU also provided funding support and assistance to organizers for collection. It also had an on-site presence the whole weekend with staff and volunteers to help with food recycling. Vendor food material was targeted, rather than scraps from the general public, since this was the first year for recycling compostables.

Festival organizers and site and city staff worked together to plot the best ways to organize food collection at existing festivals. Obstacles included having a tight footprint for containers (for kitchen containers in vendor booths and for carts for hauler pickup), high turnover of food booth employees throughout the festivals and nightly collections of material.

Program components were developed based on the specific needs of each festival. Kitchen containers (16-gallon "slim jims"), 96-gallon carts and biodegradable bags were provided to vendors to implement a uniform program for all participants. Vendors were responsible for carrying biodegradable bags full of food scraps to carts located nearby. Carts were tagged when full, and picked up nightly by the hauler after festival hours. The material was taken to Cedar Grove Composting in the Seattle region for composting. Cedar Grove only accepts biodegradable bags that it has tested for biodegradability in its composting system.

Program Challenges and Successes

Outreach materials were incorporated with other festival education materials. Vendors received an introduction to food waste collection in their packets. Once the festivals were underway, on-site personnel visited the vendors daily to assist them in participating in this brand new program. Educational materials given to businesses included stickers for containers and posters with photos of what could and could not be included.

The program was optional for vendors, but only three or four out of about 100 vendors did not participate. (The decision to pilot food recycling was made after vendors had filled out their applications and were approved. In future events, agreeing to recycle food could be part of the application process. Reasons for not participating included not having much food waste, tight booth space, and staff who felt they were too busy to sort materials. Most vendors, however, had tight space but still found room for a food waste collection container.

Top contaminants found in food waste containers included plastic gloves, plastic film and plastic utensils. Having food recycling staff (through the City of Seattle) and volunteers on-site to monitor containers helped combat these issues before they became a problem. When these items were found in kitchen containers, food compost staff let vendors know.

It was difficult to "hide" carts from the public. Although carts had large signs, some carts were in locations where festival participants (general public) walked by. Participants often put garbage in these carts. This issue was solved by turning cart lids away from easy access, and placing an easy access garbage container beside them.

Although some contaminants were found in containers, overall there was very little contamination. Only one container throughout both festivals was emptied as garbage due to noncompostables. All other carts contained clean, organic material. Contaminants were removed from the containers by staff and volunteers at the vendors' booths while they were more accessible (i.e., before the bags were tied closed and put in the 96-gallon carts).

Vendors seemed to "catch on" quickly. There were many staff members involved with each booth, so the program could be easily understood. With daily education, staff seemed to grasp the concept of the program and what materials could be included.

The collection system for both festivals worked well. Providing uniform kitchen containers and biodegradable bags and carts, maximized the available tight festival space and made the education message easier to convey. An efficient collection system helped vendor participation. Providing a "made program" eliminated issues that may have occurred if each vendor had tried to create their own system.

Collection and Survey Results

Almost six tons of food compost materials were collected from both festivals – a volume of about 40 cubic yards. Vending staff seemed excited to participate in a new program and were interested in information on composting the food scraps from the festival. Vendor staff comments included "worked really well" and "really liked the program."

Participants were surveyed after each festival. Here are some of the questions with responses:

Was food recycling easy for you? – 91 percent responded "Yes"; 5 percent responded "No". Did staff understand and participate in the program? – 89 percent responded "Yes"; 5 percent responded "No"; and 5 percent responded "Sort of".

Festival food recycling is an exciting new frontier. Utilize Seattle's experience and tips to start food recycling at your local festival. You'll not only be collecting organic materials, but you will also be helping to build a foundation to attract local businesses and residents to future programs. By taking advantage of high profile events such as festivals for food waste collection, your community can address a big garbage problem and turn it into a successful venture.

Sam Wilder, President of Wilder Environmental Consulting (www.wilderenvironmental.com), worked with the pilot food recycling trials in Seattle in 2005. She is also involved with projects at Sound Resource Management Group, Inc. (www.zerowaste.com)

Top Tips for Including Food Recycling at Festivals

Vendors have probably not participated in food recycling projects. They may be less likely to participate at their business location if they have a negative experience at a special event, such as a festival. There are a number of action items that can help make local festival food recycling a success, and most key components are related to education. These top tips can be summarized as follows:

1. Have on-site food waste staff or volunteers during the festival. Food waste collection is still very new for many people. Although vendor staff may have the right intentions, they are still unfamiliar with types of materials that can be composted. Having staff or volunteers on-site can help address these issues as they arise.
2. Provide signage for all containers. Mark all containers with signage indicating what can and cannot be put in the food collection program. This will be a reference for the vendors throughout the event and will help to provide information to employees during the festival.
3. Incorporate education materials in regular festival materials. Avoid making food recycling a separate part of the festival or an "add on" idea. If vendors need to apply to participate in the festival, include food recycling participation as one of the requirements for being part of the festival.
4. Train regular festival staff about food recycling. Festival staff should be aware of food waste containers and what can be included in the program. Vendors will have questions, and on-site staff can help provide quick answers.
5. For the first few festivals, involve people experienced in food waste collection with program set up and implementation. Compostable collection requires different considerations than garbage or regular recyclable collection. For example, staff and volunteers will need to be prepared to reach into containers and remove contaminants (which can be a messy task). Don't assume that festival staff can tackle this alone during their first few festivals with food collection. Have a person or team with food waste collection experience involved to help

ensure success. Festivals are fast paced and action-packed. There is not much room for on-site error. Problems need to be predicted and addressed prior to the festival so that when they occur (e.g., a bag breaking as the vendor removes it from the container, spilling the contents at the booth), a plan is in place to take care of it quickly.

6.   Involve the hauler with program set-up details. Make sure the hauler is involved with initial set up and kept up-to-date on program changes. Also be sure to have a way to reach the driver during the festival weekend, if any unexpected circumstances arise.

7.   Make it as easy as possible. Vendors commented that the program was easy because: They did not need to separate food waste (meat could be included); Containers, biodegradable bags and signs were provided and; Collection carts were located near their booth.

Garlic's secret armory consists of more than 33 active sulfur-containing substances that do battle with enemies such as bacteria, viruses, and fungi. Some of the more familiar compounds are allicin, alliin, cycroalliin, and diallyldisulphide. Allicin, garlic's warrior against bacteria and inflammation, is also the culprit behind its offensive odor. Garlic's antibiotic effect is attributed to alliin, the sulfur-containing amino acid responsible for the manufacture of allicin.

Alexandra Hicks, food writer and avid gardener, explains garlic's magic: "Simply stated, when a clove of garlic is cut or crushed, its extracellular membrane separates into sections. This enables an enzyme called allinase to come in contact and combine with the precursor or substrate alliin to form allicin, which contains the odoriferous constituent of garlic."

Renowned for his revelation that microscopic germs caused infection, French microbiologist and chemist Louis Pasteur was first to recognize garlic's antibacterial properties. To demonstrate garlic's amazing strength, imagine that one milliliter of raw garlic juice can be compared to a milligram of streptomycin or sixty micrograms of penicillin.

Jason and the Laundronauts

by Jason Wentworth

QUESTION: *What work do you do?*

ANSWER: I am the owner, along with my wife Sandrine, of the Washboard Eco Laundry in Portland, Maine.

How does it relate to the environment?

We have attempted to create a new model for the coin-laundry industry by designing our business around the goal of minimizing the environmental impact of cleaning clothes. We accomplish this goal in several ways: we use a solar system to generate the majority of our hot water; we have the most energy-efficient washers on the commercial market (all front-loaders); we have a comprehensive recycling program; we only sell detergents from bulk containers to reduce packaging waste; and we sell several natural, non-petroleum-based detergents and fabric softener and only offer a non-chlorine bleach alternative, called sodium percarbonate. In partnership with another local cleaner, we offer wet cleaning, which is a water-based alternative to chemical dry cleaning. Our building was remodeled using many local and low-impact materials and includes lots of windows for natural lighting, a radiant floor-heating system, four times the typical insulation found in commercial buildings, and a high-efficiency lighting system.

What are you working on at the moment?

My current project is to design a heat-recovery system for our dryers that will allow us to recoup some of the energy that is being wasted by exhausting 130-degree (Fahrenheit) air out the back of the building.

How do you get to work?

I ride my bike nearly every day, and if I have too many deliveries for my bike trailer to handle, I use our diesel VW Golf.

What long and winding road led you to your current position?

I grew up on an organic family farm that my parents started from nothing more than fields and woods. This childhood experience made me an environmentalist and activist from an early age. I've spent most of my professional life working in the public sector, serving several terms in the Maine legislature, running a nonprofit alternative-transportation advocacy group, and coordinating environmental programs at Bates College.

About five years ago I decided to try something creative in the private sector, and applying my experience with solar and energy-efficiency led me to a laundromat. Frankly, I didn't really consider that this choice would mean doing tons of laundry; I was excitedly focused on all the opportunities to reduce the environmental impact of cleaning clothes.

Where were you born? Where do you live now?

I was born in the quaint village of Kennebunkport, Maine, before the election of the first Bush filled the town with tour buses. After trying out a few other areas on the globe, I ended up in Portland.

What has been the worst moment in your professional life to date?

The most stressful was going deep in debt to start this business and then having our new machines fail in major ways. I spent the first year of operation dealing with lawyers, machine manufacturers who were slow to take responsibility, and the creditor who would have gladly taken our house had we not been able to make the payments.

What's been the best?

Seeing how popular this business has become. People have responded overwhelmingly to what we have created, and I am sure that we would not have made it in our competitive market if it were not for the environmental and community focus of the business. I am now even more convinced that making genuine environmental protection a cornerstone of a business generates deeply loyal customers who recognize that doing business with you has benefits far beyond the direct transaction.

What environmental offense has infuriated you the most?

I get very annoyed by people who claim that we can solve the terrible environmental problems facing our planet with "greener" technology. Certainly there is an important role for things like renewable energy and recycling technology, but I see far more evidence that technology ultimately leads to more consumption – and consumption is the fundamental problem. At some point, we're all going to have to accept that people need to live simpler lives with less stuff, if the planet is to recover. Ultimately, that simplicity will be forced upon us by the limits of Earth's resources, but it is not going to be an easy transition. The hope that technology can save us seems to be eating up precious time by softening our will to downsize our consumption habits.

Who is your environmental hero?

Jim Hightower has been an inspiration to me. I first heard him speak many years ago when he was Texas Commissioner of Agriculture and I was just starting my short career in politics. His sharp wit, strong ideals about local agriculture, and simple way of explaining even the most complex issues gave me hope and kept me laughing.

What's your environmental vice?

I fly to France once or twice a year to visit my wife's family and vacation. I do plan to start buying carbon offsets, which should make eating Camembert and baguette nearly guilt-free.

How do you spend your free time (if you have any)? Read any good books lately?

Before I started the business, when I had free time, I spent most of it outdoors, kayaking Casco Bay, hiking in the White Mountains, and cross-country skiing the Maine woods. Now I just think about all that while I clean laundry. I do take time to read, and am currently enjoying *Fingersmith* by Sarah Waters. David Sedaris remains one of my all-time favorite writers.

What's your favorite meal?

Lobster cream sauce on homemade ravioli with a mesclun salad from my parents' organic farm, and my wife's chocolate cream for dessert.

Which stereotype about environmentalists most fits you?

I loathe American-style consumerism. I just finished folding clothes for a family that had 50 pairs of brand-new infant socks for one baby! To me, this is a clear example of the false idea that "quantity = happiness," which sadly seems to dominate the psyche of many Americans.

What's your favorite place or ecosystem?

Acadia National Park in Maine is one of my favorite areas, but there are so many places to love.

If you could institute by fiat one environmental reform, what would it be?

Based on the theory that some human behavior can be changed by rewarding good choices and punishing bad ones, I would institute a carbon tax at the federal level. I think that the biggest challenge humans face in saving our planet is that there isn't much incentive for the individual to significantly change behaviors, because each of us contributes such a tiny bit to a huge problem. Taxing consumption based on its carbon impact might help people make a connection between their choices and the impact those choices have on global warming.

Who was your favorite musical artist when you were 18? How about now?

Looking back through my record collection, I'd have to say it was a tie between The Police, Little Feat, and Dire Straits. Today, I listen most often to a French artist named Francis Cabrel.

What's your favorite TV show? Movie?

I try to watch TV as little as possible and only get one French satellite station anyhow. As for movies, *Napoleon Dynamite* is one of my recent favorites.

Which actor would play you in the story of your life?

The only movie stars whose names I can remember are likely to be long gone before the screenplay for my life is written.

If you could have every InterActivist reader do one thing, what would it be?

Hang dry your clothes. Dryers are energy hogs, and they make it easy to own and wear way too many clothes, needing too much closet space, in a too-big house.

An eco-friendly laundromat owner answers questions asked by Grist's gritty reporter

Reprinted by permission from Grist
www.grist.org
For more environmental news and commentary
sign up for Grist's free email,
www.grist.org/signup

Narcomedusan

Before the introduction of antibiotics during World War II, garlic was the favored treatment for whooping cough and tuberculosis. During World War II, chemist Chester Cavallito reported in the *Journal of the American Chemical Society* that in his laboratory research at the Sterling-Winthrop drug company he found garlic more effective than penicillin in combating some varieties of bacteria. He also noted that garlic was effective in killing fungus.

Garlic's ability to lower serum cholesterol is attributed to diallyldisulphide-oxide. The high level of selenium in garlic is believed to prevent sticky platelets and ward off atherosclerosis and clot formation in the arteries.

Zel and Reuben Allen, *Vegetarians in Paradise*,
a monthly internet magazine (vegparadise.com)

Gardening When it Counts

by Steve Solomon

Before the 1930s, few farms had electricity. Many vegetable gardens were grown without running water. Before 1880, when 90 percent of all North Americans (and probably Australians and New Zealanders) lived on family farms or in tiny villages, it would be a fair guess that over 90 percent of all vegetable gardens were grown without running water. In those days, after a few weeks without rain, many would begin talking about drought and of how their gardens or crops were suffering. But other gardeners in the vicinity wouldn't be complaining much.

In 1911 John Widstoe wrote *Dry Farming*, a book about large-scale farming in semi-arid places. Widstoe had a different take on what a drought (or "drouth," as he called it) actually is.

He said:

> Drouth is said to be the archenemy of the dry farmer, but few agree upon its meaning. For the purposes of this volume, drouth may be defined as a condition under which crops fail to mature because of an insufficient supply of water. Providence has generally been charged with causing drouths, but under the above definition, man is usually the cause. Occasionally, relatively dry years occur, but they are seldom dry enough to cause crop failures if proper methods of farming have been practiced. There are four chief causes of drouth: (1) Improper or careless preparation of the soil; (2) failure to store the natural precipitation in the soil; (3) failure to apply proper cultural methods for keeping the moisture in the soil until needed by plants, and (4) *sowing too much seed for the available soil-moisture.*

I emphasize Widstoe's fourth point because this is the factor that most pertains to veggie gardening. I also emphasize it because choosing plant spacing is the single most important decision the gardener will make. These days, having piped water is normal. Veggie gardening styles have adapted to this situation and to the needs of suburbanites living on smaller lots, who buy most of their produce instead of growing it. This shift in vegetable-growing methods was named "intensive." The idea: put the vegetables much closer together in massed plantings on raised beds so the yield from postage-stamp-sized gardens becomes greater per square foot. The gardener loosens the bed to two feet deep (60 centimeters), supposedly so the root systems can go down instead of out. The high plant density sucks the soil dry so rapidly the gardener must water almost daily during the growing season. However, the yield from the amount of water used is supposed to be greater. And, of course, the gardener must make the soil super-fertile to support this intense growing activity.

The intensivists say that putting vegetable rows far apart is a waste of garden space and that gardeners do it only in foolish imitation of farmers, who have to do it so that machinery can work the field. This assertion is not correct. The reason people traditionally spread out their plants (and why farm machinery was designed to match this practice) was so that the vegetables could go through rainless weeks without damage or moisture stress. Most of the intensivist claims listed in the preceding paragraph are also not quite true, as I will soon demonstrate.

I expect many North American cities and towns will start to experience more severe water shortages, if only due to increases in population. This is also happening in the U.K., Australia, and New Zealand. But under economic stress, many people may again wish to grow a substantial amount of their own food. What little irrigation their gardens will get may have to be recycled household water or rainwater off the roof, trapped in tanks, which is how most rural Australians still live. Plenty of piped, chlorinated water may be available in some areas, but unless alternative and large-scale energy sources are developed, the cost of this water will increase with the inevitable increase in the price of oil.

Going back to old-style gardening won't actually be a sacrifice. In fact, it may work out to be a big gain for most people. Instead of having to water the garden constantly and finding that a veggie garden makes a problem about going on a week's holiday during summer, people will discover the old-style garden can look after itself. In my experience, the supposed advantages of intensive raised beds are largely an illusion. Instead of growing many small, crowded plants that take a longer time to harvest (and clean), people will spend less time harvesting larger, more attractive-looking, more delicious vegetables.

Species that produce an ongoing harvest, like tomatoes and cucumbers, will surprise the intensivist by yielding a lot more toward the end of the season because when these plants are crowded together, they produce well for a few short weeks and then virtually stop yielding, their root development stopped by over competition.

— From Gardening When It Counts:
Growing Food in Hard Times

Botanically known as *Allium sativum*, garlic's name is derived from two sources, the Celtic word *allium*, meaning "hot or burning," and the Latin second name *sativum* meaning "cultivated." Our familiar word garlic is from the Anglo-Saxon word *garleac*, a combination of *gar* meaning spear and *lac* that means leek.

chapter 8 : The Good Life

The following started out as an open letter from George
Schenk, founder and President of American Flatbread.

Beyond Organic:
Investing In Local Food Economies
by George Schenk

Think of a farm and what image comes to mind? A house and barn surrounded
by fields and woods. A few chickens in the yard, a big garden, a pen of pigs and a
small herd of cows in the pasture. This, or something similar is what most of us
think of because for about as long as we can remember this is what farms looked
like. They called them family farms and they functioned within the content of nature and their communities. Although far from perfect and often difficult, at a fundamental level family farming produced both delicious and nutritious foods,
conserved open space and were a durable foundation upon which democracy and
civil society flourished.

That was food's past. Today very little of our food comes from such places.

Beginning after the First World War and accelerating after the Second, small
family farms gave way to large corporate organizations that to the greatest extent
possible stripped the messy complexity of nature and humanity out of farming and
replaced them with a streamlined industrial process. Petroleum based synthetic fertilizers took the place of on-farm manures and allowed for nutrient intensive hybrid
seeds; pesticides supported monoculture cropping patterns; the routine use of antibiotics and growth hormones promoted high density feedlots and confinement
rearing of animals; machines replaced people. More recently GMOs, synthetic hormones and irradiation have further distanced food from its natural origins.

Food became a commodity: cheap, abundant, and seasonless. Flavor and nutritional integrity were sacrificed on the altar of price, appearance and convenience.
In a mad scramble to survive, neighbors valued each other's land more than their
friendships. The significant environmental costs of this new system were discounted. The social costs were hardly considered. Farming lost its innocence.

The industrial transformation of the American food supply was not an evil solely
of faceless self-serving corporations but was done with the encouragement and support of the federal and state governments and with the acquiescence of a disengaged
public who saw food as little more than fuel and valued cheap, unblemished seasonless variety over all else. In a way, business and government gave us exactly the
food we asked for. If we now find ourselves with a kind of thoughtless food it is because we have been thoughtless – and careless – about it.

Like so many systems of human design, industrial food swung past its point of
equilibrium which gave rise to a counter response that came to be known as the or-

ganic food movement. Born in idealism, organic food began as small and personal expressions of a more sustainable and nurturing food production model. For many years the model existed at the margins of the national food supply. Starting about twenty years ago, however, organic food gained more public acceptance and began a steady rise to prominence. Today organic food is the fastest growing sector of the food industry – a fact that has not been lost on "Big Food" – the large, often multinational corporations that control a great deal of what the world eats.

Ironically, though perhaps not surprisingly, organic's success is now compromising its future. Now in the big time, organic's production, processing, and distribution systems are mimicking its non-organic conventional counterparts.

Organic food is being industrialized

Large fields are all but mono-cultured; "Free-Range" poultry range on barn floors shared by 20,000 birds; labor conditions on vast irrigated fields in the American southwest echo those of conventional food. Hundreds of miles separate field from plate (the average piece of food in America travels 1,500 miles). Overpackaging and market hype are common. I think commercial organic food is better than its conventional counterpart, but it is only somewhat better.

American food is at a new crossroads. The industrial food model, be it conventional or organic, is failing us. With its long distances from farm to plate, it is failing our environment. With its reliance on some-place-else it is failing local and regional land bases. With its emphasis on "cheap at all costs" it is failing our farmers. With its concentrated processing plants, it is failing our safety. With its ever more exotic chemicals and processes exempt from labeling it is failing to be transparent. And with its problematic residues and narrow views of soil fertility it is failing our nutritional needs.

Food is important. What we eat and how it is grown intimately affects our health and the well being of the world.

Good, nutritious food is not a luxury. It is essential, and related to all that we hold dear.

What is needed, in my view, is a more local and regional perspective on food. "Locavore" as this cuisine has been called is based on the logic of eating locally.

I think the best food you can eat comes from your own garden. Following this would be food that is grown and raised on small farms in your area or region. CSAs, farm stands, and farmers markets are great sources of these foods.

One of the peculiarities of food is that it does not scale well, that is it is hard to maintain food quality and integrity with ever increasing volumes.

In the same way there is a difference between a batch of Grandma's homemade cookies and cookies that are churned out 10,000 an hour in some distant factory, there is also a difference between vegetables from a five-acre plot and those from a 5,000-acre corporate farm. And there is a difference between milk and milk products that come from a small herd of animals who pasture outdoors and are called in by name and a 3,000 head herd confined 24/7 to a concrete barn.

If we are to have better food, the kind we truly need, we need better farming. The solution is not a few mega farms; it is many small successful farms. Many farms imply many farmers. Currently less than 1% of Americans make their living in agriculture. Never before have so few tried to feed so many. How did this happen? It's simple really: People stopped farming because farming stopped paying.

And this is where you and I come in.

There are people willing to farm if only they felt confident there would be buyers of their work.

We are their customers.

If we truly want to have better, cleaner food, if we want to help conserve open areas and agricultural land bases, if we want to lessen the environmental footprint of our food supply, if we care about the dignity of our neighbors who farm – BUY THEIR FOOD!

By getting more money into local farmers' pockets we will make local farming more viable. And while we're at it…

- Give 'em a wave and smile and say thanks
- Don't quibble about the price – good local food is always worth it
- Advocate for public institutions to buy locally produced food
- Ask your favorite markets and restaurants to carry more local foods
- Join a CSA. Take seriously the farmers markets and farm stands.
- And finally, ask your elected officials to review policies and regulations that do not protect organic farmers from GMO pollen drift and that restrict or prohibit a farmer's rights to sell directly to the public.

To this last point there are many regulations that restrict Farm-Gate (farmer to public) sales. Most of these regulations revolve around animal products (raw milk and meat) and are couched in the language of public health and safety. Upon closer inspection however these concerns are antiquated, not scientifically based and inconsistent. The rules are slanted against small farmers and they are more properly understood as crutches for the industrial food model.

The Vermont Experience

Farming is a tremendously hard way to make a living and it is shameful that small farmers are yoked to such burdensome rules. Although there are ways around the rules they all ultimately are illegal and therefore criminalize the very people who are responsible for some of the most interesting, flavorful, nutritious and sustainable food produced in Vermont. This is fundamentally wrong. Far from being criminal, the work of our farmers is noble and deserving of our highest praise and respect.

Over the past several years well-intentioned and reasonable citizens have petitioned state government for Farm-Gate relief without success. Further, with disregard for the will of the Vermont Senate and House, the Governor has vetoed the Farmer Protection Act which would have held responsible the corporate manufacturers of GMO seeds for any damage or trespass GMO pollen might inflict on non-GMO fields – for these reasons, and at risk to our financial security and personal liberty, American Flatbread openly and publicly served chicken raised and farm processed by our neighbor and friend Hadley Gaylord.

American Flatbread is committed to the rule of law and to responsible citizenship. When government promulgates laws that do not serve the public interest it is the obligation and responsibility of the citizens to promote constructive change. The purpose of this public act of civil disobedience in support of local agriculture is to support our neighbor, to offer the most sustainably produced food to our customers we are able, and to stimulate a conversation in our community and across our state about our food stories: Where did it come from? How was it grown, and by whom? How was it stored or processed? What's in it? What's not? And maybe most importantly, what of the future of our food?

For more information about how to support or access local foods look for your local localization or locavore organization, farmers market, or CSA.

This article was written with the encouragement of many though I alone am responsible for its content. I know that there are some who worry for the well being of Flatbread or for their own reputations. Please know I worry too. I fear regulatory sanctions, public ridicule, and/or financial ruin (though I think all of these possibilities are remote). But more than these I fear a thoughtless acceptance of a food system that is not serving us well and surely will not well serve our children. Thank you.

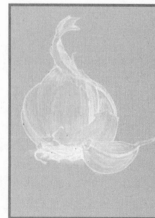

Around the globe garlic is known by many names: In China it is called *da suan*; in Korea, *taesan*; in Japan, *taisan*; in Thailand, *kratiem*; in India it may be called *lassan* or *vellay poondoo* depending on dialect. The Russians say *chesnok*, the Greeks call it *scorodon*, the Polish refer to it as *czosnek,* the Romanians call it *usturoi*. The French say *ail*, the Germans call it *knoblauch,* the Italians *aglio*, the Spanish *ajo*. In Israel the Hebrews say *shoum*, while in Arabic it is *thoum*.

Beautiful, sturdy buildings can be built using this update of a versatile, time-tested method for building post-and-beam homes. Rob Roy is the director of Earthwood Building School in West Chazy, New York

Timber Framing
by Rob Roy

Many natural building methods – such as straw bale, cordwood masonry and cob building – benefit from timber-frame construction primarily because these methods can involve infilling between the timbers that make up the building's structural framework. Unlike conventional 2-by-4 stick framing, the center-to-center spacing of timber-frame posts is somewhere between 6 and 10 feet. This makes infilling much less tedious; imagine trying to fill the narrow spaces in regular stick construction with cordwood masonry or straw bales.

Also, there is a great practical advantage in erecting a timber frame first–getting the roof on as a protective umbrella, and then infilling the structure using one or more of these natural building methods.

Yes, you can accomplish all this with "traditional" wood-on-wood – such as mortise-and-tenon and dovetail – joining methods. But these methods require intricate cuts and exact measurements, and to do it right, a great deal of time and study must be expended, and there are a few specialized tools that need to be purchased. The reality is that most farmers, contractors and owner-builders use methods of timber framing (also called post-and-beam) that they have simply picked up from colleagues, relatives or neighbors. With the advent of relatively inexpensive mechanical fasteners, most builders – contractors and owner-builders alike – rely on other methods of joining, using truss plates, screws and bolts, pole-barn nails and even gravity.

Timber Framing Advantages

Whether you go with traditional timber framing or (modern) "timber framing for the rest of us," you will discover certain advantages and disadvantages in both systems.

- STRENGTH. Timber framing by either method is strong in real structural terms. Heavy-timber frames, with or without infilling, are more resistant to trauma from earthquakes, wind uplift and heavy snow load than light-frame construction.
- CONDUCIVE TO INFILLING. Heavy-timber framing is more appropriate than stick framing for infilling with natural building techniques. With infilling, it is not critical that exact spacing be left between vertical studs or posts; masonry and cob can fit any space, and straw bales can be made to fit almost any width of space.

- AESTHETIC APPEAL. With many of the contemporary timber-frame houses, structural insulated panels (SIPS) are fastened to the outside of the frame, and the beautiful heavy timbers are exposed on the interior. On some cordwood homes, the heavy timbers are in evidence on the exterior, but not on the interior. In all cases, the exposed timbers lend character, texture and an esthetic sense of strength. All of this translates into comfort—spiritual and otherwise.

- EASE OF CONSTRUCTION. If you've never before built a timber-frame structure, you might find it easier than conventional studding, which requires fairly exact tolerances for the application of sheetrock, plywood and the like. With timber framing, far fewer pieces are handled, and tolerances, at least in the post-and-beam frame, do not need to be quite so exact.

- ECONOMY. If you are buying from a local sawmill, you will likely discover that timber framing is more economical than buying finished lumber. When buying heavy timbers from a distant source, this advantage is lost, and timber framing may become more expensive. The key to building anything economically by any method is to use local or indigenous materials.

For centuries garlic was believed to ward off the dark forces of demons, evil spirits, and vampires. It may be possible that 8th century BCE Greek poet Homer, who wrote the Iliad and the Odyssey, set the stage that elevated garlic's powers. During Odysseus's long journey, he encounters the goddess Circe, who uses sorcery to turn men into pigs. Hermes warns Odysseus not to eat the Moly, a plant in the garlic family, saving him from the porcine fate of his companions.

A 300 BCE Greek custom used by travelers for protection from evil spirits was to place garlic at a crossroads to confuse the demons and cause them to lose their way.

To learn more about timber framing, try Rob's *Timber Framing for the Rest of Us* a Mother Earth News Book for Wiser Living from New Society Publishers, 2004

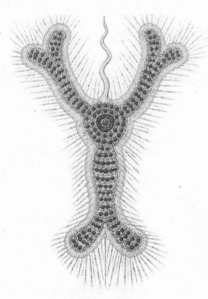

Radiolarian

The Plowboy Interview:
Euell Gibbons

Euell Gibbons (1911-1975) probably turned more people on to nature – certainly to wild foods – than any other writer. His first book about foraged fare, *Stalking the Wild Asparagus*, was (and continues to be) such a best seller that Gibbons followed its success with five more popular titles. Three – *Stalking the Healthful Herbs*, *Stalking the Blue-eyed Scallop* and *Beachcomber's Handbook* – are wild foods manuals, a fourth – *Feast on a Diabetic Diet* – tells how to do just that and the fifth – *Stalking the Good Life* – is an expansion of his *Organic Gardening Magazine* column, "The Organic Nature Lover".

Euell's books are not based on idle theory. He was known to assemble dinners from free pickin's foraged in New York City's Central Park... wild foods gathered in the arid Southwest... the bounty washed onto a tropical beach... potherbs blooming in a Chicago vacant lot... and the wildings found during a "Down East" canoe excursion. All were equally sumptious. Once, Gibbons even gathered 25 varieties of volunteer edibles within 100 feet of a supermarket.

Now and then Euell taught the techniques of wilderness living to boys and girls at the Outward Bound schools in Minnesota and Maine. A Quaker, he also taught at Pendle Hill, a Quaker center.

Euell Gibbons was well over six feet tall, had a Bob Hope nose, plenty of wavy hair and the kind of sharp features that caricaturists love. He led a colorful life as cowboy, farmer, hobo, alcoholic, carpenter, Depression-days communist and beachcomber. Only in his last years was he financially secure (*Stalking the Wild Asparagus* was published in 1962).

Gibbons and his wife, Freda, lived outside a small village in Pennsylvania-Dutch country on a piece of property called "It Wonders Me." Hal Smith conducted the following interview in the Gibbons home in 1972.

QUESTION: *I suppose everyone who meets you asks the same question... how did you learn about foraging?*

ANSWER: By practicing it as a hobby for 50 years. I was first introduced to wild foods by my mother and maternal grandmother – both of whom were fairly good foragers – and I immediately started trying to learn everything I could about such edibles. I invented my first wild food recipe by pounding together hickory nuts and berries to make a candy bar when I was five years old.

Was that when you and your family survived on foraged foods in New Mexico?

No. That period of my life – the time when my knowledge of wild foods really came in handy – was a little later . . . after I already knew quite a bit about foraging. I've simply had an interest in wild edibles for as long as I can remember. This interest is probably connected with a daydream of independence . . . of wanting to say, "Stop the world!" and then doing it. That's always been there to some extent.

My fascination with foraging has also been a handle to a great deal more than just wild foods. It's been an entry to the study of botany and nature generally. There's even a bit of one-upmanship involved when I crunch into one of nature's treats and know I'm enjoying a taste thrill that some of the wealthiest people in the world have never experienced.

I can tell you some of the things that did not lead me into wild foods. It was not an interest in the survival of lost hunters and soldiers or stupid airplane pilots. I had a friend – a very good guy – who was running the survival school at a Navy airbase in Maine. I worked with him a few times... strictly on a volunteer basis because I won't accept any job with the military. I looked over their material, visited a few times. Both of us were critical of the armed forces' manuals on survival and very critical of their teaching methods.

What was wrong with them?

You can't expect someone to remember a plant when you say, "There's something you can eat as an alternative to starvation." How much better that individual will remember if he incorporates a wild fruit or vegetable into his food right now and finds that he actually likes it.

I've found the latter approach very effective with children as a method of arousing a genuine interest in nature, which I think is the greatest value of foraging. A wrong attitude about nature is almost an integral part of our culture, and all the crying we're doing about the environment is going to come to nothing as long as such an attitude persists. We can change this misconception... but only by bringing our children into an intimate, creative relationship with nature. Let them see that they're a part of it... let them see that plants have meaning for them. I've watched this method work enough times to trust it.

I know you've long deplored the fact that many people in our culture consider nature-in-the-wild a menace. I remember when a boy near Philadelphia died from eating horse nettle berries. You sensibly pointed out that horse nettles posed far less threat to our children than the family medicine cabinet. Nevertheless, frightened people demanded that fields be sprayed with poisons, wild areas burned off with flame-throwers and open spaces paved over. Can we really change such irrational fear of nature into a feeling of oneness with it?

That's what I'm trying to do. That's what I see as the chief value of wild foods. If you take a child out to the berry bush where he can pick and eat the fruit for himself, he can't help but change his attitude. A child has to change if you lead him into seeing how he himself relates to nature.

Is it that cut and dried? That simple?

Not always. Taking kids out in the field for such a lesson sounds easy, but it can be very hard to do in today's world of six-year-olds who're already prejudiced. I took such a boy out to gather wild blackberries and he thought we were going to buy them. He was really turned off when he saw me picking the berries from a bush. It was somehow nasty to him.

How did we get ourselves into such a ridiculous position?

This anti-nature attitude in our culture comes from very respectable sources. One of those sources was Charles Darwin: he said that sometimes the "fittest" creature was the one which cooperated... but every example he gave us was an example of competition. Another source was Spencer, who first used the term "struggle for existence". Wallace too. Even Thomas Huxley claimed that each form of life is in continuous battle and competition with every other. There's nothing wrong with that statement except that it's pure bullcrap (laughter).

Nature is typified by cooperation and mutualism. It's everywhere. The production of fruit and the scattering of seed by animals is one example. Flowers and bees are another. There are thousands and thousands of examples of mutual aid... of one life form absolutely dependent on another. I find that the "fittest" is very often the life form which has best learned to cooperate with other life forms around it.

Has no one else noticed this?

Of course. Kropotkin, to name one. In 1898 he tried to refute Huxley with his book, *Mutual Aid*... and not long ago Kropotkin was writing another book to prove that there's even cooperation within a species, let alone between species. Yet – in one of his more recent books, *A Historian's Approach to Religion* – we find Arnold Toynbee saying that every form of life tries to establish itself as the center of the universe and in so doing comes into competitive rivalry with every other form of life. That's a ridiculous statement for a truly great man to make. It simply isn't true.

It's much more accurate to say that every life form, in order to survive, must come into non-competitive relationships with dozens of other life forms. Life doesn't exist alone. It exists in interdependent communities... and there are no boundaries around communities.

I read an article the other day by an ecologist who was talking about the closed community of life in a cave. Surely he ought to know there can be no such thing because there'd be no source of energy. All energy has to come from the sun and the bats are flying in and out eating the insects which eat the plants which get the sun. The bats traveling in and out are the "truck drivers" . . . all the other life forms in the cave depend on them and their manure and bodies. There's no more a closed community in a cave than anywhere else in the world. The web of life is connected from the fish in the deepest part of the ocean to the rat running along the top of the Continental Divide. It's all a unity and we're not separate from it.

Nevertheless we indiscriminately kill life forms all the time. The people who build superhighways across the country never find out what living things they're destroying. The builders don't even know the life forms' names, natures, or relationship to man . . . they just plow straight through. The people who spray the roadsides have no idea what life is being destroyed or what relationship that life has to their own. For example, if we listened to the people who say, in effect, "Let's kill all wild vegetation in the world because a boy got poisoned," . . . we'd all soon die: most of our oxygen is supplied by wild vegetation.

But what about the folks in the middle . . . the people who feel that the "hate nature" idea is wrong and who would love to know how to forage . . . but who have no "wise uncle" to instruct them in the ways of the wilds. Can such individuals learn to forage from a book?

Some of them can't. People have become so estranged from nature that a great many don't know how to go about recognizing a plant. They don't know how a plant is formed, what its essential parts are. Such people ask, "How can I tell the edible ones from the poisonous?" They want a shortcut so they don't have to learn anything . . . but there isn't any shortcut, other than growing up with or acquiring the knowledge firsthand.

Think of it this way: it would be extremely difficult – in a book – to teach someone to distinguish between a head of cabbage and a head of lettuce. Yet anyone who's raised a garden. orhas become acquainted with supermarket produce recognizes the difference quite easily. It's the same with wild foods. A book can only present information. It's up to the individual to absorb that knowledge and put it to use . . . and that takes some effort and firsthand living.

Unfortunately, many of us don't seem to want to expend the necessary energy. It's easier for a parent to just tell a child that some wild plants are poisonous and, therefore, the child should never touch a volunteer plant, look at one, get close to one, etc., etc. The parent doesn't have to learn a damn thing and the child is robbed of a tremendous heritage. As a result, we get more alienated from nature every minute. We don't even understand "The Barefoot Boy " these days because Whittier was talking about a relationship with nature that we don't have anymore.

A boy who lives near here came over once and got so excited when he found me out in the orchard gathering wild strawberries. He'd lived here all his life and never even knew they were there. My God, when I was a boy the idea of letting wild berries get past you . . . I mean, we didn't have a Coke machine at our little country school but we knew exactly where every wild nut – every wild berry – was growing and when recess came we were right out after them. To me it's a damn shame that today's kids aren't getting what's coming to them.

Which brings us back to the way we relate and interrelate with nature . . .

Right.

... and the question of how we should approach nature.

We need to develop an attitude of loving cooperation with no idea of "conquest". It's much easier to learn about a thing you love than a thing you intend to conquer or dominate. We're thinking of domination if we say "weeds", "brush" or "briars" when we're really talking about lamb's-quarters, blackhaws or blackberries. Emerson's definition was, "A weed is a plant whose virtues we have not yet discovered."

What about shooting wild animals for food? Many of today's people – especially young people – look upon hunting as another futile "conquest" of nature. Obviously you don't because you sometimes eat wild game. You're a pacifist but not a vegetarian. Does that square?

Yes, it squares. Very much so. I don't think that eating animals is a conquest of nature at all. To hunt and eat wild animals is to assume your role within nature.

Now I can see a vegetarian saying, "I won't eat commercially produced meats because this is a wasteful means of feeding people." The pig, for instance, is raised for no other purpose than so that we may eat its flesh . . . yet pigs are way up in the food chain. It takes at least 10 pounds of vegetable protein to make one pound of animal protein and it takes 10 pounds of pig to make one pound of growing child. It would be ten times more efficient, you see, for us to interrupt this food chain a step lower and eat the vegetable protein directly.

But that doesn't apply to eating sea creatures, shore creatures and other wild animals. They're already there naturally. If I'm going to relate to them, I must relate for what I am... and I'm part predator.

Take a mussel on the Maine coast. Every mussel produces about four million eggs a year for three years. That's twelve million eggs . . . and only two can be allowed to survive or else the population of mussels will change. If all those eggs survived, the world would be ten feet deep in mussels in one year. The surplus is not only available for eating, it must be eaten. Some of the excess eggs are even eaten by the mussels themselves.

The same thing in decreasing frequency holds true right on up the scale. At the present time – because we've done away and continue to do away with most other predators – the hunter is an absolutely necessary balance in nature. So I'm not anti-hunter in general, though I have nothing but contempt for the person who shoots animals and won't eat them. I would also say that – from my moral point of view – the vegetarian downgrades the life of plants by stating that it's OK to eat them but not animals. Plants are alive too.

How do you account for the fact that people – even non-vegetarians – are generally more squeamish about trying strange wild meats – such as 'possum – than about tasting exotic wild plants?

I don't know exactly how to explain it. I imagine it's partly because we have fewer animals from which we get meat. It also seems to tie into religious beliefs... whether as cause or effect is hard to say. The Hindu religion absolutely forbids beef and frowns on meat of any kind. Buddhists eat meat under certain circumstances if they can find a Muslim to butcher it for them. The Jew and Adventist won't eat pork. Ideas about "clean" and "unclean" meats are very extensive while the Bible says that "every green herb" is food for man. Well, that's quite an exaggeration because some green herbs will kill you deader than hell (laughter).

Even the American Indians – whom we sometimes think each knew all there was to know about the outdoors – had food prejudices . . . just like everyone else. No one tribe ever made full use of the wild food in their area, even when they realized that another group of Indians often ate something they were passing up. Individual tribes generally recognized that and would speak of another by saying, "They eat that but we don't." Sometimes this was just a matter of custom and sometimes it was bound up with certain real taboos... like a Jew avoiding pork or a Hindu beef.

The interesting thing about the Indians, though, is that they weren't nearly as bad as we are at putting others down for what they ate. Nor are most so-called "primitive" peoples. One might even say that individuals who live in small tribes are far more sophisticated anthropologically than the average person in our Western culture. The typical member of Western society thinks we do what we do because it's the right way... the primitive realizes that there are many solutions to a problem and that his tribe's approach is not necessarily humanity's only option.

To what extent, then, are you simply preserving the traditional eating habits of the American Indian with your books about foraging? Is much of your work original?

I suppose this will sound pretty conceited, but I know more about the use of wild plants today than any member of any one tribe ever knew . . . for the simple reason that I have access to what they all learned. I've done practically no original research in finding wild plants that have never been used for food before. Primitive man did an extremely good job of learning what was edible and what was not. I've just compiled that knowledge and used it.

The wisdom the Indians accumulated wasn't lost, you know. There's hardly a tribe that someone didn't make a report on. Those papers contain invaluable information about the eating habits and the ethno-botany of each tribe and they can all be found in the Library of Congress now. When I began my studies before the Second World War, though, the old manuscripts were very hard to find. I had to go from library to library to dig them out. That's how I first learned much of what I know about wild foods.

Is there anyone who knows more about foraging than you?

I've met one man in my life who knew more about wild foods – worldwide – than I do. Fred Irving. He's not well-known. Before his death he recorded a great deal of information about the wild food plants of Australia, Africa and the Soviet Union... areas I'm not familiar with.

I've never known anyone, however – not even Fred Irving – who was or is better at using foraged fare than I am. Fred had very little practical experience in gathering and preparing wild food, whereas I've done it regularly all my life.

Has your experience given you any rules that a novice forager can use to protect himself from being poisoned?

The only rule I have is that you know the plant before you eat it. The novice simply cannot expect to start out and immediately gather all the wild plants in his area ... but it only takes about one minute to learn to identify one plant. If you learn the winter cress today, you can pick all the winter cress you want. After you've found and eaten it a few times, you won't feel any different about foraging a particular plant than you feel about selecting a head of cabbage at a supermarket or picking lettuce from your garden.

You can start gathering wild food with very little learning and, as you accumulate more knowledge, you'll harvest both more fun and more food. If you have no one to point out edible plants to you, the Alaska Sleeping Bag Company in Portland, Oregon publishes a beautiful set of wild plant identification cards. They're really grand because they have good, helpful photographs on one side and an explanation on the other. The Western States set is $4.50 for 54 cards and 37 of them work just as well in the East as in the West. I've suggested that they expand the pack to 100 cards that would be extremely valuable anywhere in the country.

There really are no hard and fast rules. The armed forces' manuals always try to give such guides, though, and that's one of the things I have against them. For instance, such handbooks tell you to avoid plants with milky juice. Well, milkweed and dandelion are two of the most available and wholesome wild foods and they both have milky juices. Of course, some poisonous plants – like the dogbane – do have milky juices... and other plants are just as poisonous but have no milky juice at all. I'd say the rule means nothing.

Another worthless general rule would have you steer clear of any wild green that is extremely bitter... when practically all wild greens are at least a little bitter. I can imagine some poor guy tasting foraged plants and trying to decide at what point something was just not quite bitter enough to hurt him or just enough to hurt him or just a little too bitter to be safe.

In my mind, the guides that say to avoid bitterness and milky juices eliminate just about every wild plant from consideration. It's an approach that goes at the problem the wrong way 'round. I'd say that you don't have to know the poisonous plants in order to gather the edible ones... you just have to learn the plants you're eating.

What about mushrooms?

It's the same as with other plants: you only have to know one mushroom to start. As soon as you know two, you can gather two. I'm no expert on them but I'm up to about three dozen that I can hunt... and I know I'm missing a tremendous number of good mushrooms that I still don't know. I add to my knowledge each year.

And what about the mushrooms you can't identify for certain? Is there any simple test that will insure they're safe?

None whatever. This business of trying to peel a mushroom or of putting a silver spoon into a pot of cooking fungi... well, hell, the *Amanita muscaria* will peel! And while that one might not kill you in small quantities – it's used as an intoxicant in Siberia – it undoubtedly does a lot of damage to the liver and kidneys.

Here in Pennsylvania – but not in other places – it would almost work to say that if a green plant tastes good, it is good. But even that rule won't work with mushrooms. It's been reported by people – just before they died – that the Amanitas vera tastes very good. Come to think of it, the rule wouldn't work anyway... you might find a plant you think tastes good but I think tastes like hell.

You've written that herb gatherers originated the modern fields of botany and medicine. If herbal medicine was once the center of the healing arts, why has it come to such disrepute?

There are several reasons. One is that there was such a god-awful number of quacks in the field. Another was the separation of the herbalist from the doctor.

It's amazing how many diseases listed in the old herbals were really vitamin deficiencies. As long as the doctor was also the herbalist, a patient treated with freshly-gathered natural medicines got the benefit of the plants' vitamin content as well as their drug content. As soon as the doctor stopped gathering for himself, his medicinal herbs had to be dried or distilled so they could be kept. This destroyed some or all of the vitamins in the plants and the herbs were no longer as efficacious as they once were.

We should stress, though, that medicine is descended from botany and a great many herbal remedies are still in the doctor's kit. The drugs have been extracted or synthesized, but many owe their origins to the herbalist.

You argue that herbal medicine isn't nearly so steeped in superstition as some skeptics believe. For example, the folk remedy of applying bread mold to wounds to prevent infection dates back to long before scientific medicine and the discovery of penicillin. Just how much can homesteaders rely on folk cures today?

Herbal remedies can help cure most of the simple illnesses. Nature, for instance, can regulate your bowels in either direction. Cascara bark is still used in a great many commercial laxatives, such as Ex-Lax. Most of the medicines for diarrhea are based on tannin... though the natural ones don't have opiates added to relieve pain or quiet muscles. Blackberry juice, blackberry cordial, the berries themselves or a tea made from the leaves is as good as anything the doctor can give for diarrhea.

People around here use strawberry leaf tea when they get to feeling down, when they bruise easily, when cuts refuse to heal, when their teeth start getting loose... anytime they develop the symptoms of scurvy and need vitamin C. Willow scrapings or strawberry leaf, rose hip or pine needle tea will cure vitamin C deficiency beautifully.

For that matter, you can hardly find a green plant that doesn't contain ascorbic acid – or vitamin C – and an amazing number of such plants can be found in the middle of winter. I've seen kids kicking aside the snow to get wild strawberry leaves. You can make your own cough and cold medicines but when it comes to cold remedies – natural or modern – I don't think any are much good. Take your choice: if you treat a cold with herbal medicine, you'll be over it in a week... if you go to a doctor, it'll take seven days.

I believe there's another advantage to herbal remedies – over and above drugs and vitamins – that we sometimes forget. With modern medicine we often try to get rid of family troubles by sending them out to a specialist. But when a member of the family takes the time to go out, gather herbs, bring them home, prepare them and give them to a sick person... it shows the individual that he's cared for, that someone is anxious about him and wants to do something for him. That, as well as the medicine, has a curative effect.

But there seems to be so much opposition to herbal remedies today.

There is. Let me give you an example. I wrote in my first book about eating poison ivy leaves to gain immunity to the plant. I eat three of the tiny little leaves – that's one leaf with three little leaflets – when they're still red. "One every day in the month of May."

I've never had the slightest ill effect from eating those leaves and, since I've been doing it, I've never gotten poison ivy during the summer. I sometimes get it on my fingers in the early spring when I dig sassafras roots or something before I've eaten the leaves... but I no longer contract the ailment in the summer.

Now, although this old folk remedy works for me, I made it very plain in my book that I don't consider this a safe and settled scientific practice. I merely told the truth about observations on myself and other people who turned me onto the practice. Still, people – including Kingsbury, author of *Poisonous Plants in the U.S. and Canada* – have written telling me my poison ivy experiment is dangerous because some individuals are extra-sensitive to the plant.

Kingsbury said that I should not have published the information at all so I wrote back and told him that every drugstore in this state – and in most states where there's poison ivy – sells pills against it... and those pills are nothing more than poison ivy extract. They're made from the poison ivy plant, they're taken to grant immunity and it says right on the box that if you start to to break out in a rush you should immediately stop taking the the pills and see a doctor. I told Kingsbury that I was doing exactly the same thing, only I was going out and gathering my medicine instead of buying it over a drugstore counter. He wrote back the most condescending, patronizing letter you ever saw in your life. He said, "Mr. Gibbons, you apparently do not understand that this immunity pill is never given to people until they're first tested for sensitivity."

I got up and walked right downtown and three drugstores in a row sold that medicine to me. All three recommended that I take it. So I wrote back to Mr. Kingsbury and told him, "You're completely misinformed if you think everybody has to have a sensitivity test to get these pills. They're sold over the counter, no questions asked. I'll bet what's bothering you isn't the danger of what I'm doing. You're bothered because I'm going out and getting a wild plant for nothing, putting it in my mouth and eating it. You somehow feel protected if somebody is processing it, packaging it and selling it at a huge profit. Because you're brainwashed." And that's exactly where I stand.

What does Kingsbury say about some of the other things you eat?

Well, poisonous plants are his specialty but he includes anything... even if all it does is make milk taste bad. Wild onions are included in his book. I've seen one-fourth of the plants he mentions used regularly and in large quantities.

You should see some of the things this guy has written. After I did an article for *National Wildlife* they got a lot of letters about poisonous plants so they had Kingsbury do a piece and he included acorns on his danger list. He said acorns contain some kind of poison that can cause bloody stools and four or five other horrible symptoms if they're eaten in large quantities over a long period of time.

Well, I wouldn't argue with him about that. If you ate raw acorns in large quantities – maybe a bushel a day for ten years – you'd probably get something like that. But then Kingsbury ended up by saying something like, "The effect of even the smallest amount one time on a very young child is simply not known."

You see what he's done? He's thrown a hell of a scare in there for every mother in the country. I could say exactly the same thing another way: "There is no evidence whatever that a small quantity of acorns taken only one time ever had any effect on a child." That's all he really said but he said it in a way to make every woman grab her baby and run every time she sees an oak tree. I know 80-year-old Indians out west who've eaten acorns all their lives. Every year. Whole cultures depended on them. And for him to make such a ridiculous statement as that!

As far as I'm concerned, you don't have to know the poisonous plants in order to gather the edible ones. Know the ones you eat, not the ones you don't.

What about foraging in polluted streams? Are such water plants safe to eat?

Plants themselves do not take up pollution in the form of disease germs – there are no disease germs in the sap of a plant – but greens can be contaminated on the outside by polluted air or water. Such contamination can usually be washed off – some people suggest putting chlorine in the water – but I try to avoid that for aesthetic reasons. For instance, I know a stream about a mile from here that's overloaded with watercress. I don't eat that cress. Instead, I gather the plant from a spring down here in the brush. It's harder to get the water cress from this spring but I know it's not polluted and I feel better about eating it.

There is one form of air pollution that is absorbed by plants, by the way, and that's lead... mostly from automobile exhausts. Strangely enough, plants seem to love it.

Wouldn't that be a reason not to pick roadside plants?

Yeah. Ordinarily plants 10 feet or more from the road are safe, since lead is heavy even when it's in gaseous form and settles to the ground very fast. I would certainly have my doubts about anybody getting enough lead to poison him if he's careful. I suspect – I don't know anything about it – lead might even be an essential mineral for us. But our usual task is not to get too much of it.[Research is showing that "too much" lead can be very little indeed. Since estimates of our tolerance level are falling lower and the effects of lead in the system have been shown to be cumulative, 50 or even 100 feet from the road would be a safer figure – Ed.]

You spent a few years in Hawaii, out of which came the Beachcombers Handbook. Is a tropical environment better than a colder one for foraging?

I suppose it's better the year 'round because there're times when the pickin's get pretty poor in these parts. When the snow gets deep and the ground frozen, it becomes very difficult to find wild foods here. You could still survive, but in most cases you'd have to eat to live... you sure wouldn't live to eat.

There were some tribes of Indians who were reduced to such scrounging almost every year. The word "Adirondack" – the mountains were named after an Indian tribe – means "tree-eaters." There've been reports of huge areas in which all the bark was removed from the white pines. Like many other tribes, the Adirondacks ate white pine, ponderosa pine and quite a number of other barks.

How'd they prepare it?

Usually they boiled the inner bark... and if it was boiled with meat it might have had enough flavor to be good. I've never been able to fix it well, at least not pine or any of the other thicker barks.

The American Indians weren't the only people to eat bark, by the way. Laplanders, for instance, still do. They scrape off the outer layer to get the inner bark and the cambium, which is the part that produces new cells for growth. The bark is tacked on the sides of the barn or under the eaves of the house where it dries while it's insulating the building. When they need it, they grind the bark into flour and make bread with it. It has lots of starches and sugars . . . mixed with a distinct taste of turpentine.

Some of the willow barks and leaves in the Arctic are really, really tremendous. You get sugar, starch and probably more ascorbic acid than any place else in nature besides rose hips. The Eskimos eat willow around first thaw in the spring, when they need vitamin C more than any other time of the year.

Willows are one of the few trees that grow so far north. They go clear to the Arctic Sea – far beyond what's usually called the timber belt – though they may not grow more than knee-high there. In an hour or two you can gather a pound or so of bark scrapings. Despite what many explorers have written, the Eskimos have always been very good vegetable eaters... with a little help from the climate, they invented the first home freezer for fresh frozen foods.

When I was a boy we used to eat ponderosa pine for pleasure... called it "slivers." In the spring the bark is really gorged with starches and sugars and tastes quite sweet. It's also high in vitamins.

Are some areas of this country better for foraging than others?

Oh, gosh yes. Some of the best places in the world are right here in this area. Pennsylvania, West Virginia, Virginia and Maryland are tremendous for wild foods because we have an overlapping of southern and northern flora. There's even a persimmon tree right across the road. But you know, if some kids get hold of one that's particularly puckery, they get turned off. This idea that every specimen has to be perfect comes from the supermarket.

A friend of mine was visiting people who had a greengage plum tree in their back yard. When he went out and started eating plums off the tree, someone stuck his head out the window and yelled, "Don't eat those. They haven't been sprayed." The reason we get all this perfect supermarket fruit is that the bugs have better sense than we do... they they won't eat fruit that has been sprayed!

Within a given region, where do you find the best foraging?

It depends on what you're looking for, but in general, you'll find a great many more wild foods along roadsides and streams, in old fields and homesteads and around farm ponds. Burned-over and cutover areas are excellent... some plants grow only in places like these that are open to light.

Many edible plants are pantropic weeds... they're plentiful in disturbed ground but don't grow out in the real wilderness. Indians in northern Minnesota call plantain "the white man's track" because it's only found along the portage trails where canoes are carried from one lake to another. They say wherever the white man steps, it grows. I imagine a lot of people wear the same pair of pants on a canoe trip they wear at home, so their cuffs are full of plantain seed, which they scatter along the trails but not in the untraveled wilderness.

Trees, of course, compete with one another. All kinds of hickory trees grow in the forest here, but they don't bear many nuts because of the competition and the squirrels get what the trees do produce. But if a farmer leaves a hickory out in the middle of a field, he'll have nuts.

In answer to complaints that your books aren't very helpful in the semi-arid regions of the United States, you've said that if you could choose your route and time of year, you could walk from the Gulf Coast of Texas to the Pacific Coast of California living entirely on wild food... and never go hungry. What would you eat?

I've played around with that idea but I don't think I'll ever do it. It would be a pretty rugged job. Then again, I lived in the Southwest for the first 21 years of my life and I know there's a lot of food out there. We went out more than once and stayed four days living entirely on wild foods... in December. It's not that hard.

To walk from one coast to the other, I think I'd probably go up the Rio Grande Valley straight into New Mexico... then cut across to the Gila and follow it to the California coast. Most of the trip you'd have the riverside plants as well as the desert ones to keep you going.

You have an organic garden, I guess.

I haven't had an organic garden in four or five years because I'm not home enough in the summer to tend it. I'm not too wild about gardening anyway; there are some real advantages to foraging instead. I begin to gather wild food in the spring before the first person even starts to plant an organic garden. Ordinarily, in this section of the country, I gather from sometime in March to sometime in December and – if we happen to have a warm spell – I may even collect volunteer vegetables in January or February.

Of course I have done a great deal of gardening. I certainly did when I was in charge of buildings and grounds at a Quaker center called Pendle Hill, an intentional community in Indiana. At that time there were usually 60 to 80 people there and gathering wild food simply wouldn't have worked. One person just can't collect enough for a large group.

Oh, there are certain things you could gather, yes – like poke – and a few times I foraged enough wild fruits to make jams and desserts for everybody. But ordinarily you can't do it. If you need large quantities, you'd better garden. Another alternative would be to send everyone out to gather, but that's no alternative at all. Eighty people all foraging one area would be a disaster.

How important a factor can foraging be in providing someone's regular food supply? Can a small family gather wild foods in combination with gardening to noticeably cut their food budget?

Yes, you can successfully combine gardening and foraging and come out way ahead. We've always added wild foods to our diet and I've never regarded them as coarse fare to survive on or eat out of necessity... they're special seasonal treats. Not everyone feels that way, however.

The pinon nut of New Mexico, for instance, is as fine a nut as has ever been eaten... but some folks consider the pinon so tedious to shell that – they say – you could starve to death trying to eat it. Once you get used to shelling the pinon, though, it's really a fine nut and, of course, it can be shelled by machine now.

The wild strawberry. I raised garden strawberries here and I completely abandoned it. Picking the big garden berries was easy... but I had to do all the work of spading, putting out plants, weeding and pinching runners for a year in order to get each crop. By the time I got through – when I added up all my time – I could've picked more wild berries.

Now the time you put into foraging comes all at once and it seems like a rather poor return. But if you figure out every minute you put in on an ordinary strawberry patch, it adds up to a lot of time for each pint too. I honestly believe I get more strawberries by gathering the wild ones... and I never do a thing for the volunteers except harvest them. I have wild strawberries in my freezer right now and there's just no comparison in quality.

You can even combine gardening and gathering quite literally since some of the pantropic weeds – like purslane and lamb's-quarters – grow well in disturbed soil. In other words you can gather wild vegetables by weeding your garden. I've got a letter from some people in Oregon who said they learned from one of my books that lamb's-quarters was what was coming up in their spinach. They tried eating it ... and then pulled up the spinach and let the lamb's-quarters grow.

Do you think it's practical to transplant and cultivate some wild foods as part of a garden?

Yes, but very few. Poke, for instance, works well in gardens. It's been domesticated in Spain, Portugal and North Africa, although it's an American plant. There are also horticultural varieties of purslane you can raise.

Some wild foods are even marketed. Lamb's-quarters are commonly sold in Denmark. In the American South and sometimes in Pennsylvania wild poke is seen in the markets, as are dandelions. The Pennsylvania Dutch don't think they can go through the year without eating dandelions in the spring, but they're getting estranged enough from nature to have someone else gather their dandelions for them.

It seems it takes a lot more time and skill to prepare wild foods than garden vegetables.

Often there's not much more time involved than in preparing garden vegetables from the garden. When you buy produce in the supermarket, a lot of work has already been done on it. If you gather them from the garden, some vegetables are just as tedious to prepare as the wild ones. But on the whole, yes, I'd say wild vegetables are considerably more work than domestic ones.

Less than 100 years ago, 90% of the population lived on farms. That means before agriculture became so mechanized it took nine people to grow enough food to feed ten... themselves and one extra. So foraging is not more efficient than modern agriculture. If it is, we've made a big mistake (laughter).

I do think that gathering wild food is a great thing for people to do occasionally. For instance, these kids living on communes can get a huge part of their food by foraging . . . and it's a wonderful way for backpackers to relate to nature as they go along gathering a big portion of what they eat. When I go camping I carry sugar, salt, cooking oil and sometimes a little flour for thickening soup or flouring fish. But all the rest of my food is gathered, which makes it so much more fun. There's such a great challenge to foraging, and it also keeps you from having to carry a week's supplies on your back.

What's the story on sugaring? Is it possible for most homesteaders to gather their own sugar and syrup?

If there are maples around, yes. I'd say you can get sugar from any kind of maple if the trees are big enough to drill, drive a spike in and hang a bucket on to catch the sap. [The experts we've talked to all say not to tap a tree less than 10 inches in diameter measured two feet above the base. – Ed.] I know people who've even made syrup from the strappin maple and the mountain maple.

What about the nutritional value of wild foods? How do they compare with garden vegetables?

I could give you figures on that, but you can look them up in *Stalking the Healthful Herbs*. I want to make it clear that you can get perfectly good nutrition without ever eating a wild plant. Generally, though, they're more nutritious than comparable domestic plants... at least those I've had tested.

I struck nutritional gold in a number of cases with wild plants so high in food value that their domestic counterparts just couldn't compare. The common stinging nettle proved to have more protein than any leafy material ever tested, and the strawberry leaf makes a tea that's incredibly rich in vitamin C. The analysts wouldn't believe that one, so they went out and gathered their own strawberry leaves . . . they thought I'd sprinkled ascorbic acid or something on mine before I brought them in. The new tests came out almost exactly the same. Of course, the vitamin C content does depend on how long the leaves have been picked, how much they've been exposed to the air and what ground the plants grew on.

When you cook dandelions and some other wild greens, you change the water three times. Do foraged foods generally have to be cooked a great deal? What does this do to their nutritional value?

Well, I don't always change water. Greens that are mild in flavor don't need it at all. I only change water with extremely bitter plants like dandelion and milkweed.

I look at it this way: palatability is very, very important... the amount of vitamins in a plant won't help you at all if they don't get into your stomach. Our tests at Penn State showed that you only lose – at most – 35% of the vitamin C and none of the vitamin A (the two things we tested for) when you cook a wild vegetable in three waters. If you start with a plant that was maybe twice as nutritious as the comparable garden variety to begin with, you still have a better vegetable. Then too, not everyone prefers their food as bland as I do. One man wrote me asking, "Why did you say milkweed had to be boiled three times? I like it just cooked and eaten."

What do you think of the sudden popular interest in ecology? Are people really changing their attitudes toward nature?

Yes, I think so and it's very definitely a part of the general youth revolution. There's a generation growing up that's genuinely different, although the difference may not be as drastic or as original as some of them think. I was smoking pot in 1932 and was arrested for inciting to riot in 1934.

You've had some experience with intentional communities. Why do they interest you?

They've interested me for a long time, though I've done a lot more of almost-becoming-a-member than of actually joining. When we left Hawaii, we were thinking of joining a community of some Quakers – largely to get away from the draft – set up in Monte Verde, Costa Rica. We thought about another one, Macedonia, which used to be in Georgia and we even considered the Bruderhoff in Paraguay for a while... when they started near here we were pulled to them more than any other group. The Bruderhoff bunch is awfully hard to think of arguments against when you're around them. There's so much love and brotherhood in the community. But our theological differences were such that I didn't think I could become a member without either drastically changing my beliefs or lying about them. And I don't know how to change my beliefs. I have no technique for that.

Why were you first attracted to intentional communities?

Because I used to say the only way a person could serve God was in community, though now I can't even remember why I thought that. I've become very disillusioned with communes, mainly because of the amount of time you have to spend on the glue needed to hold one together. After a group reaches a certain size diminishing returns set in and it's no longer efficient at anything.

I was part of an intentional community in Indiana for a year. I couldn't see any community in the place and I never did find out what its intentions were. It looked to me like what they were doing was raising more corn to buy more machinery to raise more corn to buy more machinery. The government bought the corn, stored it in grain houses till it rotted and then bought some more. So I couldn't see that I was doing anything worthwhile. And the people I was with couldn't see anyone taking time off to go out and pick some berries. I didn't want to live my life that way.

Do you have any suggestions about reforming society or the economy to improve the ecological outlook?

Better birth control methods. All other efforts are going to fail unless that problem is solved.

We also need to get rid of the idea of throwing things away. We have to set up a planet based on recycling everything we possibly can. We're simply running through irreplaceable resources and we don't need to. When you talk about sewage, people say, "Oh, yes, let's put it through secondary and tertiary treatment systems and then turn it into the river." I say let's not run it toward the river, let's run it the other way.

One of the reasons sewage pollutes the river is that it's got too much plant food in it, and the right place for plant food is on plants. Or, if you don't want to eat plants grown in sewage, let's grow forests with it. Let trees purify the sewage and turn it into timber and oxygen. Then we wouldn't have to worry about phosphates in detergents... which is a side issue anyway.

A lot of people have the idea that if we stop using detergents, we could safely dump all our sewage in the rivers, but we couldn't. We could put in a little and, strangely enough, it would probably help – there are places in Florida where a pure spring runs out in huge quantities and for a mile or two downstream there's no aquatic life whatever, because the water's absolutely pure and there's nothing for life to live on – but if we overload the rivers they'll die.

We've got to think in terms of balances and there's no shortcut. Of course, I'm not against palliative measures. A lot more fish are living in the Susquehanna as the laws are enforced even a little bit. But palliative measures aren't enough.

In Milwaukee someone said to me, "We'll be all right if we just avoid everything chemical." I said, "You'd have to avoid all of nature... it's the greatest chemist the world's ever seen. We can't duplicate many of the tremendous chemical compound, nature can make."

We have to learn what our role is and there's no easy way to do it, no rule of thumb by which a person can run his life. We have to search for the way, and that requires application, study and experience. We can shorten the process a lot by helping one another, passing on what's discovered. But it's like passing a map to somebody: he still has to take the journey.

This article is very old, but very fresh. No one reconnected us with nature quite so single-mindedly as Euell Gibbons. This piece stands as testament to how much great information Mother Earth News has provided over the years.

Reprinted by permission from
Mother Earth News

Sea-star

Garlic's reputation as protector from evil touches nearly every continent. In Mohammed's writings, he equates garlic with Satan when he describes the feet of the Devil as he was cast out of the Garden of Eden. Where his left foot touched the earth, garlic sprang up, while onion emerged from the footprint of his right foot.

In Greece, midwives would prepare the birthing room by crushing a clove of garlic. Then, after delivering the baby, a midwife would place a necklace with a clove of garlic around the baby's neck.

Dan Chiras is an award-winning nonfiction writer who has published two dozen books, including *Lessons From Nature: Learning to Live Sustainably on the Earth, The Homeowner's Guide to Renewable Energy* and *EcoKids: Raising Children who Care for the Earth*

The Bonds That Tie

Dan Chiras

Besides lifting our spirits, improving our health, and providing inspiration for design and guidance for creating a sustainable future, visits to natural areas provide valuable opportunities to create deep and lasting connections with the life-support system of the planet. The beauty of a grand vista, the gentle curve of the feather-soft petals of a columbine, and the eerie cry of the loon through the misty morning air – these are the things that inspire awe and open young hearts to the world outside cities and suburbs.

When our hearts open, our minds quickly follow. We become allies of nature, interested in voting the conservation ticket and living our lives consistently with the love we hold for the living world. As a parent, you can open your children's hearts and minds to nature, building compassion and love for the planet by introducing them to nature, and giving them opportunities to visit often.

In the 1980s, I taught ecology as part of my general biology course at the University of Colorado at Denver. Like most other professors, I mostly lectured to my students with an occasional chalkboard drawing to illustrate some key point. During what I have come to call my "chalkboard ecology years," I described ecosystems and how they function. I talked about food chains, food webs, consumers and producers and all of the other details I thought students needed to know to understand ecology.

One day, though, it struck me that I was going about this all wrong. Sure, students seemed to be getting the information. For the most part, they did fairly well on exams, spitting back the information I'd crammed into their heads. But did they really understand what I was talking about, or was this just more abstract knowledge they were stuffing into their memories, quickly to be forgotten after the test?

I suspected the latter, and set out to change my ways.

The next summer I taught the course, I canceled class for the ecology week, and asked students to reserve the following weekend for a camping trip. I announced,"We are going to venture into nature to learn about nature." However, I wasn't about to take the naturalist approach, assiduously flitting around naming and numbering things and spewing out interesting but largely useless facts. Rather, it occurred to me that what my students really needed to know was how nature worked, what role we humans played in nature, including how we were affecting it, and how we could change our ways to better fit within nature's grand scheme.

So we headed out of Denver into the mountains of Colorado. We met on Friday evening at a National Forest campsite and sang songs around the campfire, with my amateur guitar playing helping to hold the group together. The next morning after breakfast, we hiked off into the woods and fields and immersed ourselves in nature. The first stop along the trail was at a majestic ponderosa pine tree. With the class gathering around, I asked, "What is this?"

One bright student chimed in, "It's a ponderosa pine."

I shook my head, and chided in a good-natured tone, "Oh, come on ... what is this?"

"A Douglas fir?" another student offered.

I laughed.

"You're going in the wrong direction."

"Well, it's not an aspen," another student joked.

We all laughed.

"And it is not a grizzly bear," I said. "So what is it?"

The students looked puzzled.

"Come on," I laughed. "What is this? Let me give you a hint: be more general."

Still more puzzled looks.

"A tree," one student offered nervously.

"Yes," I said, "a tree. But isn't that just a name? Do you think this tree cares what its name is? What is this?"

By now I'm sure some of the students were beginning to worry about spending the weekend in the mountains with their crazy professor. I wasn't carrying any sharp implements, so they must have figured I was okay for a while. Still, however, there were no answers.

I waited.

After a while I said, "Let me tell you. It's an oxygen producer. It cranks out tons of oxygen that the cells of your body need to break down glucose to make energy. Without it, you could not survive."

Some nods of appreciation. We'd already studied cellular energy production. "See those tiny needles? They contain chlorophyll, which you learned about in class. They are nature's solar collectors. They capture the sun's energy and use it to make plant matter: roots, branches, and limbs. Interestingly, one of the byproducts is oxygen. It's a waste product, really, but this waste is gold."

I pointed to the neighboring hillside, covered with trees. "This is what keeps all animal life going. Without it, none of you, and not one other living animal on the planet could survive. We'd all perish."

Some nods of appreciation.

"So to call it a tree really misses the point, don't you see?"

Some more nods.

"But you keep it alive, too," I announced. "The carbon dioxide you're exhaling right now, which comes from the breakdown of sugar molecules in the cells of your body to make energy, feeds this plant. The trees and all other plants on Earth and in its oceans, lakes, rivers, and streams use carbon dioxide to make plant matter. Without you, the plant kingdom could not survive."

Some smiles emerged on their faces.

Some of them had never really ever thought of a tree, or themselves, in this light – as partners in (excuse the reference to the movie Lion King) the circle of life.

I smiled too. I'd given the lecture a dozen times before on a chalkboard. Students had dutifully written notes as I blabbered on. But I'm not sure anyone really ever got it like this group.Not a word was spoken.

"So when we cut down trees in the rainforest or in the deciduous forests of the eastern United States or destroy any living plant matter for that matter ..." I stopped.

They all knew where I was going.

"You get the point," I said.

More head nodding.

We left, patting the tree, a little sign of our gratitude. You might want to try this with your children.

Illness was often considered a manifestation of the evil spirits or supernatural forces.Along with ceremonial magic, herbal remedies were linked to good spirits. Garlic, with its antibiotic properties, was often the remedy of choice. Because it was frequently successful in healing, garlic was considered the ideal weapon to battle the dark forces.

Financial Independence –
For Us Common Folk
by Jane Dwinel

What would you do with your life if you didn't have to work for money?

I faced this compelling question 13 years ago. I didn't have an answer. Sure, it would be nice to travel, spend more time with the family, and all that, but what would I do – actually do with my time – if I didn't have to work for money?

I let go of the question, and I focused on another one – what is "enough?" That is, how much "stuff" – material goods – was enough for me, and my family? How many services did we need to pay for, and how many could we handle ourselves?

It was another big question that began to shape my life.

In the meantime, I followed a process that allowed me to answer these questions – I began to keep track of every cent my family spent and took in, what we spent it on, and then asked the question – is this purchase in alignment with our values? After having considered what our "real" hourly wage was (it's not what on your paycheck), I could also figure how many hours of our life energy we spent to acquire that good or service.

Does this sound complicated? Does it sound intriguing? It's all part of a nine-step program called "Your Money or Your Life" presented in a 1992 book of the same title written by Joe Dominquez and Vicki Robin. This book changed my life.

In our busy, consumer society, it seems that so many of us just go along with our lives without taking time to consider if what we're doing – and how we spend our money – is in alignment with our values. I thought my family lived a pretty simple, honest life. We gardened and raised a good share of our food. We lived off-the-grid with solar power. Both adults were committed to working part time so that one of us would be home with the kids. We didn't buy too much stuff – or so I thought.

It turns out that, by examining our life by following the nine steps, we were able to achieve Financial Integrity, Financial Intelligence, and Financial Independence.

Here are the steps:

STEP 1: MAKING PEACE WITH THE PAST: In this step, you look at how much money you have brought in over your whole life, and what your current "balance sheet" is. Figuring out your assets and liabilities is more than adding up the worth of your house, your car, and your savings minus your mortgage, loans, and credit card debt. It's also counting everything you own, and determining the worth of all that stuff should you sell it tomorrow in a yard sale or on Ebay. This is a very enlightening step. It's the first step toward Financial Intelligence.

STEP 2: BEING IN THE PRESENT – TRACKING YOUR LIFE ENERGY: Now it's time to figure out your "real hourly wage." Determine your gross weekly or yearly income, and then deduct all the expenses that you incur with your paid work (weekly or yearly). This includes commuting costs, wardrobe, meals, the alcohol or drugs you use to wind down, the vacations you have to take to destress, the visits to the massage therapist or the psychologist or your health care practitioner to clear up "problems," and the time it takes to do all these things. Do the math, and discover your real hourly wage. It'll be a wake-up call, for sure. If you're self-employed or your income is erratic, you'll have to be creative in figuring this out.

Once you've done that, it's time to keep track of every cent that comes into or goes out of your life. Not everyone is a numbers-cruncher, and this step is a stickler for many. It may take you several months to figure out a system that works for you and your family. I've been doing it for 13 years, and my system has evolved over time. It can be done, and it is the centerpiece of the program.

STEP 3: WHERE IS IT ALL GOING?: In this step you take all those monthly figures that you've got written on scraps of paper, Post-it notes, or index cards, and tabulate them.

Create your own monthly balance sheet with income and expenses in categories that work for your situation. You'll want categories for housing, transportation, food, health care, other services, and material goods. You can make each category as general or as specific as you want.

Once you know total expenses, you can then determine how many hours of life energy (via your "real hourly wage") that it took for you to buy all that stuff.

Is this how you want to spend your life?

STEP 4: THREE QUESTIONS THAT WILL TRANSFORM YOUR LIFE: Once you know how many hours of your life energy it took to get your food, take care of your car, keep a roof over your head, and find time for some fun, ask yourself these three questions about each category of expenditures:

1.   Did I receive fulfillment, satisfaction, and value in proportion to life energy spent?

2.   Is this expenditure of life energy in alignment with my values and life purpose?

3.   How might this expenditure change if I didn't have to work for a living?

Do this with total honesty. You may discover areas of your life where you clearly want to spend less of your life energy. Conversely, you may find areas where you want to spend more. Find out what is Enough for you. Now you're building Financial Integrity.

STEP 5: MAKING LIFE ENERGY VISIBLE: Create a wall chart for yourself with a line for income, and a line for expenses. Put it in a place where you will see it every day. Make it attractive and make it big enough – you'll be watching your life change.

STEP 6: VALUING YOUR LIFE ENERGY – MINIMIZING SPENDING: If you're asking yourself the Three Questions, you will probably find your spending going down. Not buying stuff is a good first step. For the things you need, you can look into buying used, bartering, buying on sale, using the library, brown-bagging it, and making and repairing things yourself. There are oodles of ways to save money, and there are plenty of books on the subject. Be creative. It's your life energy.

STEP 7: VALUING YOUR LIFE ENERGY – MAXIMIZING INCOME: Because you value your life energy, you'll want to make sure that you're paid what you're worth. Negotiate with your employer or in any contract work that you do. Don't accept a job if you're not being paid enough (remember your "real hourly wage"). Sometimes you'll save money by not working, by working closer to home, or at a job you love (so that you don't have to pay for all those de-stressing activities).

STEP 8: CAPITAL AND THE CROSSOVER POINT: Now it gets fun. As you spend less and earn more, you will start to save money. Once you have six months of living expenses tucked away in a money market for a cushion, you can start to invest your money toward the day when you reach the Crossover Point – Financial Independence. Calculate the interest rate on your capital (using the best rate on a current Certificate of Deposit as a guesstimate), and add that line to your Wall Chart. One day your interest income will be your only income. When it reaches the same place as your expenses, you've reached Crossover, and you can leave your paid work.

STEP 9: MANAGING YOUR FINANCES: As you begin to invest, you need to educate yourself about the best choices for you. This is not the time to speculate in the stock market. You want steady and secure income. The authors of *Your Money or Your Life* recommend investing in long-term US government bonds. Not being that interested in investing in the federal government, and not trusting its security, I invest in Vermont bonds – those that finance schools, hospitals, and housing. They're tax free, too.

Educate yourself about investments. There are many good books on the subject. Talk to others about their choices, and invest your money wisely. It's still your life energy, and now it can give you Financial Independence.

Financial Independence gives my family the option to do paid work that we love (if we choose), volunteer in our community, and have plenty of time for family, friends, and avocations. It's a good life, it's a balanced life, and it's available to anybody – just follow the nine steps.

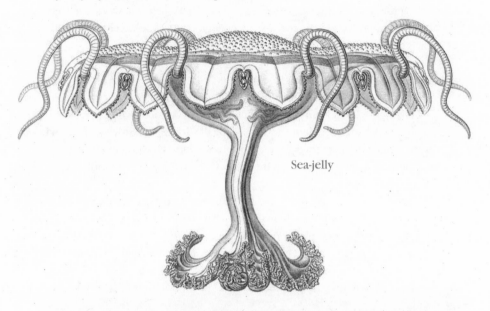

Sea-jelly

European peasants of the 1700s would attach braids of garlic to the entrance of their homes to assure evil would not enter.

As indicated in ancient Egyptian records, the pyramid builders were given beer, flatbread, raw garlic and onions as their meager food ration. Upon threatening to abandon the pyramids leaving them unfinished, they were given more garlic. It cost the Pharaoh today's equivalent of 2 million dollars to keep the Cheops pyramid builders supplied with garlic. In the ancient Middle East, bartering was common practice where a male slave in good health could be bought for 15 pounds of garlic.

Because the Roman generals believed that garlic gave their armies courage, they planted fields of garlic in the countries they conquered, believing that courage was transferred to the battlefield.

Though many ancient cultures recognized garlic's curative abilities, they were unable to comprehend its components. The "cure" was attributed to garlic's magic.

The Good Life:
The New Village People

66 The idea that there were two separate things called "humans" and "the environment" is in my opinion the single largest, most destructive misstep in history. The bizarre thought that we, by accident of being human, are somehow above or beyond the rest of our world has caused untold – and untellable – damage and destruction."

— *Ingrid Witvoet*
Managing Editor, New Society Publishers

66 The collapse of every biological system is going to force more and more humans to realize that in order to save humanity from itself, we must reject ideologies based on "us vs. them" (whether the "them" is the fundamentalists, the corporate leaders, or nature itself). We are in the early stages of an historic paradigm shift from the package that has dominated the planet for the past 500 years (money values, violence, God-is-on-our-side) to one that consists of life values, nonviolence, and a "God" that does

not take sides in intra- species conflicts. We are moving toward a working definition of Global Citizenship and planetary stewardship, which will replace silly little nationalistic, tribalistic and individualist (narrow) ideologies that grab headlines in the corporate media because they distract people from the real sources of our problems."

— *Kevin Danaher*
Global Exchange

66 My late elder brother, Kendrick Putnam, had a profound influence on me and, indeed, on our parents, with his very early espousal of pacifism (in the 1950s, as a teenager), radical social and political views, and unconventional lifestyle. Although I have not come close to emulating him, his influence remains with me 30 years after his death. Although not widely known outside a relatively small circle of New Hampshire and Vermont residents, he had a similar influence on those who knew him."

— *Spencer Putnam*
Vermont Businesses for Social Responsibility

The New Village Library

Meanwhile, Next Door to the Good Life, Jean Hay Bright, Bright Berry Press, 2003.

The New Organic Grower: A Master's Manual of Tools and Techniques for the Home and Market Gardener, Eliot Coleman. Chelsea Green, *1989.*

Four-season Harvest: How to Harvest Fresh, Organic Vegetables from Your Home Garden all Year Long. Eliot Coleman. Chelsea Green, 1992.

Walden; Or, Life in the Woods, and on the Duty of Civil Disobedience. Henry David Thoreau. Signet Classics, 1999.

Scott Nearing, a biography: The Making of a Homesteader. John Saltmarsh. Chelsea Green Publishing, 1998.

Epicurean Simplicity. Stephanie Mills. Island Press, 2002.

Mortgage Free! Radical Strategies for Home Ownership. Rob Roy. Chelsea Green Publishing, 1998.

Timber Framing for the Rest of Us: A Guide to Contemporary Post and Beam Construction. Rob Roy. New Society Publishers, 2004.

Stalking the Wild Asparagus. Euell Gibbons. David McKay Company, 1974.

Stalking the Healthy Herbs. Euell Gibbons. David McKay Company, 1974.

Your Money or Your Life: Transforming Your Relationship with Money and Acheiving Financial Independence. Joe Dominguez & Vicki Robin. Penguin Books, 1992.

Colophon
by Michael Potts

Traditionally, this is where the book designer would name the type fonts (Garamond Book, Times New Roman, and Kabel), and, in this computer age, the programs employed (Quark, Firefox, and PhotoPaint). Then the printer might tell about the printing process. (See this book's last page.) This being a non-traditional book, I have saved myself a few pages to share the experience of designing this book.

New Village Green is a hopeful plunge into a salty ocean of ideas. Working my way through, I noticed that some of the articles sparkle, and every one glows with care for our planet and for the miraculous life that surrounds us.

While admitting we stand on the shoulders of giants, we are not very good at learning from them. Lovelock, for example, perches atop William Emerson Ritter, who arrived on the scientific scene at a time (1910-1920) when the nature of life was being debated by two narrow schools. The Mechanists, holding that life is only machinery, were fond of saying things like, "the brain secretes thoughts in the same way that the kidneys secrete urine." The Vitalists argued that living things possess, or are possessed by, a vital, spiritual force. Mechanists and Vitalists agreed on very little except that theirs were the only two conceivable possibilities. Revolutionary Ritter proposed a third, Organicism, the notion that life is the inter-relationships between organisms. Now called "systems theory," Ritter's Organicism provides a scientific foundation for the work of Lovelock, Carson, the Meadows, and all of us who would preserve our species.

Diving deeper and deeper into the book, I decided this must be the first of several volumes, because some important chapters seem to be missing. Goo-powered rubber-tired vehicles dominate the North American countryside so comprehensively that a naive alien visitor might be forgiven for thinking that cars are the dominant lifeform here. Those small two-leggeds scuttling about might be their servants. In this book there is one nice short piece on why bicycles are better (page 149) and Elizabeth Courtney notes the way our culture is shaped by the combustion engine — "The Industrial Revolution started something that we are now realizing can destroy the very life it made possible." We need at least one more book to help us corral our more insatiable sacred cows.

Manichean Paranoia

As I swam through the sea of luminous articles that became *The New Village*

Green, I was constantly awash in germane ideas from outside the manuscript. John Steinbeck and Ed "Doc" Ricketts enlightened me about Ritter, whose ideas were unaccountably left out of my education; how remarkable that their *Log from the Sea of Cortez,* written in the late 1930s, would touch on so many themes found again in *The New Village Green*!

Churning through the articles, I noticed several veiled references to the 43rd President of the US, but only one author comes right out and writes his fearful name (page 85). Relaxing one evening, my hopes were stirred when Zbigniew Brzezinski, President Carter's national security adviser, visited my primary news source (Jon Stewart of *The Daily Show*). The Zbig guy summed up our recent history in stark and unflattering terms: international politics changed utterly when it became cheaper to kill a million people than to govern them. The "western powers" had a chance to make a difference during the 1990s, but we were too complacent, self-indulgent, and greedy. More recently, we surrendered to what Brzezinski calls "Manichean Paranoia" — we are good, they are evil; they are out to get us.

Possibly coming soon — in 2008 and for a short golden time thereafter — Brzezinski predicts a window of opportunity, if we can adjust our inner qualities to those prevailing in the rest of the world. After 9-11, our fearful and greedy leaders squandered the opportunity for global solidarity, and America's credibility, legitimacy, and even our power was called into question by our war of choice — apparently, we US-ers will do anything for oil, except conserve it. Even so, we are a kindly, appealing people, and the greater world would quickly forgive us if we found the humility and social responsibility required to lead. An optimist, Brzezinski believes we can achieve effective consensus, and work with the rest of the world to solve humanity's problems. "To lead," he said, "we must be willing to sacrifice." By this I do not think he meant sacrifice our courageous soldiers in a chimerical war for the enrichment of a very few.

Watching Brzezinski over and over again, I recognized the fallacy that has shaped so much of recent environmental consciousness. It will take more than 50 Simple Things and Jimmy Carter's Cardigan to work the evolution our planet requires of us. Without really having it ourselves, we pretend to export democracy to those unfortunates who are otherwise governed... provided they inhabit lands with petroleum futures. What we are really doing, is crusading to infect the world with our own rampant consumerism... even as the planetary well runs dry.

A Real Green Village

I settled my family several decades ago in the tiny coastal California village of Caspar "the friendly ghost town" — a redwood company town where the Victorian-era mill fortunately shut down before millworkers started pouring toxic chemicals on the ground. In our backyard the mill rusts and rots benignly as Nature slowly reclaims the land.

The mill closed in 1955, and the town was repopulated by a new breed, Casparados. We worked ourselves into lathers resisting offshore oil drilling, large subdivisions, aerial spraying, clearcutting ancestral forests: a village of reactionaries. Practically islanders, separated from the mainland by mountains and twisty roads, all we could agree on was that we did not like what was happening "out there." Privately, we also admitted we did not like each other much either. Reaction is spirit-draining work.

In 1989 the mill land went on the market, and visions of ticky-tack assailed us — we did not need to look far to see our future; just across the bay stands a chaotic, over-dense subdivision. "Maybe we better build some community, in case we need it one day," someone said. Someone else floated the idea that democracy tends, as has repeatedly been proven, toward dysfunctional stalemate, and government regulation institutionalizes paralysis. Could we secede from *Roberts Rules* and try another kind of governance, like consensus? Everyone knows consensus takes too long... but we quickly agreed that taking time to work things out thoughtfully would be a welcome change. Some time later, our resident songwriter sang us a ballad about our village a hundred years from now — happy, sustainable, healthy, diverse, self-sufficient, embraced by and embracing nature — then challenged us to think backwards and remember what we did to get there. We committed to a Hundred Year Plan, conveniently long enough so not a one of us will see the results, and therefore a wonderful test similar to the "unto the seventh generation" goal proposed in the Precautionary Principle (page 166).

Caspar gathered successes and press so that by the end of the millennium our isolationists were worried that fame would ruin us. Italy's *la Repubblica* asked if we were "*La città più 'verde'*?" — the greenest city, and the *Times* on both coasts excitedly featured our work. With the folks in the subdivision across the bay in the vanguard, we saved our beach and sacred headlands (the old mill site) from cookie-cutter privatization. "We don't want to look out our windows and see anything like US!" they confessed. We bought our old schoolhouse and turned it into a community center. We learned to be unblinkingly proactive, to anticipate future consequences of hasty actions, to think with each others' heads... including those of our neighbors the Osprey, Foxes, Kites, and Grey Whales. We learned to build consensus by hearing out the hysterical blocker who opposes progress, finding the seed of important insight in his rant, and nurturing it into a productive element of a better plan. Again and again we achieved consensus, more easily each time. We even started liking each other.

Governing Caspar — accepting inevitable change, reaching consensus on new ideas — is still like herding cats. But in the time that neighboring communities have institutionalized polarization and scuttled opportunities, we have managed to fulfill, in the short term at least, our stated mission of improving the quality of all life in Caspar.

Too Many Monkeys?

"Is Caspar replicable?" we are asked. Perhaps, but it is certainly not scalable; more than 300 people may not be able to get to Yes through face-to-face consensus building. For the larger, Continental Consensus, the one we need so badly, we must start with agreement on some fundamental principles, and screw up our courage to be Draconian in abandoning "modern" behaviors, strategies, and luxuries that cannot be sustained and shared globally. To lead, we must, quite literally, change our minds.

Why not look closely at places in our lives where the fabric of civilization is so frayed that suicidal behavior results? What are the causes? A culture that practices warfare and amuses its young with *Grand Theft Auto IV* has lost its ethical center, and needs to heal.

How can we be so busy and selfish that we have no time for our children, gardening, meditation, correspondence, friendship, a good book and an old idea in a new setting?

What is so intoxicating about speed? Millions of commuters driving one per car an hour to work and an hour home while yapping on the cell suggests that too many of us are worker ants in some profiteer's greed-hive.

What were we thinking when we accepted Corporations – deathless, heartless, fixated on profit – as our equals? Do we even remember why we work, or is it only "I owe, I owe, so Off to Work I go"? Can we wean ourselves from government subsidies, and forswear our entrenched sense of entitlement? Governance that is not of, by, and for all people in the broadest and most inclusive sense – the Global sense – only benefits the powerful few. As long as one village anywhere is without potable water, we have important work ahead.

When did we agree to make money our sole measure of success? Not so long ago, a lifetime ambition was often stated as the hope of leaving the world a better place. In 1950, when the American Dream of owning a house was coming true, the average new home was 1,300 square feet. In 2000, it was nearing 3,000. Did we get bigger? Our families shrank. There continue to be differing interpretations of the Good Life. Even the editors of *The New Village Green* disagreed about whether "Living Large" belonged in the same sub-title as Living Light and Living Local.

Just as I was finishing the book, a wave washed over me that almost drowned me. One reviewer of *Your Money or Your Life* writes, "I believe most of us are teaching our children we'd rather be consumers than parents." As a youngster, I played outside every moment I could, but now children shun the outside — there are no outlets there, and terrorists steal children. How can we live in harmony with other living creatures, thrive on current solar income, generate no waste, and encourage diversity, if our imaginations and experience are virtual and delivered by electrons? Somewhere about a century ago, our people made some wrong choices. Much of what we have achieved since that time is valuable, precious, even ennobling. But there is also much that is suicidal and murderous. We and our heirs have a brief opportunity for a do-over. Othewise, here's a bit of good news: extinctions happen all the time.

In *Thinking Like a Mountain* Aldo Leopold wrote, "just as a deer herd lives in mortal fear of its wolves, so does a mountain live in mortal fear of its deer." This idea is strange to an indoor culture accustomed to dominion. Leopold ended his famous essay with these words:

> We all strive for safety, prosperity, comfort, long life, and dullness. The deer strives with his supple legs, the cowman with trap and poison, the statesman with pen, the most of us with machines, votes, and dollars, but it all comes to the same thing: peace in our time. A measure of success in this is all well enough, and perhaps is a requisite to objective thinking, but too much safety seems to yield only danger in the long run. Perhaps this is behind Thoreau's dictum: In wildness is the salvation of the world. Perhaps this is the hidden meaning in the howl of the wolf, long known among mountains, but seldom perceived among men.

Despite being the dirtiest creatures ever, humans are the first life form to be able to choose our evolution, and so far... well, we can do better. Global warming and its lesser known but equally potent sidekicks global dimming and global weirding may presage an end to our holocene, consumerist age; we may be an infection that this mighty and glorious organism Gaia may be preparing to shake off. Corporatism, Globalism, Scientism, and a whole pack of bloodthirsty Isms have led us astray, but simple, sustainable pleasures – children, family, neighbors, books, Nature – persist, and may, if we pay attention, help us find a way out.

Can we find the will and courage? While recovering from a hard day Quarking through this book, I opened the March/April 2007 issue of *Orion* to an article by Curtis White, "The Idols of Environmentalism," wherein White wonders how long environmentalists will conspire against their own best interests. At the end of his bleak article he writes,

> Even when we are trying to aid the environment, we are not willing as individuals to leave the system that we know in our heart of hearts is the cause of our problems. We are even further from knowing how to take the collective risk of leaving this system entirely and ordering our societies differently. We are not ready. Not yet, at least.

Nor am I sure we can be ready in time. Even so, we must try. Every article in this book opens a pathway to a new way of working, thinking, living. Each may only be a small beginning, a sketchy line on a map to a sustainable future, but as Euell Gibbons said in 1972 (quoted on page 245), we still have to make the journey.

Out my window, spouts and great heaving backs show that the Grey Whale migration is at its peak. When we moved here, these magnificent mammals were endangered, but in four decades of mindful stewardship they have rebounded. Nature is insanely, reassuringly regenerative, so much so that we who live with Her every day can forget how disconnected most Americans are. Yet the Caspar Dump now collects half as much for recycling as for trash, up from zero two decades ago. We are a fantastically imaginative, capable, protean species, and we can evolve faster if only we get our bearings and strive. Writing at the same time as Steinbeck, when most of us were young or not yet born, Robinson Jeffers knew The Answer, a poem ending with these lines:

> Organic wholeness, the wholeness of life and things,
> the divine beauty of the universe. Love that, not man
> Apart from that, or else you will share man's pitiful confusions,
> or drown in despair when his days darken.

How The New Village Green was created

Picture the lonely writer sitting in front of the keyboard, staring at a blank screen, awaiting the divine inspiration that will channel through his hands, spewing poetry onto the page.

That's not how this book happened.

It began with three emails, one to Paul Freundlich, founder of Co-op America, another to Chris Morrow, proprietor of the Northshire Book Store in Manchester Center, Vermont, and a third to Chris and Judith Plant of New Society Publishers. The request was simple enough "Who are some interesting people in your address book who might have provocative thoughts on the most important ideas that have shaped our current environmental situation." The people they nominated were then solicited for their thoughts on the books, events, and ideas that have shaped our living history.

This eclectic group included musicians, writers, farmers, executives, and a few people impossible to categorize. Their responses resulted in most of the quotations that grace these pages, and, in turn, pointed to more interesting individuals to solicit. The circle expands.

Our chapters were named to honor ideas, originating in books, that appeared most frequently in the emailed responses. (This might be considered the *American Idol* method of creating a book.)

With eight seminal ideas to give us an organizing principle, we then sought contemporary expressions of these ideas in action.

We are living in a golden age of re-publishing. Our research led us to a variety of other publishers to share the information that they had originated. Some were traditional (*HopeDance*, *BioCycle*, *Mother Earth News*, *The New York Times Review of Books*), others were electron-based (*Truthdig*, *Grist*, *New Southerner*), and others swing both ways (*Vermont Commons*). To say that we were overwhelmed by the cooperation and generosity that we received is an understatement. Not a single request for permission to reprint was turned down.

The final stage was one of public information. Here the warehouses of words and images were mined to provide the critical linkages. Wikipedia, Amazon, and Google divulged their secrets to become the threads that hold together the fabric of *The New Village Green*. All that is missing is the alchemy of design.

The lonely writer crumples his sheet of paper and throws it in disgust. Not in this case. This entire text was created without sacrificing a single tree, and just a few trees will be sustainably harvested for the physical package of *The New Village Green*.

That lonely writer should come out and join the party.

The New Village People Index

About Green Living

Created in 1990, *Green Living: A Practical Journal for Friends of the Environment* has been published quarterly for the tri-state area of Vermont, Massachusetts, and New Hampshire known locally as the Pioneer Valley.

Regular topics include organic gardening, green building, health, eco-careers and right livelihood, outdoors/sports, socially responsible investing, econotes, questions and answers, book reviews, and features on topical environmental issues. Our focus is on the practical and positive: most articles focus on how the reader can help the environment or improve their health. We make important information friendly and readable.

In 2006 we published our first remote edition in Southern Oregon/Northern California under the watchful eye of Local Publisher Linda Pinkham. We are seeking additional LPs (which stands for both "Local Publisher" and "Linda Pinkham") in other territories. Requirements are entrepreneurial zeal and a commitment to the environmental community. To inquire:

Green Living
100 Gilead Brook Road
Randolph, Vermont 05060
802.234.9101
email: Stephen@thepublicpress.com
For the latest *Green Living* news, visit our website:
greenlivingjournal.com

About The Public Press

Green Living is a publication of The Public Press, LLC. The Public Press was created to provide a platform for books too specialized, too controversial, or too experimental for the conventional publishing world. The guiding principle has been to reconfigure the author/publisher relationship to reduce the distance between the author's creative concept and the finished work.

Address Publisher Stephen Morris at the coordinates shown above.

For more information, visit the website:
thepublicpress.com

If you have enjoyed *The New Village Green* you might also enjoy other

BOOKS TO BUILD A NEW SOCIETY

Our books provide positive solutions for people who want to
make a difference. We specialize in:

Environment and Justice • Conscientious Commerce • Sustainable Living
Ecological Design and Planning • Natural Building & Appropriate Technology
New Forestry • Educational and Parenting Resources • Nonviolence
Progressive Leadership • Resistance and Community

New Society Publishers

ENVIRONMENTAL BENEFITS STATEMENT

New Society Publishers has chosen to produce this book on recycled paper made with
100% post consumer waste, processed chlorine free, and old growth free.

For every 5,000 books printed, New Society saves the following resources:[1]

31	Trees
2,831	Pounds of Solid Waste
3,115	Gallons of Water
4,063	Kilowatt Hours of Electricity
5,146	Pounds of Greenhouse Gases
22	Pounds of HAPs, VOCs, and AOX Combined
8	Cubic Yards of Landfill Space

[1]Environmental benefits are calculated based on research done by the Environmental Defense Fund and
other members of the Paper Task Force who study the environmental impacts of the paper industry.

For a full list of NSP's titles, please call 1-800-567-6772 or check out our website at:

www.newsociety.com

NEW SOCIETY PUBLISHERS